CBSE 10

MATHEMATICS

12 + 1 SAMPLE PAPERS

MOHIT TRIPATHI

EDUCATOR

B.Sc. (Maths), MCA, GNIIT

STRICTLY IN ACCORDANCE WITH
THE SAMPLE PAPER RELEASED BY THE
CBSE ON 16TH SEPTEMBER 2022

Title : CBSE Class 10 Mathematics

Author Name : Mr. Mohit Tripathi

Published By : EduGorilla Community Pvt. Ltd.

Publishers Address : Sector-12/651, First Floor Opp. Arvindo Park, Near Jama Masjid, Indira Nagar, Lucknow, Uttar Pradesh-226016, India

Copyright

ISBN: 9789355564887

+91-63932 16806, +91-78000 04200
book@edugorilla.com
www.edugorilla.com

Disclaimer

Although the author and publisher have made every effort to ensure the accuracy of information in this book, we do not assume any responsibility to errors and hereby disclaim any liability to any party for any loss, damage, or disruption caused by errors or omissions, whether such errors or omissions result from negligence, accident, or any other cause.

Created & Compiled by EduGorilla Publication

Printed by EduGorilla Community Pvt. Ltd.

CBSE X MATHEMATICS

MIND MAP

TO GET FREE ACCESS SCAN THE QR CODE

* PREVIOUS YEAR PAPERS
* TOPPERS ANSWER SHEET
* STUDY NOTES & VIDEO LECTURES
* VIDEO SOLUTION OF SELF-ASSESSMENT PAPERS
* LIVE DISCUSSION ON MEQ (MOST EXPECTED QUESTIONS)

COURSE STRUCTURE CLASS –X

Units	Unit Name	Marks
I	NUMBER SYSTEMS	06
II	ALGEBRA	20
III	COORDINATE GEOMETRY	06
IV	GEOMETRY	15
V	TRIGONOMETRY	12
VI	MENSURATION	10
VII	STATISTICS & PROBABILITY	11
	Total	**80**

UNIT I: NUMBER SYSTEMS

REAL NUMBER **(15) Periods**

Fundamental Theorem of Arithmetic - statements after reviewing work done earlier and after illustrating and motivating through examples, Proofs of the irrationality of$\sqrt{2}, \sqrt{3}, \sqrt{5}$

UNIT II: ALGEBRA

1. **POLYNOMIALS** **(8) Periods**

   Zeros of a polynomial. Relationship between zeros and coefficients of quadratic polynomials.

2. PAIR OF LINEAR EQUATIONS IN TWO VARIABLES **(15) Periods**

   Pair of linear equations in two variables and graphical method of their solution, consistency/inconsistency.

   Algebraic conditions for a number of solutions. Solution of a pair of linear equations in two variables algebraically - by substitution, by elimination. Simple situational problems.

3. **QUADRATIC EQUATIONS** **(15) Periods**

   A standard form of a quadratic equation $ax^2 + bx + c = 0, (a \neq 0)$. Solutions of quadratic equations (only real roots) by factorization, and by using the quadratic formula.

   Relationship between discriminant and nature of roots.

   Situational problems based on quadratic equations related to day-to-day activities are to be incorporated.

4. **ARITHMETIC PROGRESSIONS** **(10) Periods**

Motivation for studying Arithmetic Progression Derivation of the nth term and sum of the first n terms of A.P. and their application in solving daily life problems.

UNIT III: COORDINATE GEOMETRY

Coordinate Geometry **(15) Periods**

Review: Concepts of coordinate geometry, graphs of linear equations. Distance formula. Section formula (internal division).

UNIT IV: GEOMETRY

1. TRIANGLES **(15) Periods**

Definitions, examples, and counter examples of similar triangles.

1. (Prove) If a line is drawn parallel to one side of a triangle to intersect the other two sides in distinct points, the other two sides are divided in the same ratio.

2. (Motivate) If a line divides two sides of a triangle in the same ratio, the line is parallel to the third side.

3. (Motivate) If in two triangles, the corresponding angles are equal, their corresponding sides are proportional and the triangles are similar.
4. (Motivate) If the corresponding sides of two triangles are proportional, their corresponding angles are equal and the two triangles are similar.

5. (Motivate) If one angle of a triangle is equal to one angle of another triangle and the sides including these angles are proportional, the two triangles are similar.

2. CIRCLES **(10) Periods**

Tangent to a circle at, the point of contact

1. (Prove) The tangent at any point of a circle is perpendicular to the radius through the point of contact.

2. (Prove) The lengths of tangents drawn from an external point to a circle are equal.

UNIT V: TRIGONOMETRY

1 INTRODUCTION TO TRIGONOMETRY **(10) Periods**

Trigonometric ratios of an acute angle of a right-angled triangle. Proof of their existence (well defined); motivate the ratios whichever are defined at 0 and 90. Values of the trigonometric ratios of $30°, 45°$ and $60°$. Relationships between the ratios.

2 TRIGONOMETRIC IDENTITIES (15) Periods

Proof and applications of the identity $\sin^2 A + \cos^2 A = 1$. Only simple identities to be given.

3 HEIGHTS AND DISTANCES: Angle of elevation, Angle of Depression. (10) Periods

Simple problems on heights and distances. Problems should not involve more than two right triangles. Angles of elevation/depression should be only $30°, 45°$, and $60°$.

UNIT VI: MENSURATION

1 AREAS RELATED TO CIRCLES **(12) Periods**

Area of sectors and segments of a circle. Problems based on areas and perimeter/circumference of the above-said plane figures. (In calculating the area of a segment of a circle, problems should be restricted to a central angle of $60°, 90°$ and $120°$ only.

2 SURFACE AREAS AND VOLUMES **(12) Periods**

Surface areas and volumes of combinations of any two of the following: cubes, cuboids, spheres, hemispheres, and right circular cylinders/cones.

UNIT VII: STATISTICS AND PROBABILITY

1 STATISTICS **(18) Periods**

Mean, median, and mode of grouped data (bimodal situation to be avoided).

2 PROBABILITY **(10) Periods**

The classical definition of probability. Simple problems in finding the probability of an event.

Mind Map : Arithmetic Progression

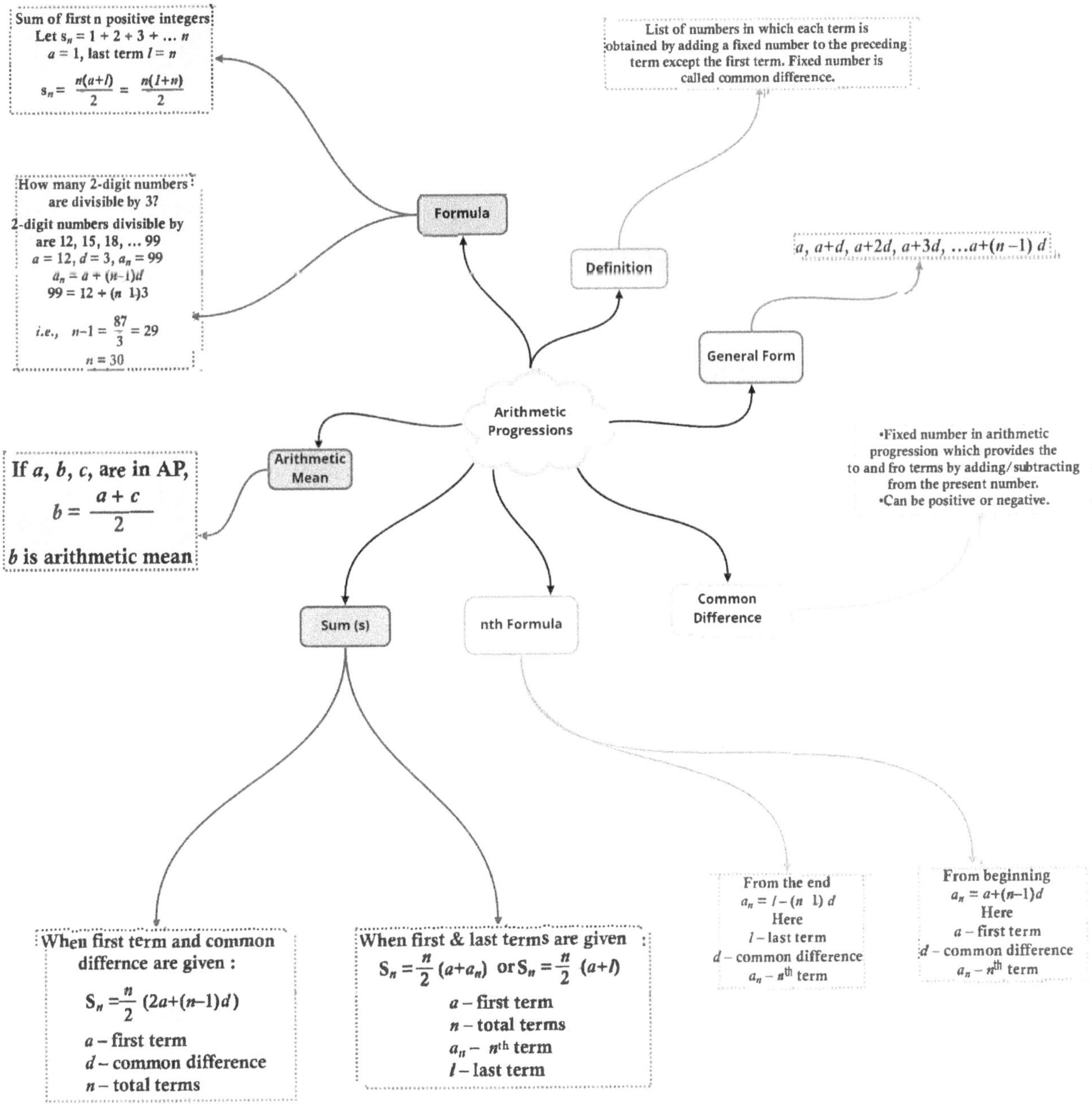

Arithmetic Progressions

Formula

Sum of first n positive integers
Let $s_n = 1 + 2 + 3 + \ldots n$
$a = 1$, last term $l = n$

$$s_n = \frac{n(a+l)}{2} = \frac{n(l+n)}{2}$$

How many 2-digit numbers are divisible by 3?
2-digit numbers divisible by 3 are 12, 15, 18, … 99
$a = 12, d = 3, a_n = 99$
$a_n = a + (n-1)d$
$99 = 12 + (n-1)3$

$$i.e., \quad n-1 = \frac{87}{3} = 29$$

$n = 30$

Definition

List of numbers in which each term is obtained by adding a fixed number to the preceding term except the first term. Fixed number is called common difference.

General Form

$a, a+d, a+2d, a+3d, \ldots a+(n-1)d$

Arithmetic Mean

If a, b, c, are in AP,

$$b = \frac{a+c}{2}$$

b is arithmetic mean

Common Difference

- Fixed number in arithmetic progression which provides the to and fro terms by adding/subtracting from the present number.
- Can be positive or negative.

Sum (s)

When first term and common differnce are given :

$$S_n = \frac{n}{2}(2a+(n-1)d)$$

a – first term
d – common difference
n – total terms

When first & last terms are given :

$$S_n = \frac{n}{2}(a+a_n) \text{ or } S_n = \frac{n}{2}(a+l)$$

a – first term
n – total terms
a_n – n^{th} term
l – last term

nth Formula

From the end
$a_n = l - (n-1)d$
Here
l – last term
d – common difference
a_n – n^{th} term

From beginning
$a_n = a+(n-1)d$
Here
a – first term
d – common difference
a_n – n^{th} term

Mind Map : Area Combination of figures

Areas Related to Circles

Area Combination of figures

Meaning

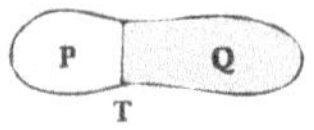

P | Q

T

Area of T = Area of P + Area of Q

Formula

Area = Area of the corresponding sector− Area of the corresponding triangle

$= \frac{\theta}{360^\circ} \times \pi r^2 -$ area of ΔOAB

$= \frac{\pi r^2 \theta}{360^\circ} - \frac{1}{2} r^2 \sin\theta$

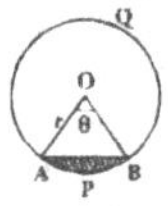

Area of Sector $= \frac{1}{2} \times L \times r$

Circle

- Circumference = $\pi \times$ diameter = $2\pi r$
- Area = πr^2

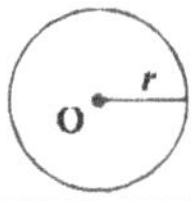

Sector

Meaning

Portion of the circular region enclosed by two radius and the corresponding arc

Major Sector

Minor Sector

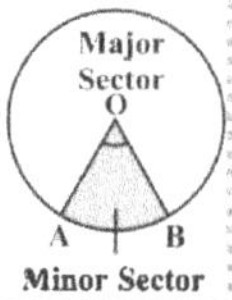

Formula

Length of arc

$L = \frac{\theta}{360^\circ} \times$ circumference

$L = \frac{\theta}{360^\circ} \times 2\pi r$

Area

$A = \frac{\theta}{360^\circ} \times$ area of circle

$A = \frac{\theta}{360^\circ} \times \pi r^2$

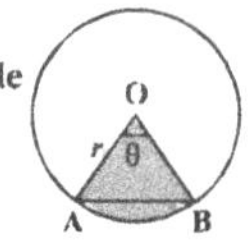

Segment

Meaning

Portion of the circular region enclosed between a chord and the corresponding arc

Major Segment

Minor Segment

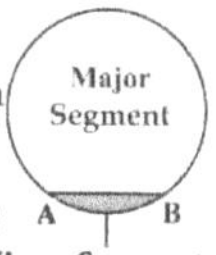

Example

Find Area of shaded region

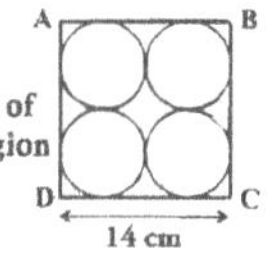

14 cm

Area of square ABCD = 14×14 cm^2

$= 196$ cm^2

Diameter of each circle, $D = \frac{14}{2} = 7$ cm

For each circle, radius $(r) = \frac{7}{2}$ cm

Area of 1 circle = πr^2

Area of 4 circles $= 4 \times \frac{22}{7} \times \left(\frac{7}{2}\right)^2$ cm^2

$= \frac{154}{4} \times 4$ cm^2

$= 154$ cm^2

Area of shaded region = Area of ABCD− Area of 4 circles

$= (196 - 154) = 42$ cm^2

Mind Map : Circles

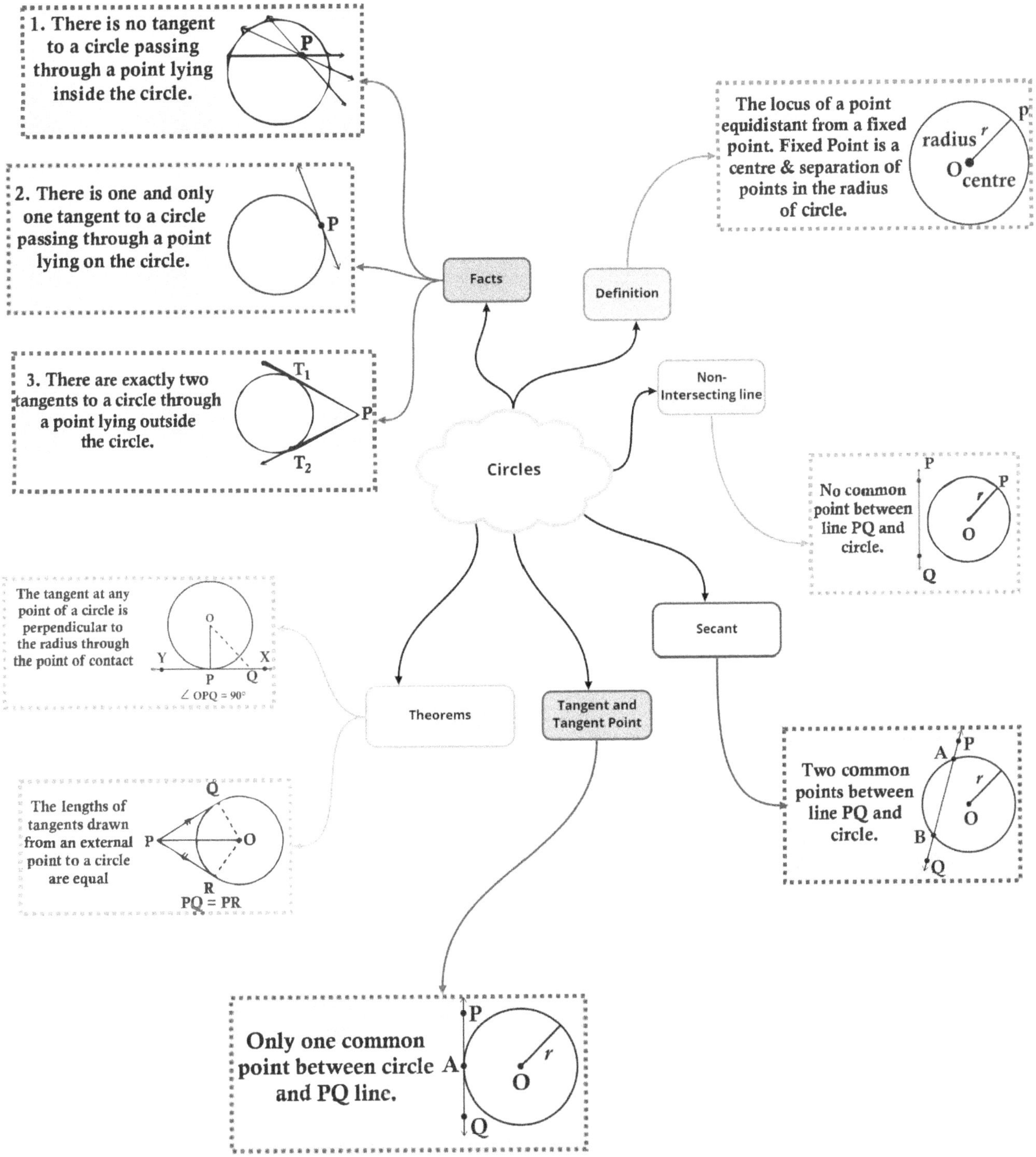

Circles

Facts

1. There is no tangent to a circle passing through a point lying inside the circle.

2. There is one and only one tangent to a circle passing through a point lying on the circle.

3. There are exactly two tangents to a circle through a point lying outside the circle.

Definition

The locus of a point equidistant from a fixed point. Fixed Point is a centre & separation of points in the radius of circle.

Non-Intersecting line

No common point between line PQ and circle.

Secant

Two common points between line PQ and circle.

Tangent and Tangent Point

Only one common point between circle and PQ line.

Theorems

The tangent at any point of a circle is perpendicular to the radius through the point of contact

$\angle OPQ = 90°$

The lengths of tangents drawn from an external point to a circle are equal

PQ = PR

Mind Map : Coordinate Geometry

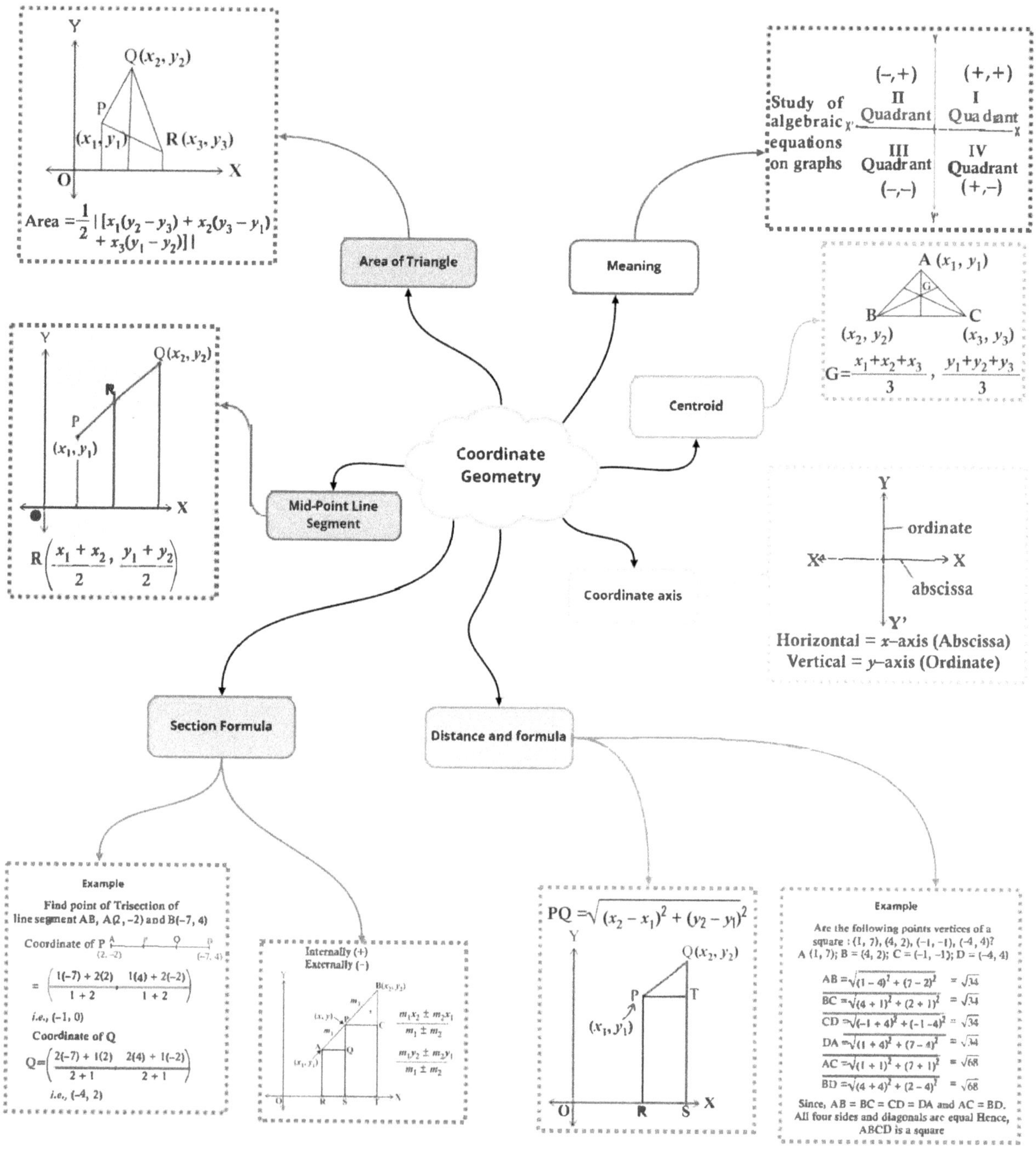

Coordinate Geometry

Area of Triangle

Y, X, O
$Q(x_2, y_2)$
P (x_1, y_1)
$R(x_3, y_3)$

Area $= \frac{1}{2} \mid [x_1(y_2 - y_3) + x_2(y_3 - y_1) + x_3(y_1 - y_2)] \mid$

Meaning

Study of algebraic equations on graphs

(–,+) II Quadrant	(+,+) I Quadrant
III Quadrant (–,–)	IV Quadrant (+,–)

X', X, Y, Y'

Centroid

$A(x_1, y_1)$
G
B (x_2, y_2)
C (x_3, y_3)

$G = \frac{x_1 + x_2 + x_3}{3}, \frac{y_1 + y_2 + y_3}{3}$

Mid-Point Line Segment

Y, X
$Q(x_2, y_2)$
R
P (x_1, y_1)

$R\left(\frac{x_1 + x_2}{2}, \frac{y_1 + y_2}{2}\right)$

Coordinate axis

Y
ordinate
X' X
abscissa
Y'

Horizontal = x–axis (Abscissa)
Vertical = y–axis (Ordinate)

Section Formula

Example

Find point of Trisection of line segment AB, A(2, –2) and B(–7, 4)

Coordinate of P — A (2, –2), P, Q, B (–7, 4)

$= \left(\frac{1(-7) + 2(2)}{1 + 2}, \frac{1(4) + 2(-2)}{1 + 2}\right)$

i.e., (–1, 0)

Coordinate of Q

$Q = \left(\frac{2(-7) + 1(2)}{2 + 1}, \frac{2(4) + 1(-2)}{2 + 1}\right)$

i.e., (–4, 2)

Internally (+)
Externally (–)

Y, X, O, R, S, T
$B(x_2, y_2)$, m_2, (x, y) P, C, m_1, A (x_1, y_1), Q

$\frac{m_1 x_2 \pm m_2 x_1}{m_1 \pm m_2}$

$\frac{m_1 y_2 \pm m_2 y_1}{m_1 \pm m_2}$

Distance and formula

$PQ = \sqrt{(x_2 - x_1)^2 + (y_2 - y_1)^2}$

Y, X, O, R, S
$Q(x_2, y_2)$, T
P (x_1, y_1)

Example

Are the following points vertices of a square : (1, 7), (4, 2), (–1, –1), (–4, 4)?
A (1, 7); B = (4, 2); C = (–1, –1); D = (–4, 4)

$AB = \sqrt{(1-4)^2 + (7-2)^2} = \sqrt{34}$
$BC = \sqrt{(4+1)^2 + (2+1)^2} = \sqrt{34}$
$CD = \sqrt{(-1+4)^2 + (-1-4)^2} = \sqrt{34}$
$DA = \sqrt{(1+4)^2 + (7-4)^2} = \sqrt{34}$
$AC = \sqrt{(1+1)^2 + (7+1)^2} = \sqrt{68}$
$BD = \sqrt{(4+4)^2 + (2-4)^2} = \sqrt{68}$

Since, AB = BC = CD = DA and AC = BD. All four sides and diagonals are equal Hence, ABCD is a square

Mind Map : Polynomials

Polynomials

Division Algorithm

If $p(x)$ and $g(x)$ are two polynomials with $g(x) \neq 0$, then –
$p(x) = g(x) \times q(x) + r(x)$
where, $r(x) = 0$ or degree of $r(x)$ < degree of $g(x)$

Relationship-Zeroes and Coefficient of Polynomials

Quadratic

α and β are zeroes of Quadratic Polynomial
$ax^2 + bx + c$
Then, Sum of zeroes,
$\alpha + \beta = -\frac{b}{a}$
Product of zeroes
$\alpha\beta = \frac{c}{a}$

Cubic

α, β and γ are zeroes of Cubic Polynomial
$ax^3 + bx^2 + cx + d$
Sum of zeroes,
$\alpha + \beta + \gamma = -\frac{b}{a}$
Sum of products of the zeroes taken two at a time
$\alpha + \beta + \gamma = -\frac{b}{a}$
Sum of products of the zeroes taken two at a time
$\alpha\beta + \beta\gamma + \gamma\alpha = \frac{c}{a}$
Product of zeroes
$\alpha\beta\gamma = -\frac{d}{a}$

Graphical Representation Quadratic Polynomials

Parabola

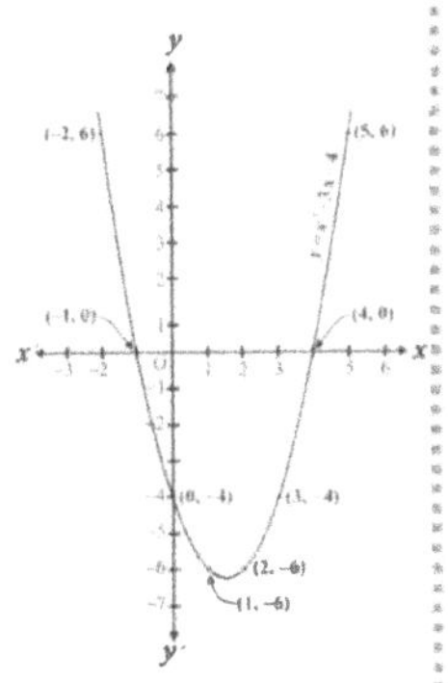

(−2, 6), (5, 6), (−1, 0), (4, 0), (0, −4), (3, −4), (2, −6), (1, −6)

$y = x^2 - 3x - 4$

Degree of Polynomials

Highest power of x in Polynomial, $p(x)$

Types

Polynomial	Degree	General Form
Linear	1	$ax+b$
Quadratic	2	ax^2+bx+c, $a \neq 0$
Cubic	3	ax^3+bx^2+cx+d, $a \neq 0$

Zeroes of Polynomial Graphically

Case 1 - Graph cuts x-axis at 2 points

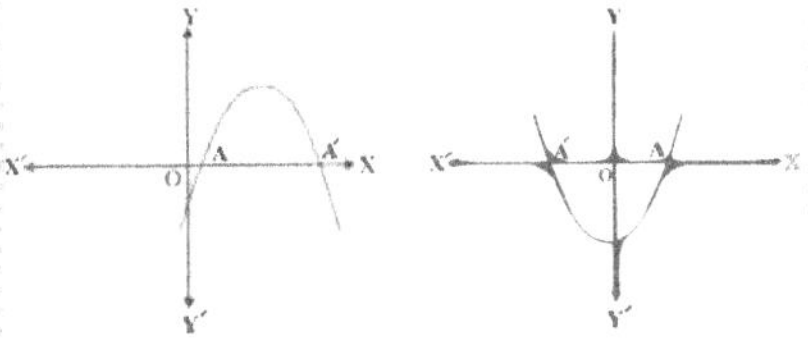

Numbers of Zeroes 2

Case 2 - Graph cuts x-axis at exactly one point

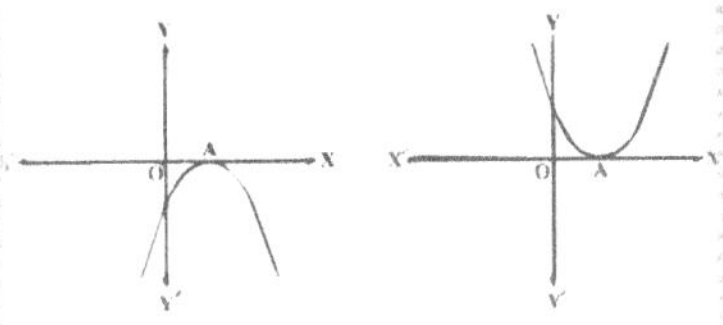

Numbers of Zeroes 1

Case 3 - Graph does not cut x-axis

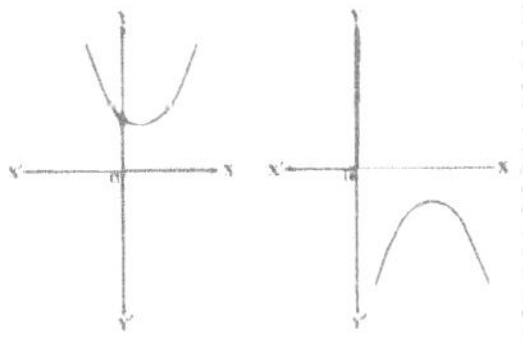

Numbers of Zeroes 0

Mind Map : Probability

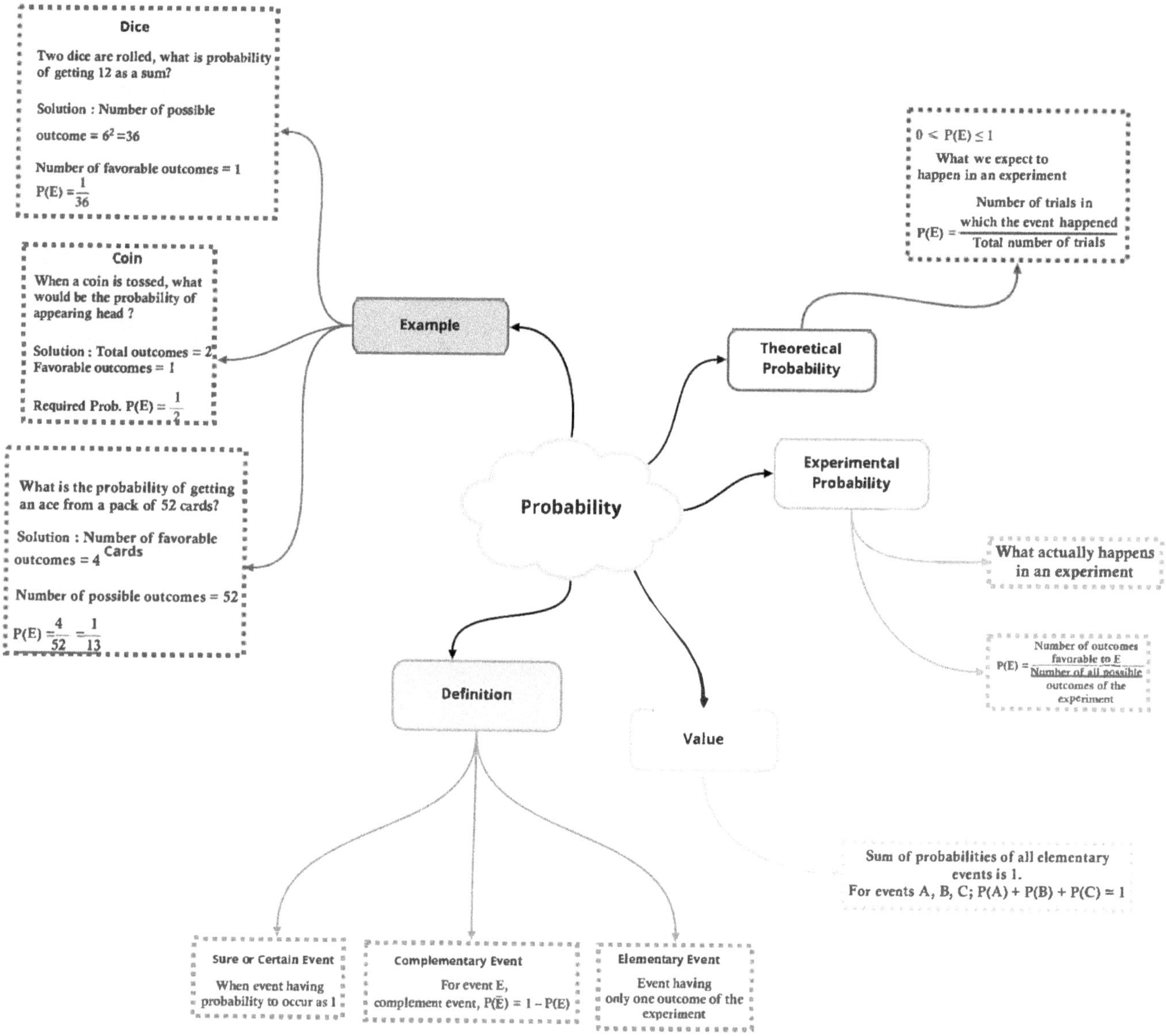

Probability

- **Example**
  - **Dice**
    Two dice are rolled, what is probability of getting 12 as a sum?
    Solution : Number of possible outcome = $6^2 = 36$
    Number of favorable outcomes = 1
    $P(E) = \frac{1}{36}$
  - **Coin**
    When a coin is tossed, what would be the probability of appearing head ?
    Solution : Total outcomes = 2
    Favorable outcomes = 1
    Required Prob. $P(E) = \frac{1}{2}$
  - **Cards**
    What is the probability of getting an ace from a pack of 52 cards?
    Solution : Number of favorable outcomes = 4
    Number of possible outcomes = 52
    $P(E) = \frac{4}{52} = \frac{1}{13}$
- **Theoretical Probability**
  - $0 < P(E) \leq 1$
    What we expect to happen in an experiment
    $P(E) = \frac{\text{Number of trials in which the event happened}}{\text{Total number of trials}}$
- **Experimental Probability**
  - What actually happens in an experiment
  - $P(E) = \frac{\text{Number of outcomes favorable to E}}{\text{Number of all possible outcomes of the experiment}}$
- **Definition**
  - **Sure or Certain Event**
    When event having probability to occur as 1
  - **Complementary Event**
    For event E, complement event, $P(\bar{E}) = 1 - P(E)$
  - **Elementary Event**
    Event having only one outcome of the experiment
- **Value**
  - Sum of probabilities of all elementary events is 1.
    For events A, B, C; $P(A) + P(B) + P(C) = 1$

Mind Map : Quadratic Equation

Quadratic Equations

Meaning

Equation of degree 2, in one variable

General Formula

$ax^2+bx+c=0$
a, b, c – real numbers
$a \neq 0$

Quadratic Formula

Roots of $ax^2+bx+c=0$ are given by

$$\frac{-b \pm \sqrt{b^2-4ac}}{2a}$$

Nature of Roots

For quadratic equation
$ax^2+bx+c=0$,
b^2-4ac is Discriminant (D)

1. D > 0
Two distinct real root

2. D = 0
Two equal real roots

3. D < 0
No real roots (imaginary)

Solution of a Quadratic Equation

By Completing the Square

Solve: $2x^2-5x+3=0$

Solution: $2x^2-5x+3=0$

$$x^2-\frac{5}{2}x+\frac{3}{2}=0$$

$$\left(x-\frac{5}{4}\right)^2-\left(\frac{5}{4}\right)^2+\frac{3}{2}=0 \Leftrightarrow \left(x-\frac{5}{4}\right)^2-\frac{1}{16}=0$$

$$\left(x-\frac{5}{4}\right)^2=\frac{1}{16} \Leftrightarrow x-\frac{5}{4}=\pm\frac{1}{4}$$

$$x=\frac{5}{4}+\frac{1}{4} \text{ or } x=\frac{5}{4}-\frac{1}{4}$$

$$x=\frac{3}{2} \text{ or } x=1$$

Find roots of $6x^2-x-2=0$

Solution: $6x^2+3x-4x-2=0$

$3x(2x+1)-2(2x+1)=0$

$(3x-2)(2x+1)=0$

The roots of $6x^2-x-2=0$

$(3x-2)=0$ or $(2x+1)=0$

$$x=\frac{2}{3} \text{ or } x=\frac{-1}{2}$$

Roots are $\frac{2}{3}, \frac{-1}{2}$

Mind Map : Real Numbers

Real Numbers

Theorems

1. Let p be a prime number. If p divides a^2, then p divides a, where a is a positive integer

2. $\sqrt{2}, \sqrt{3}$ are irrational

3. Let x be a rational number whose decimal expansion terminates. Then x can be expressed in the form, $\frac{p}{q}$ where p & q are coprime, the prime factorisation of q is of the form $2^n 5^m$ where n, m are non-negative integers

4. Let $x = \frac{p}{q}$ be a rational number such that the prime factorisation of q is of the form $2^n 5^m$ where n, m are non-negative integers. Then, x has a decimal expansion which terminates.

5. Let $x = \frac{p}{q}$ be a rational number, such that the prime factorisation of q is not of the form of $2^n 5^m$ where n, m are non-negative integers. Then, x has a decimal expansion which is non-terminating repeating

Euclid's

Division Lemma

Given positive integers a and b, there exist unique integers q and r satisfying $a = bq + r$; $0 \leq r < b$

Division Algorithm

Given positive integers a and b, there exist unique integers q and r satisfying $a = bq + r$; $0 \leq r < b$

Steps to obtain the HCF of two positive integers, say c and d, with $c > d$

Step 1: Apply Euclid's Division Lemma, to c & d. $c = dq + r$

Step 2: If r = zero, d is the HCF of c and d If $r \neq 0$, apply Euclid' s Division to d and r

Step 3: Continue the process till the remainder is zero

Prime Factorization Method

For any two positive integers, a and b
HCF (a, b) × LCM (a, b) = $a \times b$
For Example
$f(x) = 3x^2y$
$g(x) = 6xy^2$
HCF = $3xy$
LCM = $6x^2y^2$

Fundamental Theorem of Arithmetic

Every composite number can be expressed as a product of primes, and this factorisation is unique, apart from the order in which the prime factors occur

Composite Number $x = P_1 \times P_2 \times P_3 \ldots \times P_n$, where $P_1 P_2 \ldots P_n$ are prime numbers

Mind Map : Surface Areas and Volumes

Surface Areas and Volumes

Frustum of Cone

Curved Surface Area

CSA = $\pi l (r_1 + r_2)$

where $l = \sqrt{h^2 + (r_1 - r_2)^2}$

Surface Area

Sum of all of the surface areas of the faces of solid.

Volume

Quantity of 3-D space enclosed by a hollow/closed solid.

Conversion of Solids

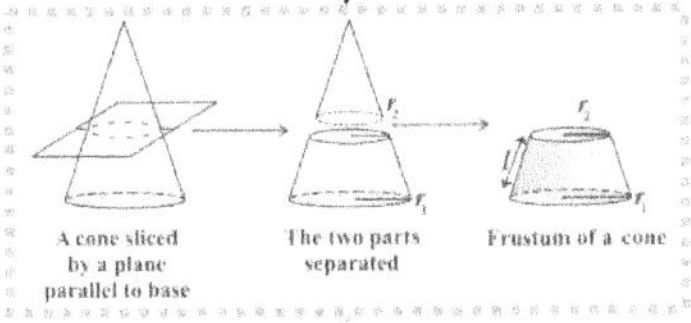

A cone sliced by a plane parallel to base → The two parts separated → Frustum of a cone

Total Surface Area

TSA = $\pi l (r_1 + r_2) + \pi(r_1^2 + r_2^2)$

Volume

$V = \frac{1}{3}\pi h(r_1^2 + r_2^2 + r_1 r_2)$

Combination of Solids

A copper rod – Diameter 1cm, length 8cm converted into a wire of length 18m. Find the thickness of the wire.

Solution : Volume of the rod = $\pi\left(\frac{1}{2}\right)^2 \times 8\text{cm}^3$

$= 2\pi \text{ cm}^3$

Let, r is the radius of cross-section of the wire, volume = $\pi \times r^2 \times 1800 \text{ cm}^3$

$\therefore \quad \pi \times r^2 \times 1800 = 2\pi$

$r^2 = \frac{1}{900}$

$r = \frac{1}{30}$ cm

Thickness = Diameter of the crosssection

$= \frac{1}{15}$ cm = 0.07 cm

Given – Inner diameter of the Cylindrical glass = 5 cm

Height = 5 cm

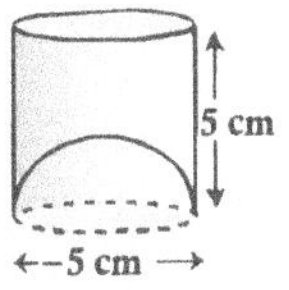

5 cm

←5 cm →

Find – Actual capacity of Cylindrical glass

Solution :– Apparent capacity of the glass = $\pi r^2 h$

= 3.14 × 2.5 × 2.5 × 5 cm^3

= 98.125 cm^3

Volume of hemisphere = $\frac{2}{3}\pi r^3$, if r = 2.5cm

$= \frac{2}{3} \times 3.14 \times (2.5)^3 \text{ cm}^3 = 32.71 \text{ cm}^3$

Actual capacity = Apparent capacity – Volume of hemisphere

= 98.125 – 32.71

= 65.42 cm^3

Mind Map : Triangles

Triangles

Theorems

In ΔABC, let DE ∥ BC. Then,

(i) $\frac{AD}{DB} = \frac{AE}{EC}$

(ii) $\frac{AB}{DB} = \frac{AC}{EC}$

(iii) $\frac{AD}{AB} = \frac{AE}{EC}$

1. If a line is drawn parallel to one side of a triangle to intersect the other two sides in distinct points, the other two sides are divided in the same ratio. If, DE || BC then $\frac{AD}{DB} = \frac{AE}{EC}$

2. If a line divides any two sides of a triangle in the same ratio, then the line is parallel to the third side. If $\frac{AD}{DB} = \frac{AE}{EC}$ then, DE || BC

3. If in two triangles, corresponding angles are equal, then their corresponding sides are in the same ratio (or proportion) and hence the two triangles are similar. (AAA criterion) If $\angle A = \angle D$, $\angle B = \angle E$, $\angle C = \angle F$ then, $\frac{AB}{DE} = \frac{BC}{EF} = \frac{AC}{DF}$ $\Delta ABC \sim \Delta DEF$

4. If in two triangles, sides of one triangle are proportional to (*i.e.*, in thesame ratioof) the sides of the other triangle, then their corresponding angles are equal and hence the two triangles are similiar.(SSS criterion) If $\frac{AB}{DE} = \frac{BC}{EF} = \frac{CA}{FD}$ then, $\angle A = \angle D$, $\angle B = \angle E$, $\angle C = \angle F$ $\Delta ABC \sim \Delta DEF$

5. If one angle of a triangle is equal to one angle of the other triangle and the sides including these angles are proportional, then the two triangles are similar. (SAS criterion) If $\frac{AB}{DE} = \frac{AC}{DF}$ & $\angle A = \angle D$ then, $\Delta ABC \sim \Delta DEF$

Right angled triangle theorem Pythagoras

1. If a perpendicular is drawn from the vertex of the right angle of a right triangle to the hypotenuse then triangles on both sides of the perpendicular are similar to the whole triangle and to each other.

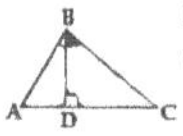

In right ΔABC, $BD \perp AC$, then, $\Delta ADB \sim \Delta ABC$, $\Delta BDC \sim \Delta ABC$, $\Delta ADB \sim \Delta BDC$

2. In a right triangle, the square of the hypotenuse is equal to the sum of the squares of the other two sides.

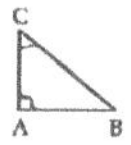

In right ΔABC, $BC^2 = AB^2 + AC^2$

3. In a triangle, if square of one side is equal to the sum of the squares of other two sides, then the angle opposite the first side is a right angle.

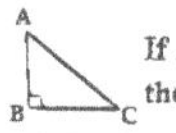

If $AC^2 = AB^2 + BC^2$ then, $\angle B = 90°$

Area of Similar Triangles

The ratio of the areas of two similar triangles is equal to the square of the ratio of their corresponding sides

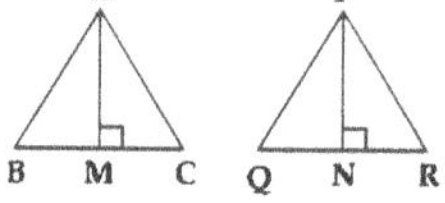

Here $\Delta ABC \sim \Delta PQR$

$$\frac{ar(ABC)}{ar(PQR)} = \left(\frac{AB}{PQ}\right)^2 = \left(\frac{BC}{QR}\right)^2 = \left(\frac{CA}{RP}\right)^2$$

Similarity

(i) Corresponding angles are equal

(ii) Corresponding sides are in the same ratio

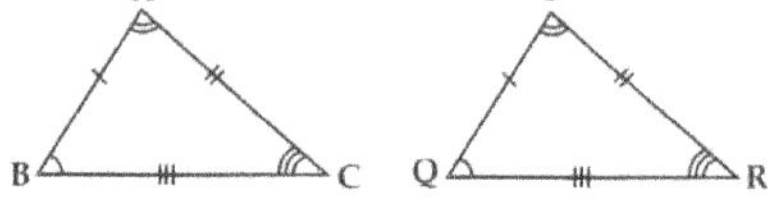

$\Delta ABC \sim \Delta PQR$

Mind Map : Introduction to Trigonometry

Introduction to Trigonometry

Example

Express tan A, cos A in terms of sin A

Solution : Since, $\cos^2 A + \sin^2 A = 1$

$$\cos^2 A = 1 - \sin^2 A \text{ i.e. } \cos A = \sqrt{1 - \sin^2 A}$$

$$\tan A = \frac{\sin A}{\cos A} = \frac{\sin A}{\sqrt{1 - \sin^2 A}}$$

Trigonometric Identities

$$\cos^2 A + \sin^2 A = 1$$

$$1 + \tan^2 A = \sec^2 A; 0 \le A \le 90^\circ$$

$$\cot^2 A + 1 = \text{cosec}^2 A; 0 \le A \le 90^\circ$$

Trigonometry

Study of relationships between the sides & angles of a right triangle

Trigonometry Ratio

Sine of $\angle A = \frac{BC}{AC}$

Cosine of $\angle A = \frac{AB}{AC}$

Tangent of $\angle A = \frac{BC}{AB}$

Cosecant of $\angle A = \frac{AC}{BC}$

Secant of $\angle A = \frac{AC}{AB}$

Cotangent of $\angle A = \frac{AB}{BC}$

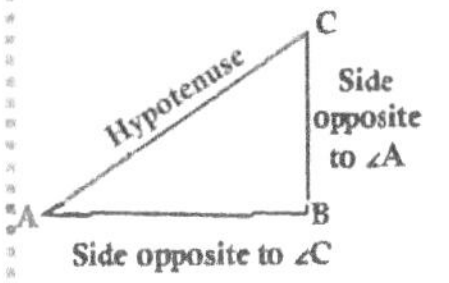

Complementary Angles

$\sin (90^\circ - A) = \cos A$

$\cos (90^\circ - A) = \sin A$

$\tan (90^\circ - A) = \cot A$

$\cot (90^\circ - A) = \tan A$

$\sec (90^\circ - A) = \text{cosec} A$

$\text{cosec} (90^\circ - A) = \sec A$

Note: How to learn the relation

"Some people have" $\sin\theta = \frac{P}{H}$

"Curly Brown Hair" $\cos\theta = \frac{B}{H}$

"through proper Brushing" $\tan\theta = \frac{P}{B}$

Values

∠A	0°	30°	45°	60°	90°
sin A	0	$\frac{1}{2}$	$\frac{1}{\sqrt{2}}$	$\frac{\sqrt{3}}{2}$	1
cos A	1	$\frac{\sqrt{3}}{2}$	$\frac{1}{\sqrt{2}}$	$\frac{1}{2}$	0
tan A	0	$\frac{1}{\sqrt{3}}$	1	$\sqrt{3}$	Not (∞) defined
cosec A	Not (∞) defined	2	$\sqrt{2}$	$\frac{2}{\sqrt{3}}$	1
sec A	1	$\frac{2}{\sqrt{3}}$	$\sqrt{2}$	2	Not (∞) defined
cot A	Not (∞) defined	$\sqrt{3}$	1	$\frac{1}{\sqrt{3}}$	0

EDUGORILLA PUBLICATION

SOLVED SAMPLE PAPER

Class- X Session- 2022-23

Mathematics (Standard)

Sample Question Paper

Time Allowed: 3 Hrs. **Maximum Marks: 80**

General Instructions:

1. This Question Paper has 5 Sections A-E.
2. Section **A** has 20 MCQs carrying 1 mark each
3. Section **B** has 5 questions carrying 02 marks each.
4. Section **C** has 6 questions carrying 03 marks each.
5. Section **D** has 4 questions carrying 05 marks each.
6. Section **E** has 3 case-based integrated units of assessment (04 marks each) with subparts of the values of 1, 1, and 2 marks each respectively.
7. All Questions are compulsory. However, an internal choice in 2 Qs of 5 marks, 2 Qs of 3 marks, and 2 Questions of 2 marks has been provided. An internal choice has been provided in the 2marks questions of Section E
8. Draw neat figures wherever required. Take π =22/7 wherever required if not stated

SECTION-A

(Section A consists of 20 questions of 1 mark each)

1. Let a and b be two positive integers such that $a = p^3p^4$ and $b = p^2p^3$, where p and q are prime numbers. If HCF$(a, b) = p^m q^n$ and LCM$(a, b) = p^r q^s$, then $(m+n)(r+s) =$

(a) 15

(b) 30

(c) 35

(d) 72

Solution: Option (c)

$$a \times b = \text{HCF}(a, b) \times \text{LCM}(a, b)$$

$$p^3q^4 \times p^2q^3 = p^m q^n \times p^r q^s$$

So $(m + n)(r + s) = (3+4)(2+3) = 7 \times 5 = 35$

2. Let p be a prime number. The quadratic equation has its roots as factors of p is

(a) $x^2 - px + p = 0$

(b) $x^2 - (p+1)x + p = 0$

(c) $x^2 + (p+1)x + p = 0$

(d) $x^2 - px + p + 1 = 0$

Solution: Option(b)

As p is a prime number so its factors are 1 and p

So quadratic is given by $x^2 -$ (sum of factors)$x +$ product of factors

$$x^2 - (p+1)x + p = 0$$

3. If α and β are the zeros of a polynomial $f(x) = px^2 - 2x + 3p$ and $\alpha + \beta = \alpha\beta$, then p is
(a) $-2/3$
(b) $2/3$
(c) $1/3$
(d) $-1/3$
Solution: Option (b)

$$f(x) = px^2 - 2x + 3p$$

$$a = p, b = -2 \text{ and } c = 3p$$

As $\alpha + \beta = \alpha\beta$ [given]

$$-\frac{b}{a} = \frac{c}{a}$$

$$-\frac{(-2)}{p} = \frac{3p}{p} \Rightarrow p = \frac{2}{3}$$

4. If the system of equations $3x + y = 1$ and $(2k - 1)x + (k - 1)y = 2k + 1$ is inconsistent, then $k =$
(a) -1
(b) 0
(c) 1
(d) 2
Solution: Option (d)
If the system of equations is $a_1x + b_1y + c_1 = 0$ and $a_2x + b_2y + c_2 = 0$ and they are inconsistent, then it satisfies the following:

$$\frac{a_1}{a_2} = \frac{b_1}{b_2} \neq \frac{c_1}{c_2}$$

From the given system

$$a_1 = 3, b_1 = 1, c_1 = -1 \text{ and } a_2 = (2k - 1), b_2 = (k - 1), c_2 = -(2k + 1)$$

$$\frac{3}{2k-1} = \frac{1}{k-1} \neq \frac{-1}{-(2k+1)}$$

$$3k - 3 = 2k - 1 \Rightarrow k = 2$$

5. If the vertices of a parallelogram PQRS were taken in order are $P(3,4), Q(-2,3)$, and $R(-3,-2)$, then the coordinates of its fourth vertex S are
(a) $(-2,-1)$
(b) $(-2,-3)$
(c) $(2,-1)$
(d) $(1,2)$
Solution: Option(c)
Let coordinates of S (a, b)
If taken in order diagonals PR and QS bisect each other.
So using the midpoint formula $(x, y) = \{\frac{x_1+x_2}{2}, \frac{y_1+y_2}{2}\}$

$$\frac{3+(-3)}{2} = \frac{-2+x}{2} \Rightarrow x = 2$$

Since only option (c) has the x coordinate = 2 so no need to find y. S $(2, -1)$

6. ΔABC~ΔPQR. If AM and PN are altitudes of ΔABC and ΔPQR respectively and $AB^2: PQ^2 = 4:9$, then $AM: PN =$
(a) 3: 2
(b) 16: 81
(c) 4: 9
(d) 2: 3
Solution: Option(d)

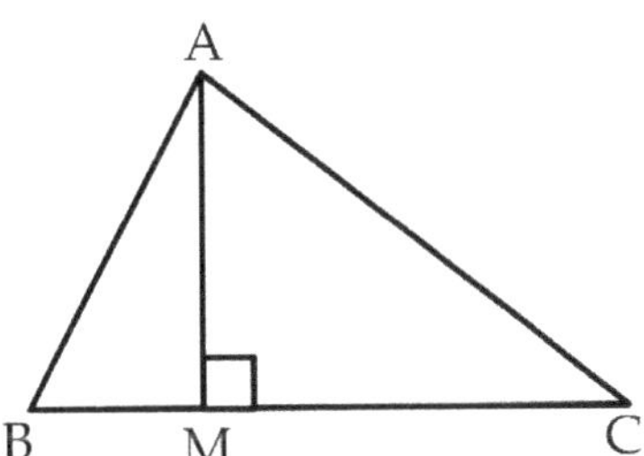

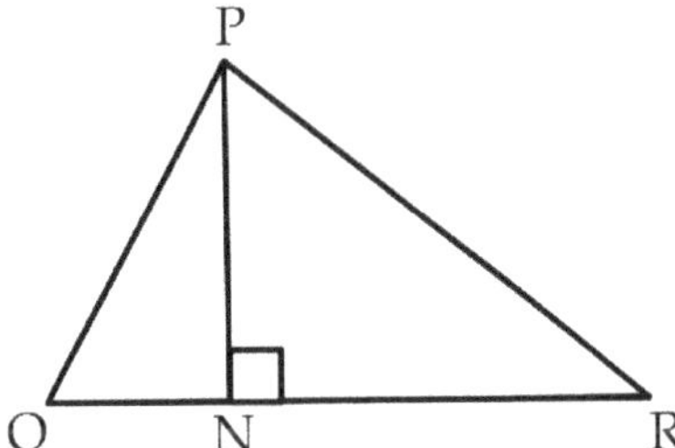

As $\Delta ABC \sim \Delta PQR$ so $\angle A = \angle P, \angle B = \angle Q$ and $\angle C = \angle R$ [corresponding angles of similar triangles]

So $\Delta ABM \sim \Delta PQN$ are also similar to AA rule as $\angle M = \angle N$ (90 each)

So $\frac{\text{AB}}{\text{PQ}} = \frac{\text{AM}}{\text{PN}}$ [corresponding sides of similar triangles are proportional]

If $\frac{\text{AB}^2}{\text{PQ}^2} = \frac{4}{9} \Rightarrow \frac{\text{AB}}{\text{PQ}} = \frac{2}{3}$ so $\frac{\text{AM}}{\text{PN}} = \frac{2}{3}$

7. If $x \tan 60° \cos 60° = \sin 60° \cot 60°$, then $x =$
(a) cos30°
(b) tan30°
(c) sin30°
(d) cot 30°
Solution: Option(b)

$x \tan 60° \cos 60° = \sin 60° \cot 60°$

$x\sqrt{3} \times \frac{1}{2} = \frac{\sqrt{3}}{2} \times \frac{1}{\sqrt{3}}$

$x = \frac{1}{\sqrt{3}} = \tan 30°$

8. If $\sin\theta + \cos\theta = \sqrt{2}$, then $\tan\theta + \cot\theta =$
(a) 1
(b) 2
(c) 3
(d) 4
Solution: Option(b)

$\sin\theta + \cos\theta = \sqrt{2}$

$(\sin\theta + \cos\theta)^2 = (\sqrt{2})^2$ [squaring both sides]

$\sin^2\theta + \cos^2\theta + 2\sin\theta\cos\theta = 2$

$2\sin\theta\cos\theta = 2 - 1$ $\quad [\sin^2\theta + \cos^2\theta = 1]$

$\sin\theta\cos\theta = \frac{1}{2}$ ....(i)

$\tan\theta + \cot\theta = \frac{\sin\theta}{\cos\theta} + \frac{\cos\theta}{\sin\theta} => \frac{1}{\sin\theta\cos\theta} = 2$ (from (i))

9. In the given figure, $DE \parallel BC, AE = a$ unit, $EC = b$ units, $DE = x$ units, and $BC = y$ units. Which of the following is true?

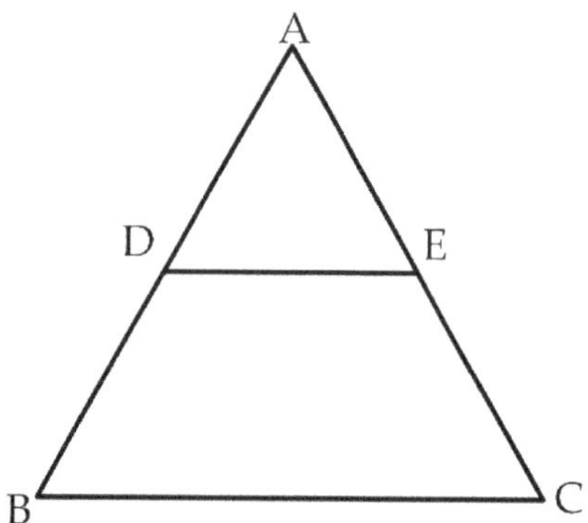

(a) $x = \frac{a+b}{ab}$

(b) $y = \frac{ax}{a+b}$

(c) $x = \frac{ax}{a+b}$

(d) $\frac{x}{y} = \frac{a}{b}$

Solution: Option(c)

$\Delta ADE \sim \Delta ABC$ by *AA* rule [as DE | | BC]

$\frac{AE}{AC} = \frac{DE}{BC} => \frac{a}{a+b} = \frac{x}{y} => x = \frac{ay}{a+b}$

10. ABCD is a trapezium with AD ∥ BC and AD = 4cm. If the diagonals AC and BD intersect each other at O such that $\frac{AO}{OC} = \frac{DO}{OB} = \frac{1}{2}$, then $BC =$

(a) 6cm

(b) 7cm

(c) 8cm

(d) 9cm

Solution: Option(c)

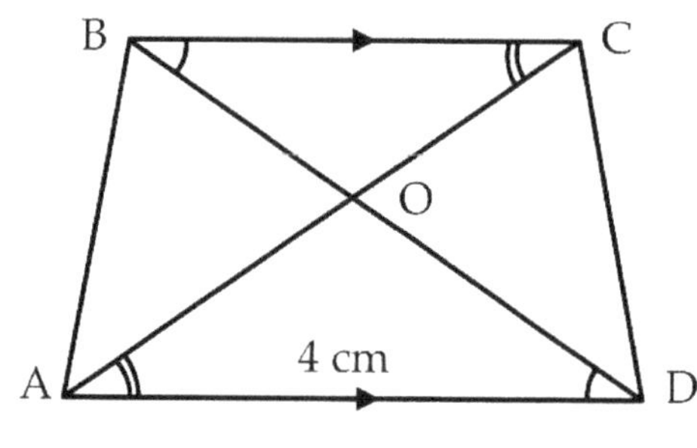

$\Delta AOD \sim \Delta COB$ by *AA* rule

$\frac{AO}{OC} = \frac{OD}{OB} = \frac{AD}{CB}$ [corresponding sides of similar triangles are proportional]

$\frac{1}{2} = \frac{4}{CB} \Rightarrow BC = 8 \text{ cm}$

11. If two tangents inclined at an angle of 60° are drawn to a circle of radius 3cm, then the length of each tangent is equal to

(a) $\frac{3\sqrt{3}}{2}$ cm

(b) 3cm

(c) 6cm

(d) $3\sqrt{3}$cm

Solution: Option(d)

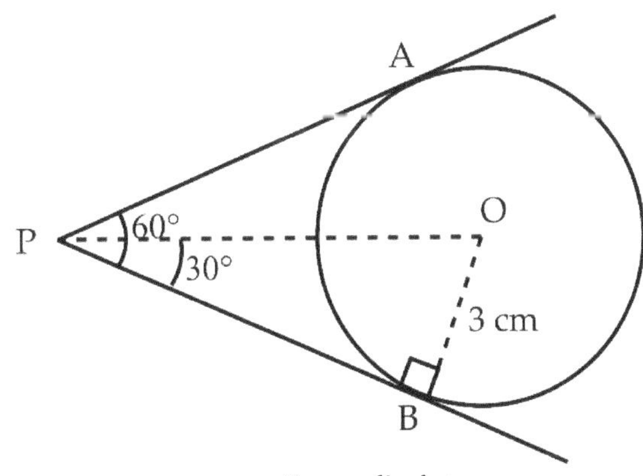

In ΔOBP $\tan 30° = \frac{OB}{PB}$ [$\tan\theta = \frac{\text{Perpendicular}}{\text{Base}}$]

$\frac{1}{\sqrt{3}} = \frac{3}{PB} \Rightarrow PB = 3\sqrt{3}$

12. The area of the circle that can be inscribed in a square of 6cm is

(a) $36\pi \text{ cm}^2$

(b) $18\pi \text{ cm}^2$

(c) $12\pi \text{ cm}^2$

(d) $9\pi \text{ cm}^2$

Solution: Option(d)

Diameter of a circle that can be inscribed in a square of 6 cm = 6 cm

So, radius $r = 3$ cm.

So, the area of the circle = $\pi r^2 = 9\pi \text{ cm}^2$

13. The sum of the length, breadth, and height of a cuboid is $6\sqrt{3}$cm and the length of its diagonal is $2\sqrt{3}$cm. The total surface area of the cuboid is

(a) 48 cm^2

(b) 72cm^2

(c) 96 cm^2

(d) 108 cm^2

Solution: Option(c)

Let length = l cm, breadth = b cm, height = h cm

$l + b + h = 6\sqrt{3}$

length of diagonal of cuboid = $2\sqrt{3}$

$\sqrt{l^2 + b^2 + h^2} = 2\sqrt{3} => l^2 + b^2 + h^2 = 12$

$(l + b + h)^2 = (6\sqrt{3})^2$

$l^2 + b^2 + h^2 + 2(lb + bh + hl) = 108$

$2(lb + bh + hl) = 108 - 12 = 96$ cm^2

14. If the difference between the Mode and Median of the data is 24, then the difference between the median and mean is

(a) 8

(b) 12

(c) 24

(d) 36

Solution: Option(b)

As we know mode = 3 medians − 2 mean

mode − median = 2 medians − 2 mean

24 = 2(Median − mean)

So median − mean = 12.

15. The number of revolutions made by a circular wheel of radius 0.25m in rolling a distance of 11km is

(a) 2800

(b) 4000

(c) 5500

(d) 7000

Solution: Option(d)

No of revolutions = $\frac{\text{distance travelled}}{\text{circumference of wheel}} = \frac{11000 \times 7}{2 \times 22 \times 0.25}$ = 7000 revolutions

16. For the following distribution,

Class	0 – 5	5 – 10	10 – 15	15 – 20	20 – 25
Frequency	10	15	12	20	9

the sum of the lower limits of the median and modal classes is

(a) 15

(b) 25

(c) 30

(d) 35

Solution: Option(b)

Cumulative frequency: 10 25 37 57 68

n = 68 (even) so median class = $(\frac{68}{2})$th = $34th$

and cumulative frequency 37 contains the $34th$ term so the lower limit of median class = 1

the highest frequency is 20 so the lower limit of modal class = 15

so sum = 10 + 15 = 25.

17. Two dice are rolled simultaneously. What is the probability that 6 will come up at once?

(a) 1/6

(b) 7/36

(c) 11/36

(d) 13/36

Solution: Option(c)

Favourable events = $\{(1,6),(2,6),(3,6),(4,6),(5,6),(6,1),(6,2),(6,3),(6,4),(6,5),(6,6)\}$

Number of favourable events = 11

Total number of outcomes in rolling two dice = 36

So the probability of the event P(E) = $\frac{\text{no of favorable outcomes}}{\text{total no of outcomes}} = \frac{11}{36}$

18. If $5\ tan\beta = 4$, then $\frac{5\sin ß - 2COSß}{5\sin ß + 2COSß}$

(a) 1/3

(b) 2/5

(c) 3/5

(d) 6

Solution: Option(a)

$\tan\beta = \frac{4}{5}$

$\frac{5\sin\beta - 2\cos\beta}{5\sin\beta + 2\cos\beta} = \frac{(5\sin\beta - 2\cos\beta) \div \cos\beta}{(5\sin\beta + 2\cos\beta) \div \cos\beta}$ [divide by cos β in both numerator and denominator]

$= \frac{5\tan\beta - 2}{5\tan\beta + 2} = \frac{5(\frac{4}{5}) - 2}{5(\frac{4}{5}) + 2} = \frac{\frac{20-10}{5}}{\frac{20+10}{5}} = \frac{1}{3}$

DIRECTION: In question number 19 and 20, a statement of **assertion (A)** is followed by a statement of **Reason (R).**

Choose the correct option

19. Statement A (Assertion): If a product of two numbers is 5780 and their HCF is 17, then their LCM is 340

Statement R(Reason): HCF is always a factor of LCM

(a) Both assertion (A) and reason (R) are true, and reason (R) is the correct explanation of assertion (A)

(b) Both assertion (A) and reason (R) are true, and reason (R) is not the correct explanation of assertion (A)

(c) Assertion (A) is true, but reason (R) is false.

(d) Assertion (A) is false, but reason (R) is true.

Solution: Option(b)

So, a product of two numbers = HCF × LCM

So, LCM = $\frac{5780}{17} = 340$ [Assertion A is true]

And 17 (HCF) is a factor of $340(LCM)$ [Reason (R) is true]

But Reason(R) is not the explanation of Assertion (A).

20. Statement A (Assertion): If the co-ordinates of the mid-points of the sides AB and AC of ΔABC are $D(3,5)$ and $E(-3,-3)$ respectively, then BC = 20 units

Statement R(Reason): The line joining the midpoints of two sides of a triangle is parallel to the third side and equal to half of it.

(a) Both assertion (A) and reason (R) are true, and reason (R) is the correct explanation of assertion (A)

(b) Both assertion (A) and reason (R) are true, and reason (R) is not the correct explanation of assertion (A)

(c) Assertion (A) is true, but reason(R) is false.

(d) Assertion (A) is false, but reason(R) is true.

Solution: Option(a)

$DE = \sqrt{(3+3)^2 + (5+3)^2} = 10$

And $DE = \frac{1}{2}$ of $20 = 10$ units

SECTION- B

(Section B consists of 5 questions of 2 marks each)

21. If $49x + 51y = 499, 51x + 49y = 501$, then find the value of x and y

Solution:

Given equations are: $49x + 51y = 499$ and $51x + 49y = 501$

Adding the two equations we get: $100x + 100y = 1000 \Rightarrow x + y = 10$ ....(i)

Subtracting the two equations we get: $-2x + 2y = -2 \Rightarrow -x + y = -1$

Solving these two new equations, we get, $x = 11/2$ and $y = 9/2$

22. In the given figure $\frac{AD}{AE} = \frac{AC}{BD}$ and $\angle 1 = \angle 2$ below, show that: $\Delta BAE \sim \Delta CAD$

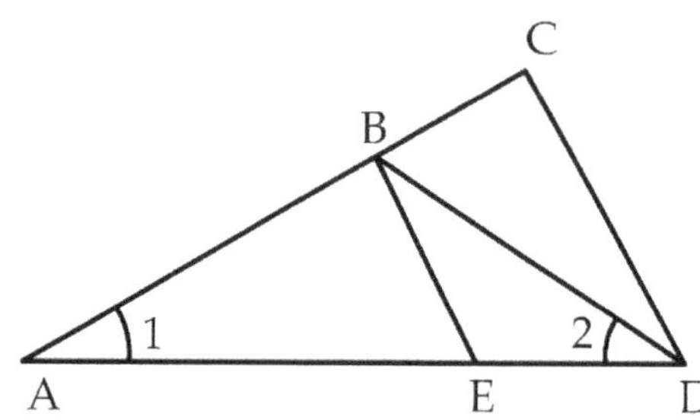

Solution:

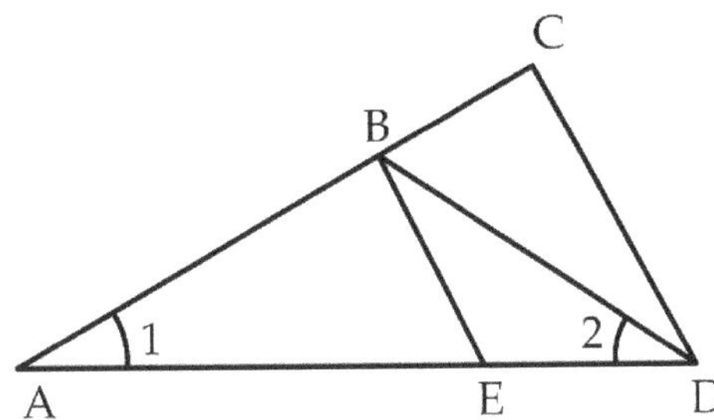

In $\Delta ABC, \angle 1 = \angle 2 \therefore AB = BD$ ....(i)

Given, $\frac{AD}{AE} = \frac{AC}{BD} \rightarrow \frac{AD}{AE} = \frac{AC}{AB}$ [as from(i) AB = BD ....(ii)

So, in ΔBAE and ΔCAD, by equation (ii), $\frac{AD}{AE} = \frac{AC}{AB}$ and $\angle A = \angle A$ (common)

$\therefore \Delta DAE \sim \Delta CAD$ [By SAS similarity criterion]

23. In the given figure, O is the center of the circle. Find ∠AQB, given that PA and PB are tangents to the circle and $\angle APB = 75°$.

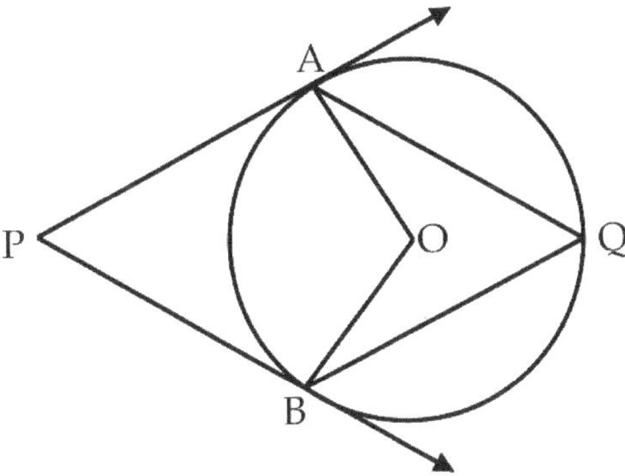

Solution:

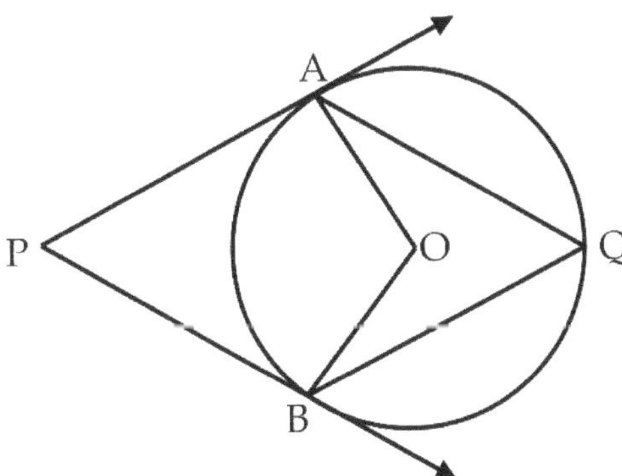

$\angle PAO = \angle PBO = 90°$ (Angle b/w radius and tangent)

$\angle AOB = 105°$ (By angle sum property of a quadrilateral)

So $\angle AQB = \frac{1}{2} \times 105° = 52.5°$

(Angle at the remaining part of the circle is half the angle subtended by the arc at the center)

24. The length of the minute hand of a clock is 6cm. Find the area swept by it when it moves from 7: 05 p.m. to 7: 40 p.m.

OR

In the given figure, arcs have been drawn of radius 7cm each with vertices A, B, C, and D of quadrilateral ABCD as centres. Find the area of the shaded region.

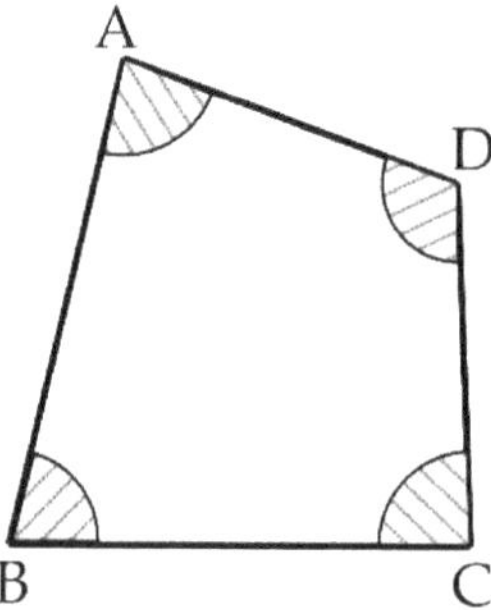

Solution:

We know that, in 60 minutes, the tip of the minute hand moves 360°

In 1 minute, it will move $= \frac{360°}{60} = 6°$

$\therefore$ From 7: 05 pm to 7: 40 pm i.e., 35 min, it will move through $= 35 \times 6° = 210°$

$\therefore$ Area of such sector with angle $210° = \pi r^2 \frac{\theta}{360}$

$$= \frac{22}{7} \times 36 \times \frac{210}{360}$$

$$= 66 \text{ cm}^2$$

OR

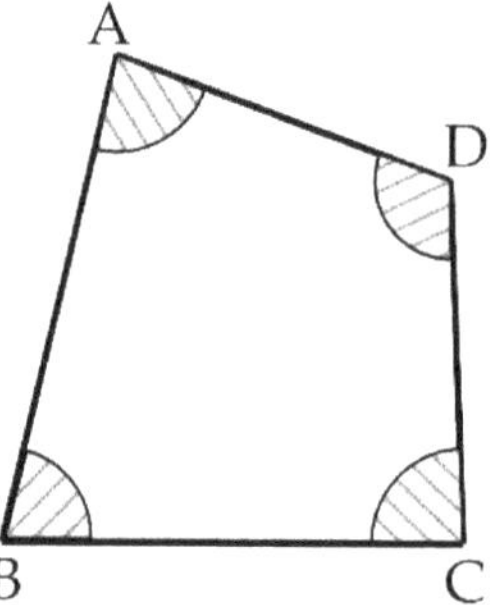

As $\angle A + \angle B + \angle C + \angle D = 360^o$ [sum of interior angles of quadrilateral]

And an area of the sector by angle $\theta = \pi r^2 \frac{\theta}{360}$

Area of shaded region $= \pi r^2 \frac{\angle A}{360} + \pi r^2 \frac{\angle B}{360} + \pi r^2 \frac{\angle C}{360} + \pi r^2 \frac{\angle D}{360}$

$$= \pi r^2 \left(\frac{\angle A}{360} + \frac{\angle B}{360} + \frac{\angle C}{360} + \frac{\angle D}{360}\right)$$

$$= \pi r^2 \left(\frac{\angle A + \angle B + \angle C + \angle D}{360}\right)$$

$$= \pi r^2 \left(\frac{360}{360}\right) = \pi r^2 = \frac{22}{7} \times 49 = 154 \text{ cm}^2$$

25. If $\sin(A + B) = 1$ and $\cos(A - B) = \frac{\sqrt{3}}{2}, 0° < A + B \leq 90°$ and $A > B$, then find the measures of angles A and B.

OR

Find an acute $\frac{cos\theta - sin\theta}{cos\theta + sin\theta} = \frac{1-\sqrt{3}}{1+\sqrt{3}}$ angle θ when

Solution:

$\sin(A + B) = 1 = \sin 90, \text{so } A + B = 90$ .... (i)

$\cos(A - B) = \frac{\sqrt{3}}{2}, = \cos 30, \text{so } A - B = 30$ ....(ii)

From (i) & (ii) $2\angle A = 120$ so $\angle A = 60°$

Substitute the value of ∠A in equation (i) we get $\angle B = 30°$

OR

Given that: $\frac{\sin\theta - \cos\theta}{\sin\theta + \cos\theta} = \frac{1-\sqrt{3}}{1+\sqrt{3}}$

$\sin 0 \mid \sqrt{3}\sin 0 \quad \cos 0 \quad \sqrt{3}\cos 0 = \sin\theta \quad \sqrt{3}\sin\theta \mid \cos\theta \quad \sqrt{3}\cos\theta$

$$\sqrt{3}\sin\theta - \cos\theta = -\sqrt{3}\sin\theta + \cos(\theta)$$

$$\sqrt{3}\sin\theta + \sqrt{3}\sin\theta = \cos(\theta) + \cos(\theta)$$

$$2\sqrt{3}\sin\theta = 2\cos(\theta)$$

$\sqrt{3}\sin\theta = \cos\theta \Rightarrow \frac{\sin\theta}{\cos\theta} = \frac{1}{\sqrt{3}} \rightarrow \tan\theta = \frac{1}{\sqrt{3}} = \tan 30^{0}$ so $\theta = 30^{0}$

SECTION -C

(Section C consists of 6 questions of 3 marks each)

26. Given that $\sqrt{3}$ is irrational, prove that $5 + 2\sqrt{3}$ is irrational.

Solution:

Let us assume $5 + 2\sqrt{3}$is rational, then it must be in the form of $\frac{p}{q}$

[where p and q are co-prime integers and $q \neq 0$]

i.e., $5 + 2\sqrt{3} = \frac{p}{q}$ So $\sqrt{3} = \frac{p-5q}{2q}$ ....(i)

Since $p, q, 5$, and 2 are integers and $q \neq 0, \frac{p-5q}{2q}$ is rational but $\sqrt{3}$ which is irrational. This is not possible. This contradiction has arisen due to our wrong assumption that $5 + 2\sqrt{3}$ is rational. So, $5 + 2\sqrt{3}$ is irrational.

27. If the zeroes of the polynomial $x^2 + px + q$ is double in value to the zeroes of the polynomial $2x^2 - 5x - 3$, then find the values of p and q.

Solution:

Let α and β be the zeros of the polynomial $2x^2 - 5x - 3$

Then the sum of zeroes: $\alpha + \beta = \frac{5}{2}$ and

product of zeroes: $\alpha\beta = -\frac{3}{2}$.

Let 2α and 2β be the zeros $x^2 + px + q$, then

$2\alpha + 2\beta = -p \rightarrow 2(\alpha + \beta) = -p$

$2 \times \frac{5}{2} = -p$ So $p = -5$ and $2\alpha \times 2\beta = q \rightarrow 4\,\alpha\beta = q$

So $q = 4\,x - \frac{3}{2} = -6$

So, $p = -5$ and $q = -6$

28. A train covered a certain distance at a uniform speed. If the train would have been 6 km/h faster, it would have taken 4 hours less than the scheduled time. And, if the train were slower by 6 km/hr; it would have taken 6 hours more than the scheduled time. Find the length of the journey.

OR

Anuj had some chocolates, and he divided them into two lots A and B. He sold the first lot at the rate of ₹2 for 3 chocolates and the second lot at the rate of ₹1 per chocolate and got a total of ₹400. If he had sold the first lot at the rate of ₹1 per chocolate, and the second lot at the rate of ₹4 for 5 chocolates, his total collection would have been ₹460.
Find the total number of chocolates he had.

Solution:

Let the actual speed of the train be x km/hr and let the actual time taken by y hours. The distance covered is xy km [distance = speed × time]

when the speed is $(x + 6)$km/hr, the time of journey is $(y - 4)$ hours.

∴ Distance covered: $(x + 6)(y - 4) = xy$

$\Rightarrow \quad xy - 4x + 6y - 24 = xy$

$\Rightarrow \quad -4x + 6y - 24 = 0$

$\Rightarrow \quad -2x + 3y - 12 = 0$

$\Rightarrow \quad -2x + 3y = 12$ ....(i)

when speed is $(x - 6)km/hr$, the time of journey is $(y + 6)$ hours.

∴ Distance covered: $(x - 6)(y + 6) = xy$

$\Rightarrow \quad xy + 6x - 6y - 36 = xy$

$\Rightarrow \quad 6x - 6y - 36 = 0$

$\Rightarrow \quad x - y - 6 = 0$

$\Rightarrow \quad x - y = 6$ ....(ii)

$x = 6 + y$ and put this value in equation (i)

$-2(6 + y) + 3y = 12$

$-12 - 2y + 3y = 12 \rightarrow y = 24$

So $x = 6 + 24$

$=> 30$

So distance = (30 × 24)km = 720km.

Hence, the length of the journey is 720km.

OR

Let the number of chocolates in lot A be x

And let the number of chocolates in lot B be y

$\therefore$ total number of chocolates $= x + y$

Price of 1 chocolate = $Rs\ \frac{2}{3}$, so for x chocolates = $\frac{2x}{3}$

price of y chocolates at the rate of Rs. 1 per chocolate = y.

$\therefore$ by the given condition $\frac{2x}{3} + y = 400 \Rightarrow 2x + 3y = 1200$ ....(i)

Similarly, $x + \frac{4y}{5} = 460 \Rightarrow 5x + 4y = 2300$ .... (ii)

Multiply (i) by 4 and (ii) by 3 and subtract we get

$$8x + 12y = 4800$$
$$15x + 12y = 6900$$
$$8x - 15x = 4800 - 6900$$
$$-7x = -2100$$
$$x = 300$$

Substitute x in equation (i) we get y = 200

$\therefore x + y = 300 + 200 = 500$ So, Anuj had 500 chocolates.

29. Prove the following -

$$\frac{\tan^3\theta}{1+\tan^2\theta} + \frac{\cot^3\theta}{1+\cot^2\theta} = \sec\theta\ \text{cosec}\ \theta - 2\sin\theta\cos\theta$$

Solution:

LHS:

$$\frac{\tan^3\theta}{1+\tan^2\theta} + \frac{\cot^3\theta}{1+\cot^2\theta}$$
$$= \frac{\tan^3\theta}{\sec^2\theta} + \frac{\cot^3\theta}{\text{cosec}^2\theta}$$
$$= \frac{\sin^3\theta}{\cos^3\theta\ \sec^2\theta} + \frac{\cos^3\theta}{\sin^3\theta\ \text{cosec}^2\theta}$$
$$= \frac{\sin^3\theta}{\cos\theta} + \frac{\cos^3\theta}{\sin\theta} = \frac{\sin^4\theta + \cos^4\theta}{\sin\theta\cos\theta}$$
$$= \frac{\sin^4\theta + \cos^4\theta + 2\sin^2\theta\cos^2\theta - 2\sin^2\theta\cos^2\theta}{\sin\theta\cos\theta}$$
$$= \frac{(\sin^2\theta + \sin^2\theta)^2 - 2\sin^2\theta 2\cos^2\theta}{\sin\theta\cos\theta}$$
$$= \frac{1 - 2\sin^2\theta 2\cos^2\theta}{\sin\theta\cos\theta} \qquad [\sin^2\theta + \sin^2\theta = 1]$$
$$= \frac{1}{\sin\theta\cos\theta} - \frac{2\sin^2\theta 2\cos^2\theta}{\sin\theta\cos\theta} = \text{cosec}\ \theta\sec\theta - 2\sin\theta\cos\theta \quad \text{RHS.}$$

30. Prove that a parallelogram circumscribing a circle is a rhombus

OR

In the figure XY and X'Y' are two parallel tangents to a circle with center O and another tangent AB with a point of contact C interesting XY at A and X'Y' at B, what is the measure of $\angle AOB$.

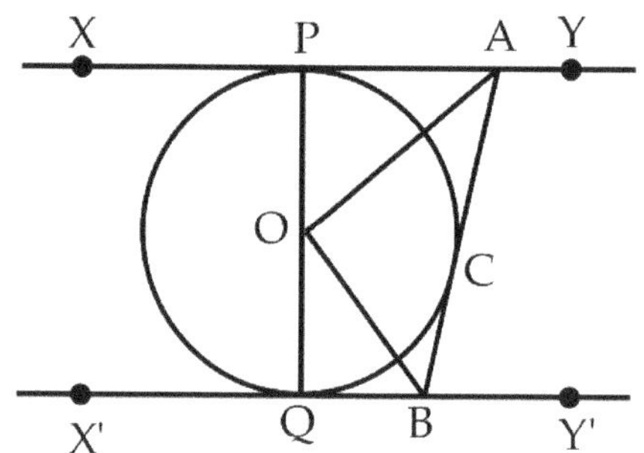

Solution:

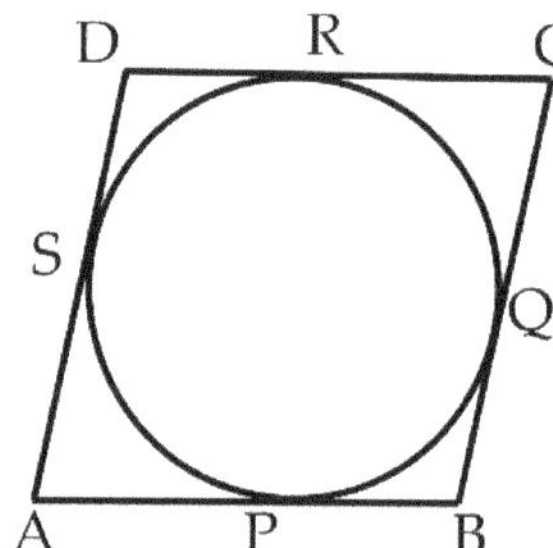

Let ABCD be the parallelogram circumscribing the circle with center O, such that AB, BC, CD, and DA touch the circle at points P, Q, R, and S respectively.

We know that the tangents drawn to a circle from an exterior point are equal in length.

$\therefore AP = AS$ .... (i)

$BP = BQ$ .... (ii)

$CR = CQ$ .... (iii)

$DR = DS$ .... (iv)

Adding (1), (2), (3), and (4) we get:

$$AP + BP + CR + DR = AS + BQ + CQ + DS$$

$$(AP + BP) + (CR + DR) = (AS + DS) + (BQ + CQ)$$

$\therefore$ $AB + CD = AD + BC$ ....(v)

Since $AB = DC$ and $AD = BC$ (opposite sides of parallelogram ABCD)

putting in (5) we get, $2AB = 2AD$ *or* $AB = AD$.

$\therefore$ $AB = BC = DC = AD$

If adjacent sides of a parallelogram are equal, it is a rhombus

Or

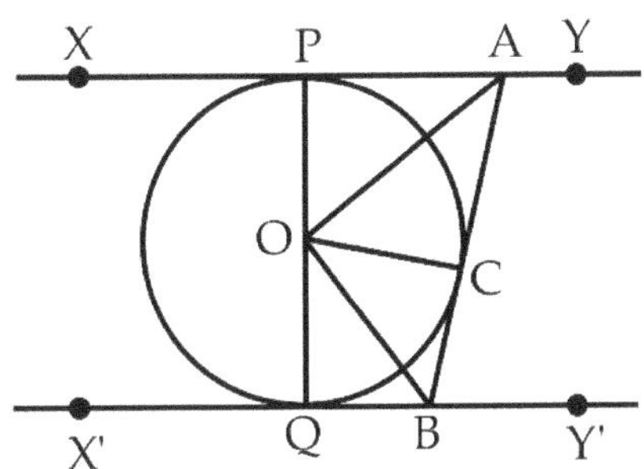

Join OC

In ΔOPA and ΔOCA

$OP = OC$ [radii]

$AP = AC$ [tangents from external point]

$OA = OA$ [common]

$\Delta OPA \cong \Delta OCA$ [SSS congruency rule]

Hence $\angle POA = \angle COA$ [cpct]

Similarly, ΔOQB ≅ ΔOCB [SSS congruency rule]

Hence $\angle QOB = \angle COB$ [cpct]

$$\angle POA + \angle COA + \angle QOB + \angle COB = 180^o$$

$$2\angle COA + 2\angle COB = 180^o$$

$$2(\angle COA + \angle COB) = 180^o$$

$$\angle AOB = 90^o$$ Hence proved

31. Two coins are tossed simultaneously. What is the probability of getting

(i) At least one head?

(ii) At most one tail?

(iii) A head and a tail?

Solution:

When two coins are tossed simultaneously total possible outcomes are:

$\{(H,H),(H,T),(T,H),(T,T)\}$

Total no of outcomes = 4

P(E)=$\frac{\text{No.of favorable outcomes}}{\text{total no of outcomes}}$

(i) P (at least one head) = $\{(H,H),(H,T),(T,H)\} = \frac{3}{4}$

(ii) P (at most one tail) = $\{(H,H),(T,H),(T,H)\} = \frac{3}{4}$

(iii) P (A head and a tail) = $\{(H,T),(T,H)\} = \frac{2}{4} = \frac{1}{2}$

SECTION -D

(Section D consists of 4 questions of 5 marks each)

32. To fill a swimming pool two pipes are used. If the pipe of a larger diameter is used for 4 hours and the pipe of a smaller diameter for 9 hours, only half of the pool can be filled. Find, how long it would take for each pipe to fill the pool separately if the pipe of smaller diameter takes 10 hours more than the pipe of larger diameter to fill the pool.

OR

In a flight of 600km, an aircraft was slowed down due to bad weather. Its average speed for the trip was reduced by 200 km/hr from its usual speed and the time of the flight increased by 30 min. Find the scheduled duration of the flight.

Solution:

Let the time taken by the larger pipe alone to fill the tank = x hours

So, the time is taken by the smaller pipe = $(x + 10)$ hours

Water filled by the larger diameter pipe for 4 hours = $\frac{4}{x}$ liters

Water filled by the smaller diameter pipe for 9 hours = $\frac{9}{x+10}$ liters

So $\frac{4}{x}+\frac{9}{x+10}=\frac{1}{2}$

$\frac{4x+40+9x}{x(x+10)}=\frac{1}{2}$

=> $x^2 + 10x = 26x + 80$

=> $x^2 + 10x - 26x - 80 = 0$

=> $x^2 - 16x - 80 = 0$

=> $x^2 - 20x + 4x - 80 = 0$

=> $x(x - 20) + 4(x - 20) = 0$

=> $(x - 20)(x + 4) = 0$

=> $x = 20, -4$

time can't be negative

so time is taken by smaller diameter pipe = 20 hours

time is taken by larger diameter pipe = 30 hours

OR

Distance travelled = 600km

Let the average speed $= x$ km/hr

Reduced speed = $(x - 200)$ km/hr

Using the formula time = $\frac{\text{distance}}{\text{speed}}$

Therefore $\frac{600}{x-200}-\frac{600}{x}=\frac{1}{2}$

$\Rightarrow \quad 600\left[\frac{x-x+20}{(x-200)x}\right]=\frac{1}{2}$

$\Rightarrow \quad x^2-200x-24000=0$

$\Rightarrow \quad (x-600)(x+400)=0$

$\Rightarrow \quad x = 600\text{km/hr}$ or $x = -400\text{km/hr}$

[this is not possible as speed cannot be negative]

Therefore, the normal duration of flight = $\frac{600}{600}$ = 1hr

33. Prove that if a line is drawn parallel to one side of a triangle intersecting the other two sides in distinct points, then the other two sides are divided in the same ratio.
Using the above theorem proves that a line through the point of intersection of the diagonals and parallel to the base of the trapezium divides the non-parallel sides in the same ratio.

Solution:

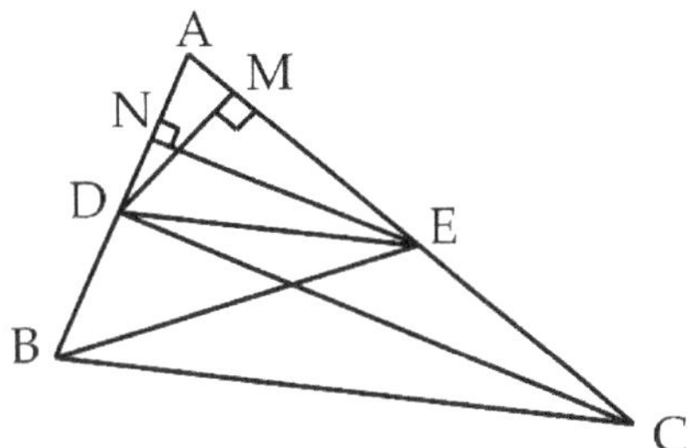

Let ABC is the triangle in which DE || BC so that it meets AB at D and AC at E.

To prove: $\frac{AD}{DB} = \frac{AE}{EC}$

Construction:

Drop $DM \perp AE$ and $EN \perp AD$

Area of triangle $= \frac{1}{2} \times$ base $\times$ height

Area $(\Delta ADE) = \frac{1}{2} \times AD \times EN$ ....(i)

Area $(\Delta DBE) = \frac{1}{2} \times BD \times EN$ ....(ii)

$\frac{\text{Area }(\Delta ADE)}{\text{Area }(\Delta DBE)} = \frac{\frac{1}{2} \times AD \times EN}{\frac{1}{2} \times BD \times EN} = \frac{AD}{DE}$ ....(iii)

Area $(\Delta ADE) = \frac{1}{2} \times AE \times DM$ ....(i)

Area $(\Delta ECD) = \frac{1}{2} \times EC \times DM$ ....(ii)

$\frac{\text{Area }(\Delta ADE)}{\text{Area }(\Delta ECD)} = \frac{\frac{1}{2} \times AE \times DM}{\frac{1}{2} \times EC \times DM} = \frac{AE}{EC}$ ....(iii)

As area (ΔDBE) = area (ΔECD) [triangles on the same base and between the same parallel lines are equal in area.]

$\frac{\text{Area }(\Delta ADE)}{\text{Area }(\Delta DBE)} = \frac{\text{Area }(\Delta ADE)}{\text{Area }(\Delta ECD)}$

So $\frac{AD}{BD} = \frac{AE}{EC}$

Hence proved

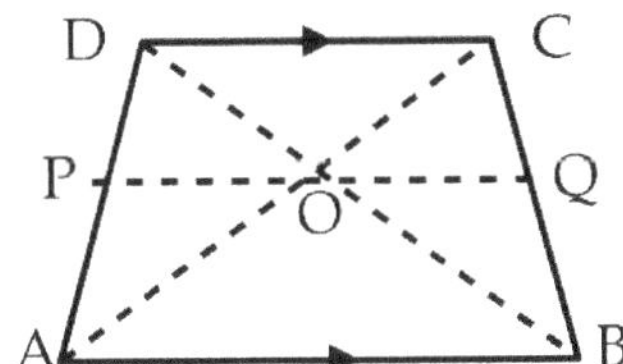

Let ABCD is a trapezium, $DC \parallel AB$ and $PQ \parallel AB$ so $PQ \parallel DC$

To prove: $\frac{DP}{PA} = \frac{CQ}{QB}$

Construction: join AC and BD, and meets PQ at O.

Proof:

In ΔABC, we have $OQ \parallel AB$

So $\frac{CO}{OA} = \frac{CQ}{QB}$ [BPT] ....(i)

In ΔADC, we have $PO \parallel AB$

So $\frac{CO}{OA} = \frac{DP}{PA}$ [BPT] ....(ii)

From (i) and (ii) we get

$\frac{DP}{PA} = \frac{CQ}{QB}$ Hence proved.

34. Due to heavy floods in the state, thousands were rendered homeless. 50 schools collectively decided to provide a place and canvas for 1500 tents and share the whole expenditure equally. The lower part of each tent is cylindrical with a base radius of 2.8 m and height of 3.5 m and the upper part is conical with the same base radius but of height 2.1 m. If the canvas used to make the tents costs ₹120 per m², find the amount shared by each school to set up the tents.

OR

There are two identical solid cubical boxes of sides 7cm. From the top face of the first cube, a hemisphere of diameter equal to the side of the cube is scooped out. This hemisphere is inverted and placed on the top of the second cube's surface to form a dome. Find

(i) The ratio of the total surface area of the two new solids formed

(ii) Volume of each new solid formed.

Solution:

The radius of the base of the cylinder = radius of the base of the cone = $2.8m$

Height of cylinder (h) = $3.5\ m$

Height of cone(H) = $2.1\ m$

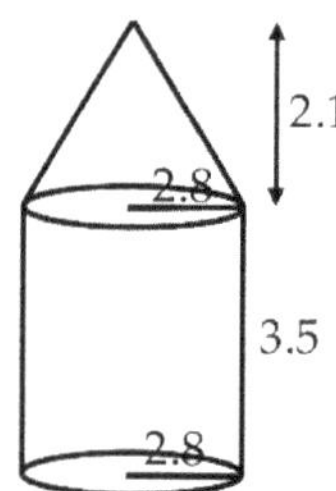

Slant height of cone (l) $= \sqrt{H^2 + r^2}$

$= \sqrt{2.1^2 + 2.8^2}$

$= \sqrt{4.41 + 7.84}$

$= \sqrt{12.25} = 3.5\ m$

Area of canvas required to make tent = CSA of cone + CSA of cylinder

$= \pi rl + 2\pi rH$

$= \frac{22}{7} \times 2.8 \times 3.5 + 2 \times \frac{22}{7} \times 2.8 \times 3.5$

$= 30.8 + 61.6 = 92.4\ \text{cm}^2$

Area of 1500 such tent = $1500 \times 92.4 = 138600\ cm^2$

Cost of a tent at Rs. 120 per square m. = $138600 \times 120 = Rs. 16{,}632{,}000$

Share of each school to set up the tents = $16{,}632{,}000/2 = Rs. 332{,}640$Ans.

OR

First Solid

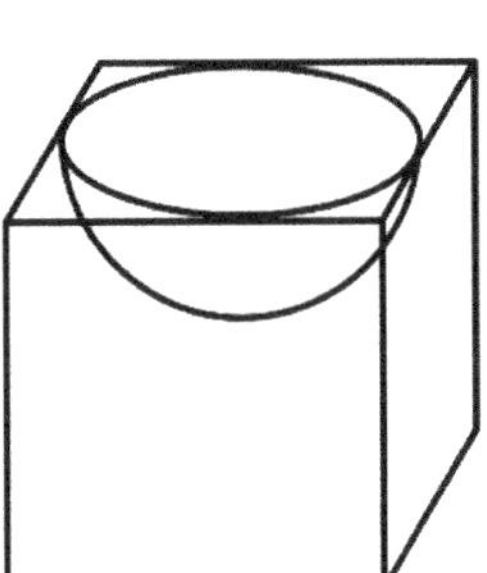

Second Solid

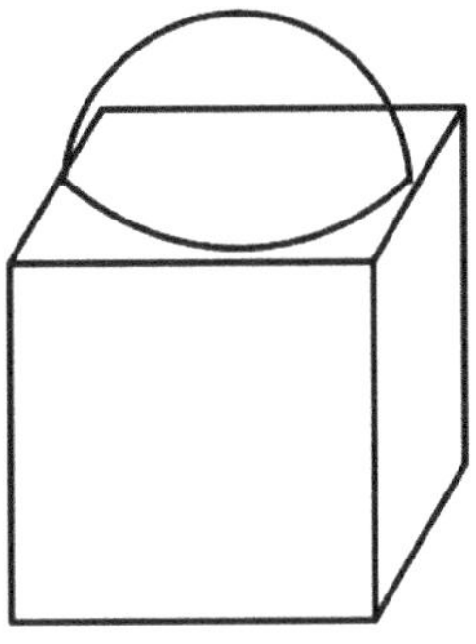

Side of cube = 7 cm

Radius of hemisphere = $7/2 = 3.5$ cm

Surface area first solid (after scooped out) = $6\,(\text{side})^2 - \pi r^2 + 2\pi r^2 = 6\,(\text{side})^2 + \pi r^2$

$$= 6\,(7)^2 + \frac{22}{7}(3.5)^2 = 294 + 38.5$$

$$= 332.5\ cm^2$$

So ratio of total surface area of both solids = $332.5 : 332.5 = 1 : 1$

Volume of first new solid = volume of a cube – a volume of a hemisphere

$$= 7^3 - \frac{2}{3} \times \frac{22}{7} \times 3.5^3$$

$$= 343 - \frac{539}{6}$$

$$= \frac{1519}{6}$$

$$= 253\frac{1}{6}\ cm^3$$

Volume of first new solid = volume of cube + volume of a hemisphere

$$= 7^3 + \frac{2}{3} \times \frac{22}{7} \times 3.5^3$$

$$= 343 + \frac{539}{6} = \frac{2597}{6}$$

$$= 432\frac{5}{6}\ \text{cm}^3$$

35. The median of the following data is 525. Find the values of x and y, if the total frequency is 100

Class interval	Frequency
0 – 100	2
100 – 200	5
200 – 300	x
300 – 400	12
400 – 500	17

500 – 600	20
600 – 700	y
700 – 800	9
800 – 900	7
900 – 1000	4

Solution:

Class Interval	Frequency	Cumulative Frequency
0 – 100	2	2
100 – 200	5	7
200 – 300	x	$7 + x$
300 – 400	12	$19 + x$
400 – 500	17	$36 + x$
500 – 600	20	$56 + x$
600 – 700	y	$56 + x + y$
700 – 800	9	$65 + x + y$
800 – 900	7	$72 + x + y$
900 – 1000	4	$76 + x + y$
	$N = 76 + x + y$	

Given, Median = 525

So median class = 500 – 600

$$76 + x + y = 100$$

$$x + y = 24 \qquad \text{..................(i)}$$

$$\mathrm{L} = 500, \mathrm{h} = 200 - 100 = 100, \mathrm{f} = 20, \mathrm{cf} = 36 + \mathrm{x}$$

$$\text{Median} = \mathrm{l} + \frac{\frac{\mathrm{N}}{2} - \mathrm{cf}}{\mathrm{f}} \times \mathrm{h}$$

$$525 = 500 + \frac{50-(36-\mathrm{x})}{20} \times 100$$

$$\Rightarrow 525 - 500 = 50 - 36 + x$$

$$\Rightarrow \quad x = 25 - 14 = 9$$

Substitute x in (i) we get $y = 24 - 9 = 15$

So, value of $x = 9$ and $y = 15$

36. A tiling or tessellation of a flat surface is the covering of a plane using one or more geometric shapes, called tiles, with no overlaps and no gaps. Historically, tessellations were used in ancient Rome and in Islamic art. You may find tessellation patterns on floors, walls, paintings, etc. Shown below is a tiled floor in the archaeological Museum of Seville, made using squares, triangles, and hexagons.

A craftsman thought of making a floor pattern after being inspired by the above design. To ensure accuracy in his work, he made the pattern on the Cartesian plane. He used regular octagons, squares, and triangles for his floor tessellation pattern

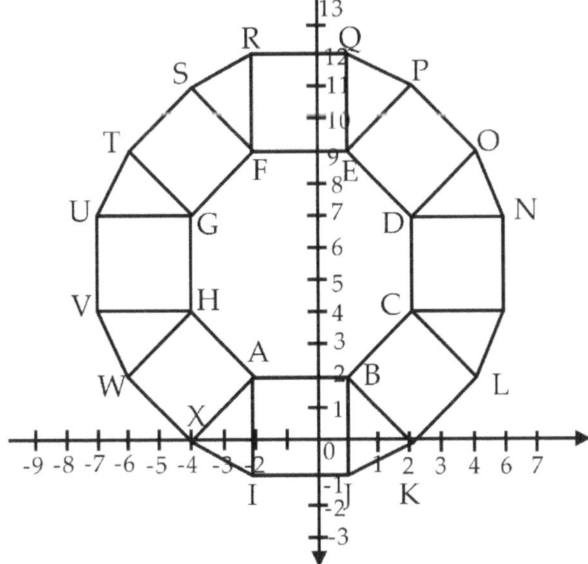

Use the above figure to answer the questions that follow:

(i) What is the length of the line segment joining points B and F?

(ii) The Centre 'Z' of the figure will be the point of intersection of the diagonals of quadrilateral WXOP. Then what are the coordinates of Z?

(iii) What are the coordinates of the point on the y-axis equidistant from A and G?

OR

What is the area of Trapezium AFGH?

Solution:

(i) Co-ordinates of $B\ (1, 2)$

Co-ordinates of $F\ (-2, 9)$

$$\text{Length of line segment BF} = \sqrt{(x_1 - x_2)^2 + (y_1 - y_2)^2}$$

$$= \sqrt{(1+2)^2 + (2-9)^2}$$

$$= \sqrt{9+49} = \sqrt{58} \text{ units}$$

(ii)

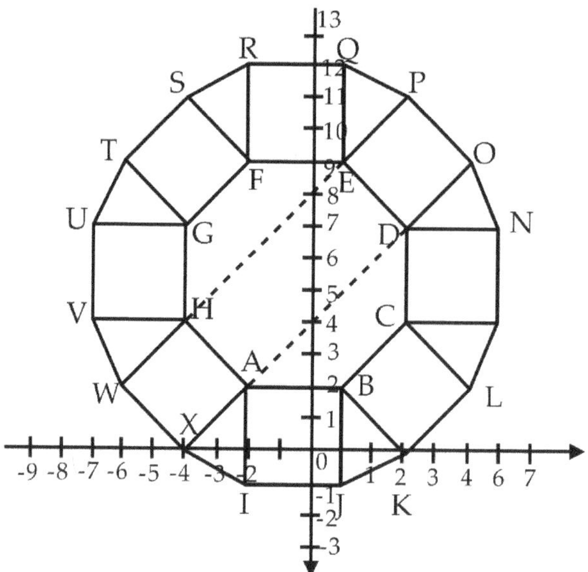

W $(-6, 2)$, X$(-4, 0)$, O$(5, 9)$ and P$(3, 11)$ forms a ||gm.

And the point of intersection of ||gm is the mid-point of any diagonal. So required point Z is the

mid-point of XP: $(x, y) = (\frac{x1+x2}{2}, \frac{y1+y2}{2})$

$= (\frac{-4+3}{2}, \frac{0+11}{2}) = (\frac{-1}{2}, \frac{11}{2})$

(iii) Co-ordinates of $A(-2, 2)$ and coordinates of $G\ (-4, 7)$

Let the point of the y-axis is P $(0, y)$ which is equidistant from A and G

$PA = PG$

$\sqrt{(0+2)^2 + (y-2)^2} = \sqrt{(0+4)^2 + (y-7)^2}$

$4 + y^2 - 4y + 4 = 16 + y^2 - 14y + 49$ [squaring both sides]

$-4y + 8 = -14y + 65$

$10y = 65 - 8 = 57$

$y = 5.7$, so, the required point P $(0, 5.7)$

OR

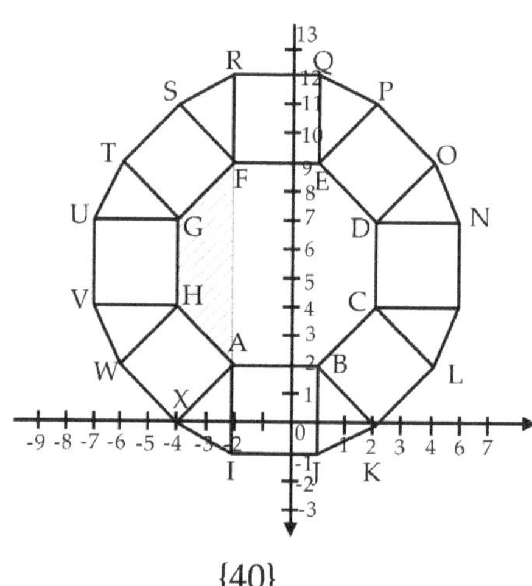

Area of trapezium $= \frac{1}{2}(sum\ of\ parallel\ sides)height$

$AF \parallel GH,$ AF = 9 - 2 = 7 units

GH = 7 - 4 = 3 units

Ans height of trapezium = 2 units

Area of trapezium $= \frac{1}{2}(7+3)2 =$ 10 square units

37. The school auditorium was to be constructed to accommodate at least 1500 people. The chairs are to be placed in a concentric circular arrangement in such a way that each succeeding circular row has 10 seats more than the previous one.

(i) If the first circular row has 30 seats, how many seats will be there in the 10th row?

(ii) For 1500 seats in the auditorium, how many rows need to be there?

OR

If 1500 seats are to be arranged in the auditorium, how many seats are still left to be put after $10th$ row?

(iii) If there were 17 rows in the auditorium, how many seats will be there in the middle row?

Solution:

(i) Seats in first row (a) = 30

Common difference (d) = 10

So seats in 10th row (T_{10}) $= a + 9d = 30 + 9 \times 10 = 120 Ans$

(ii) $s_n = \frac{n}{2}[2a + (n-1)d]$

$$1500 = \frac{n}{2}[2 \times 30 + (n-1)10]$$

$$3000 = 50n + 10n^2$$

$$n^2 + 5n - 300 = 0$$

$$n^2 + 20n - 15n - 300 = 0$$

$$n\,(n+20) - 15(n+20) = 0$$

$$(n+20)(n-15) = 0$$

$n = -20$ (not possible), 15

no. of rows = 15

No. of seats till the 10th row

$s_n = \frac{n}{2}[2a + (n-1)d]$

$s_{10} = \frac{10}{2}[60 + 90] = 750$

So the number of seats left = 1500 - 750 = 750 seats

(iii) If no of rows = 17

Then the middle row = $\frac{(17+1)}{2}$ = $9th$ row

So no of seats in $9th$ row $(T_9) = a + 8d$

$= 30 + 8 \times 10$

$= 110$ seats

38. We all have seen airplanes flying in the sky but might have not thought of how they reach the correct destination. Air Traffic Control (ATC) is a service provided by ground-based air traffic controllers who direct aircraft on the ground and through a given section of controlled airspace and can provide advisory services to aircraft in non-controlled airspace. All this air traffic is managed and regulated by using various concepts based on coordinate geometry and trigonometry.

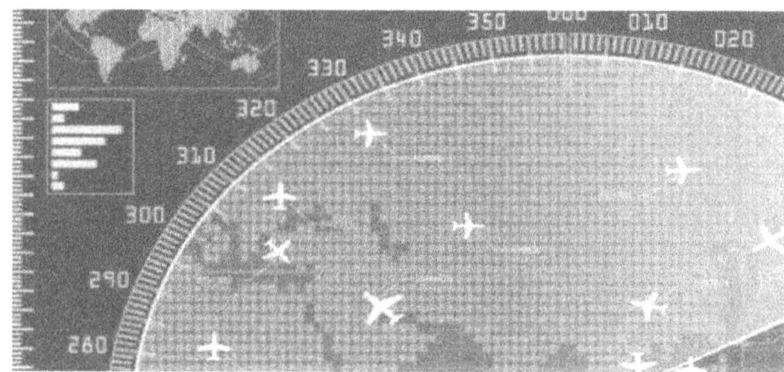

At a given instance, ATC finds that the angle of elevation of an airplane from a point on the ground is 60°. After a flight of 30 seconds, it is observed that the angle of elevation changes to 30°. The height of the plane remains constant at $3000\sqrt{3}$ m. Use the above information to answer the questions that follow-

(i) Draw a neat, labelled figure to show the above situation diagrammatically.

(ii) What is the distance travelled by plane in 30 seconds?

OR

Keeping the height constant, during the above flight, it was observed that after $15(\sqrt{3} - 1)$ seconds, the angle of elevation changed to 45°. How much is the distance travelled in that duration?

What is the speed of the plane in km/hr?

Solution:

(i)

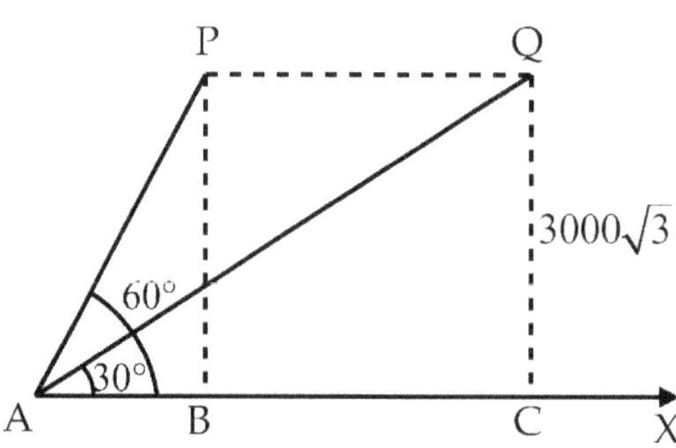

P and Q are the two positions of the plane flying at a height of $3000\sqrt{3}$ m.

A is the point of observation.

(ii) In $\triangle$ PAB, $\tan 60^\circ = \frac{PB}{AB}$

Or $\sqrt{3} = \frac{3000\sqrt{3}}{AB}$

So $AB = 3000$ m

$\tan 30^\circ = \frac{QC}{AC}$

$\frac{1}{\sqrt{3}} = \frac{3000\sqrt{3}}{AC}$

AC = 9000 mdistance covered = 9000 − 3000

= 6000 m.

OR

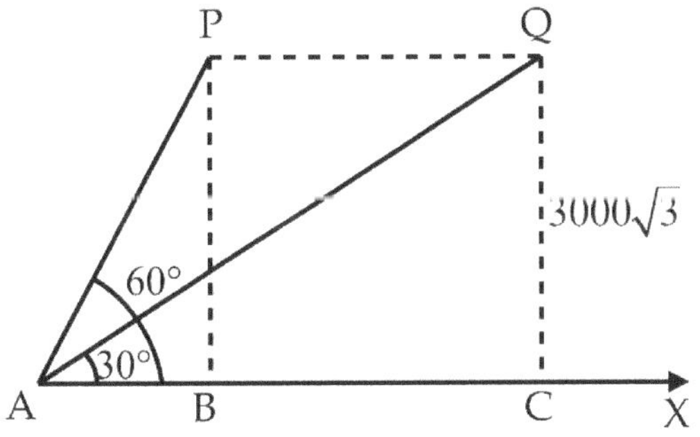

P Q

3000√3

60°

30°

A B C X

In $\triangle$ PAB, $\tan 60^\circ = PB/AB$

Or $\sqrt{3} = 3000\sqrt{3}/AB$

So $AB = 3000$ m

$\tan 45^\circ = RD/AD$

$1 = 3000\sqrt{3}/AD$

$AD = 3000\sqrt{3}$ m

distance covered $= 3000\sqrt{3} - 3000$

$= 3000(\sqrt{3} - 1)$m.

(iii) Speed = 6000/30

= 200 m/s

= 200 × 3600/1000

= 720 km/hr

Alternatively: speed $= \frac{3000(\sqrt{3}-1)}{15(\sqrt{3}-1)}$

= 200 m/s

= 200 × 3600/1000

= 720 km/hr

Class- X Session- 2022-23

SAMPLE PAPER-1

Sample Question Paper

Time Allowed: 3 Hrs. **Maximum Marks: 80**

General Instructions:

1. This Question Paper has 5 Sections A-E.
2. Section **A** has 20 MCQs carrying 1 mark each
3. Section **B** has 5 questions carrying 02 marks each.
4. Section **C** has 6 questions carrying 03 marks each.
5. Section **D** has 4 questions carrying 05 marks each.
6. Section **E** has 3 case-based integrated units of assessment (04 marks each) with subparts of the values of 1, 1, and 2 marks each respectively.
7. All Questions are compulsory. However, an internal choice in 2 Qs of 5 marks, 2 Qs of 3 marks, and 2 Questions of 2 marks has been provided. An internal choice has been provided in the 2marks questions of Section E
8. Draw neat figures wherever required. Take π =22/7 wherever required if not stated

SECTION -A

(Section A consists of 20 questions of 1 mark each)

1. Given that HCF (253,440) = 11 and LCM (253,440) = 253 × R. The value of R is:

(a) 400

(b) 40

(c) 440

(d) 253

Answer. (b)

2. If α, β are the zeros of polynomial $f(x) = x^2 - p(x + 1) - c$, then $(\alpha + 1)(\beta + 1) =$

(a) $c - 1$

(b) $1 - c$

(c) c

(d) $1 + c$

Answer. (b)

3. The pair of linear equations $x - 2y = 5$ and $2x - 4y = 1$ have:

(a) Many solutions

(b) No solution

(c) One solution

(d) Two solutions

Answer. (b)

4. Which of the following is not a quadratic equation?
(a) $2(x-2)^2 = 4x^2 - 2x + 1$
(b) $2x - x^2 = x^2 - 5$
(c) $(\sqrt{2}x + \sqrt{3})^2 + x^2 = 3x^2 - 5x$
(d) $(x^2 + 1)^2 = x^4 + 3 + 4x^2$
Answer. (c)

5. In Fig., if DE || BC, then x equals:

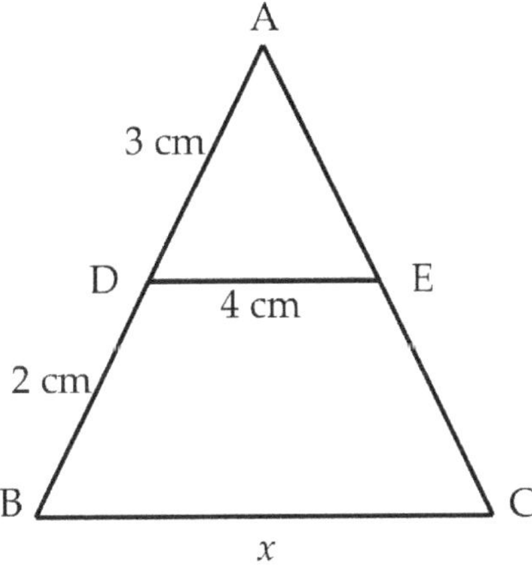

(a) 3cm
(b) 2cm
(c) 4cm
(d) 6.7cm
Answer. (d)

6. The point on the x-axis which is equidistant from points $(-1, 0)$ and $(5, 0)$ is:
(a) $(0, 2)$
(b) $(2, 0)$
(c) $(3, 0)$
(d) $(0, 3)$
Answer. (b)

7. A line that is perpendicular to the radius of the circle through the point of contact is called a:
(a) Tangent
(b) Chord
(c) Normal
(d) Segment
Answer. (a)

8. A ladder 15m long just reaches the top of a vertical wall. If the ladder makes an angle of 60° with the wall, then the height of the wall is:
(a) $15\sqrt{3}$m
(b) $\frac{15\sqrt{3}}{2}$m

(c) $\frac{15}{2}$m

(d) 15m

Answer. (b)

9. If the difference between the circumference and the radius of a circle is 37cm, then using $\pi = \frac{22}{7}$, the circumference (in cm) of the circle is:

(a) 154

(b) 44

(c) 14

(d) 7

Answer. (b)

10. $\triangle$ ABC is such that AB = 3cm, BC = 2cm, and CA = 2.5cm. If $\triangle$ DEF ~$\triangle$ ABC andEF = 4cm, then the perimeter of $\triangle$ DEF is

(a) 5cm

(b) 15cm

(c) 22.5cm

(d) 30cm

Answer. (b)

11. The value of $\sin^2 45 + \cos^2 45$ is:

(a) -1

(b) 1

(c) 0.5

(d) $\frac{2}{\sqrt{2}}$

Answer. (b)

12. Area of a quadrant of a circle, whose circumference is 22cm, is $\left(\pi = \frac{22}{7}\right)$:

(a) 3.5cm^2

(b) 13.5cm^2

(c) 9.625cm^2

(d) 17.25cm^2

Answer. (c)

13. A Test tube used for chemical tests has the shape of the combination of :

(a) A cylinder and a sphere

(b) A sphere and a cone

(c) A cylinder and a cone

(d) A hemisphere and a cylinder

Answer. (d)

14. If the mean of observations $x1, x2, x3, \ldots\ldots, xn$ is, then the mean of $x1 + a, x2 + a, \ldots, xn + a$ is:

(a) $a\bar{x}$

(b) $\bar{x} - a$

(c) $\bar{x} + a$

(d) $\frac{\bar{x}}{a}$

Answer. (c)

15. If $\tan^2 45° - \cos^2 30° = x \sin^2 45° \cos^2 45°$, then $x =$

(a) 2

(b) -2

(c) $-\frac{1}{2}$

(d) $\frac{1}{2}$

Answer. (d)

16. If the following figure, point D divides AB in the ratio 3: 5. Then the value of $\frac{AD}{AB}$ is

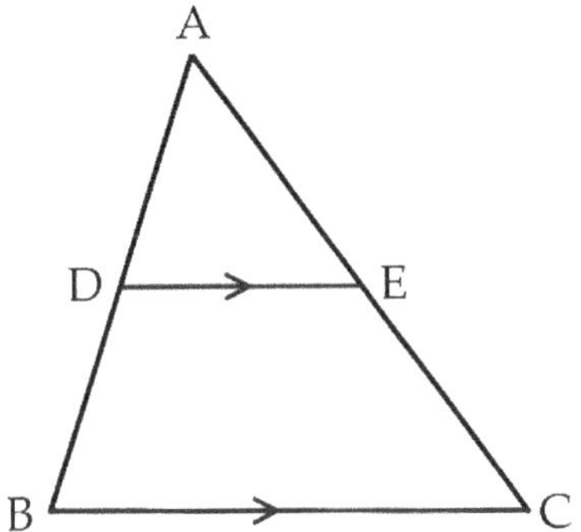

(a) $\frac{5}{8}$

(b) $\frac{3}{8}$

(c) $\frac{3}{5}$

(d) $\frac{5}{3}$

Answer. (b)

17. A box contains cards numbered 6 to 50. A card is drawn at random from the box. The probability that the drawn card has a number that a perfect square, is:

(a) $\frac{1}{45}$

(b) $\frac{2}{15}$

(c) $\frac{1}{9}$

(d) $\frac{4}{45}$

Answer. (c)

18. If the arithmetic mean of $x, x+3, x+6, x+9$, and $x+12$ is 10, the $x =$

(a) 1

(b) 2

(c) 6

(d) 4

Answer. (d)

Direction: In the following questions, a statement of Assertion (A) is followed by a statement of Reason (R). Mark the correct choice as:

(a) Both Assertion (A) and Reason (R) are true, and Reason (R) is the correct explanation of Assertion (A).

(b) Both Assertion (A) and Reason (R) are true, but Reason (R) is not the correct explanation of Assertion (A).

(c) Assertion (A) is true, but Reason (R) is false.

(d) Assertion (A) is false, but Reason (R) is true.

19. Assertion: The H.C.F. of two numbers is 16 and their product is 3072. Then their $\text{L. C. M.} = 162$.

Reason: If a and b are two positive integers, then $\text{H. C. F.} \times \text{L. C. M.} = a \times b$.

Answer. (d) Assertion (A) is false, but Reason (R) is true.

Explanation: Since $\text{HCF} \times \text{LCM} = a \times b$

$\Rightarrow \quad 3072 = 16 \times 162$

$\Rightarrow \quad 3072 \neq 2592$

20. Assertion: 3 is an example of a rational number.

Reason: The square roots of all positive integers are irrational numbers.

Answer. (c)

Explanation: Here, the reason is false. As $\sqrt{25} = \pm 5$, which is not an irrational number."

SECTION- B

(Section B consists of 5 questions of 2 marks each)

21. Solve the following system of linear equations-

$mx - ny = m^2 + n^2$

$x + y = 2m$

Solution:

$mx - ny = m^2 + n^2$ ....(i)

$x + y = 2m$ ... .(ii)

Multiply equation (ii) by n on both sides we get

$nx + ny = 2mn$ ....(iii)

Add equations (i) and (iii) we get

$mx + nx = m^2 + n^2 + 2mn$

$x(m+n) = (m+n)^2$

$x = m+n$

Substitute x in equation (i) we get

$m+n+y = 2m$

$y = 2m - m - n$

$y = m - n$

Hence $x = m + n$ and $y = m - n$

22. PQR is a triangle. S is a point on the side QR of triangle PQR such that∠PSR = ∠QPR. Given QP = 8 cm, PR = 6 cm and SR = 3 cm.

(a) Prove that: ΔPQR ~ ΔSPR

(b) Find the length of QR and PS.

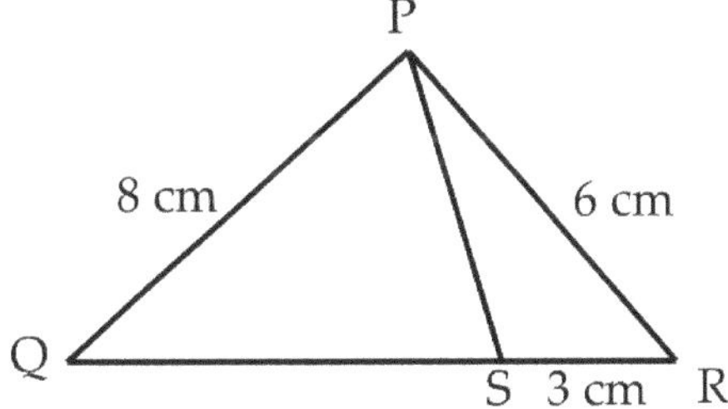

Solution:

In Δ PQR and Δ SPR

∠QPR = ∠PSR (Given)

∠QRP = ∠ PRS (common)

So Δ PQR ~ Δ SPR (AA similarity criterian)

$\frac{PQ}{SP} = \frac{QR}{PR} = \frac{PR}{SR}$ (Corresponding sides of similar triangles are proportional)

$\frac{8}{SP} = \frac{QR}{6} = \frac{6}{3}$

$\frac{QR}{6} = \frac{6}{3} \Rightarrow QR = \frac{36}{3} = 12\ cm$

$\frac{8}{SP} = \frac{6}{3} \Rightarrow SP = \frac{24}{6} = 4\ cm$

23. Prove the identity $(\text{cosec}^2 A - 1)(\sec A + 1)(\sec A - 1) = 1$

Solution:

LHS

$= (\text{cosec}^2 A - 1)(\sec A + 1)(\sec A - 1)$

$= (\text{cosec}^2 A - 1)(\sec^2 A - 1)$

$= \cot^2 A \times \tan^2 A$ [as $1 + \tan^2 A = \sec^2 A$ and $1 + \cot^2 A = \text{cosec}^2 A$]

$= \frac{1}{\tan^2 A} \times \tan^2 A$

$= 1$

$=$ RHS

24. In the given figure AD = 8cm, AC = 6cm, and TB is the tangent at B to the circle with the centre O. Find OT, if BT is 4cm.

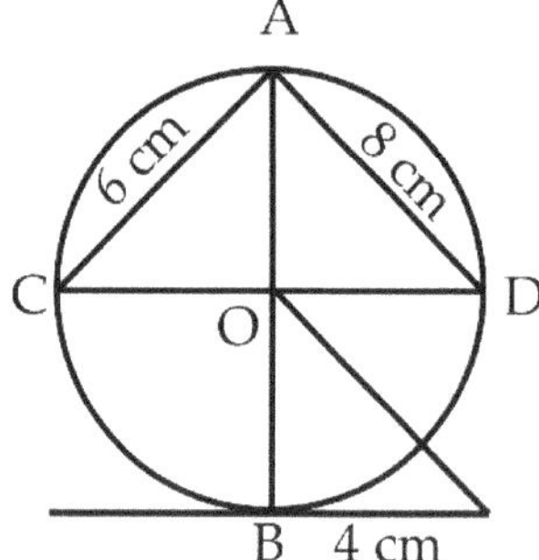

Solution:

$\angle CAD = 90°$ (Angle in a semi-circle)

So, $CD^2 = AC^2 + AD^2 = 36 + 64 \Rightarrow CD = 10cm$

Therefore, $OC = OD = OB = \frac{10}{2} cm = 5cm$

Now, $\angle OBT = 90°$ (Angle between radius and tangent)

So, $OT^2 = OB^2 + BT^2 = 25 + 16 = 41$

$\Rightarrow$ $OT = \sqrt{41} cm$

25. If the area and circumference of a circle are numerically equal, then find the radius of the circle.

Solution.

Let r be the radius of the circle

Its circumference = $2\pi r$ units

Its area = πr^2 sq. units

So $2\pi r = \pi r^2 \Rightarrow r = 2$ units

SECTION -C

(Section C consists of 6 questions of 3 marks each)

26. The area of a rectangle gets reduced by 9 square units if its length is reduced by 5 units and its breadth is increased by 3 units. If we increase the length by 3 units and the breadth by 2 units,

the area increases by 67 square units. Find the dimensions of the rectangle.

Solution:

Let the length of the rectangle be x

and the breadth of the rectangle be y

According to question

$\therefore$ Area of rectangle = xy

$(x - 5)(y + 3)\ xy - 9$

$xy - 5y + 3x - 15 = xy - 9$

$3x - 5y - 15 + 9 = 0$

$\therefore \quad 3x - 5y - 6 = 0$ ....(i)

and $(x+3)(y+2) = xy + 67$

$xy + 3y + 2x + 6 = xy + 67$

$2x + 3y + 6 - 67 = 0$

$\therefore 2x + 3y - 61 = 0$ (1)

Multiplying (i) by 2 and (ii) by 3 and then subtracting.

$$\begin{array}{l} 6x - 10y - 12 = 0 \\ 6x + 9y - 183 = 0 \\ - \quad - \quad + \\ \hline -19y + 171 = 0 \end{array}$$

$-19y = -171$

$\therefore \quad y = 9$

Putting the value y = 9 in (i)

$3x - 5 \times 9 = 6$

$3x - 45 = 6$

$3x = 51$

$\therefore x = 17$

So, the dimensions of a rectangle are 17 and 9 units.

27. Prove that $\sqrt{2}$ is irrational.

Solution:

Let us assume that $\sqrt{2}$ is rational.

So, $\sqrt{2} = \frac{a}{b}$, [where a and b are co-primes as they do not have any common factor except 1 and b $\neq$ 0.]

$\Rightarrow \quad b\sqrt{2} = a$

$\Rightarrow \quad 2b^2 = a^2$ [squaring both sides]

$\Rightarrow \quad$ 2 divides a^2

$\Rightarrow \quad$ 2 divides a [$\because$ 2 is a prime and divides a^2]

So 2 is a factor of a ....(i)

Let $a = 2c$

Putting $a = 2c$ in (i) we get

$2b^2 = 4c^2$

$\Rightarrow b^2 = 2c^2$

$\Rightarrow$ 2 divides b^2

$\Rightarrow$ 2 divides b[$\because$ 2 is a prime and divides b^2]

So 2 is a factor of b ....(ii)

Thus (i) and (ii) a and b have a common factor 2.

This contradicts the fact that a and b have no common factor other than 1.

This contradiction has arisen because of our incorrect assumption that $\sqrt{2}$ is rational.

Hence, $\sqrt{2}$ is an irrational number.

28. If α and β are zeroes of $x^2 - 3x + q$. What is the value of q, if $2\alpha + 3\beta = 15$?

Solution.

Given, α, and β are the zeroes of $x^2 - 3x + q$.

$\therefore \alpha + \beta = \frac{-b}{a} = -\left(\frac{-3}{1}\right) = 3$

$\Rightarrow \alpha + \beta = 3$ ... (i)

Also, $2\alpha + 3\beta = 15$ [given] ...(ii)

On multiplying Eq. (i) by 2 and subtracting Eq. (i) from Eq. (ii), we get

$$\beta = 9$$

On putting $\beta = 9$ in Eq. (1), we get

$$\alpha + 9 = 3$$

$\Rightarrow$ $\alpha = -6$

Now, $\alpha\beta = \frac{c}{a} = q$

$\Rightarrow$ $q = (-6)(9)$

$\Rightarrow$ $q = -54$

29. $\frac{1}{\tan A + \cot A} = \cos A \cdot \sin A$

Solution:

LHS

$= \dfrac{1}{\tan A + \cot A}$

$= 1 \div \left(\dfrac{\sin A}{\cos A} + \dfrac{\cos A}{\sin A}\right)$

$= 1 \div \left(\dfrac{\sin^2 A + \cos^2 A}{\cos A \cdot \sin A}\right)$

$= 1 \div \left(\dfrac{1}{\cos A \cdot \sin A}\right)$ $[\sin^2 A + \cos^2 A = 1]$

$= 1 \times \dfrac{\cos A \cdot \sin A}{1}$

$= \cos A \cdot \sin A$ RHS

30. PQ is a diameter of a circle and PR is the chord such that $\angle RPQ = 30°$. The tangent at R intersects

PQ produced at S. Prove that RQ = QS.

Solution:

Given:PQ is the diameter and PR is the chord of the circle with center 0.

$\angle RPQ = 30°$

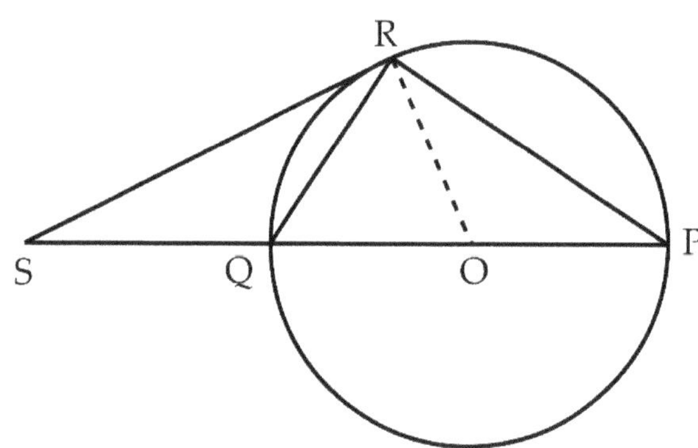

To prove: RQ = QS

Construction: Join OR.

Proof:

$\angle ORS = 90^o$ [Radius and tangents are perpendicular at point of contact]

$\angle PRQ = 90^o$ [Angles on semi-circle]

In ΔPQR

$\angle RPQ + \angle PRQ + \angle PQR = 180^o$ [Angle sum property]

$30^o + 90^o + \angle PQR = 180^o$

$\angle PQR = 60^o$

In ΔOQR

$OQ = OR$ [Radii]

$\angle OQR + \angle ORQ = 60^o$ [Angles opposite to equal sides are equal]

$\angle QRS = \angle ORS - \angle ORQ$

$= 90^o - 60^o = 30^o$

In ΔQRS

$\angle QSR + \angle QRS = \angle OQR$ [Exterior angle property of triangle]

$\angle QSR + 30^o = 60^o$

$\angle QSR = 30^o$

In ΔQRS

$\angle QRS = \angle QSR = 30^o$

$\therefore QR = QS$ [sides opposite to equal angles are equal]

Hence proved

31. Three unbiased coins are tossed together. What is the probability of getting

(i) Two heads,

(ii) At least two heads,

(iii) At most two heads.

Solution:

Possible outcomes are {HHH, HHT, HTH, THH, HTT, THT, TTH, TTT}

No. of total outcomes = 8

(i) For two heads, favourable outcomes are {HHT, HTH, THH)

No. of favourable outcomes = 3

So, P(E) = $\frac{\text{No.of favorable outcomes}}{\text{Total no.of outcomes}}$ => $\frac{3}{8}$

(ii) For at least two heads, favourable outcomes are {HHH, HHT, HTH, THH}

No. of favourable outcomes = 4

So, P(E) = $\frac{\text{No.of favorable outcomes}}{\text{Total no.of outcomes}}$ => $\frac{4}{8} = \frac{1}{2}$

(iii) For at most two heads, favourable outcomes are {HHT, HTH, THH, HTT THT, TTH, TTT}

No. of favourable outcomes = 7

So, P(E) = $\frac{\text{No.of favorable outcomes}}{\text{Total no.of outcomes}}$ => $\frac{7}{8}$

SECTION -D

(Section D consists of 4 questions of 5 marks each)

32. If roots of a quadratic equation $(b - c)x^2 + (c - a)x + (a - b) = 0$ are real and equal, then prove that $2b = a + c$.

Solution:

Since roots are equal so discriminant $b^2 - 4ac = 0$

$$(c - a)2 - 4(b - c)(a - b) = 0$$
$$c2 - 2ca + a2 - 4(ba - b2 - ca + cb) = 0$$
$$c2 - 2ca + a2 - 4ba + 4b2 + 4ca - 4cb = 0$$
$$c2 + 2ca + a2 - 4ba + 4b2 - 4cb = 0$$
$$a2 + 4b2 + c2 + 2ca - 4ba - 4cb = 0$$
$$a2 + (-2b)2 + c2 + 2ca - 4ba - 4cb = 0$$
$$(a - 2b + c)2 = 0[(a + b + c)2$$
$$= a2 + b2 + c2 + 2ab + 2bc + 2ac]$$
$$a - 2b + c = 0$$
$$a + c = 2b$$

Hence Proved.

33. Find the median wage in the following table.

Wages	0 – 10	10 – 20	20 – 30	30 – 40	40 – 50	50 – 60	60 – 70	70 – 80
No. of workers	12	20	30	38	24	16	12	8

Solution:

From the given distribution, first, find the cumulative frequency of all classes and $\frac{n}{2}$:

Wages	**No. of workers**	**cumulative frequency**
0 – 10	12	12
10 – 20	20	32
20 – 30	30	62
30 – 40	38	100
40 – 50	24	124
50 – 60	16	140
60 – 70	12	152
70 – 80	8	160
	$n = 160$	

In the distribution above $n = 160$, so $\frac{n}{2} = 80$. Now 30 – 40 is the class whose cumulative frequency of 100 is greater than (and nearest) to $\frac{n}{2}$, i.e., 80, so according to the formula

$$\text{median} = 1 + \left(\frac{\frac{n}{2} - cf}{f}\right) \times h$$

lower limit of median class (l) = 30
number of observation (n) = 160
cumulative frequency of class preceding the median class (cf) = 62
frequency of the median class (f) = 38
class size (assuming class size to be equal) (h) = 10
substituting these values in the formula above

$$\text{median} = 30 + \left(\frac{80-62}{38}\right) \times 10$$

$$\text{median} = 30 + \left(\frac{17}{38}\right) \times 10$$

$$\text{median} = 30 + 4.473$$

$$\text{median} = 34.47 \text{ (approx.)}$$

34. The length of the shadow of a tower standing on a level plane is found to be $2y$ meters longer when the sun's altitude is 30° then when it was 45°. Prove that the height of the tower is $y(\sqrt{3}+1)$ meters.

Solution:

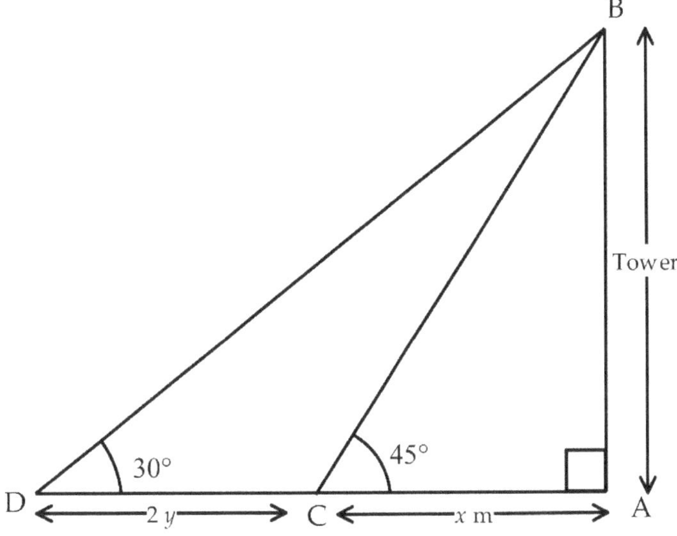

In the figure, AB is the tower, and its shadow is AC when the altitude is 45° it is 2y meters longer when the altitude changes to 30°.

In triangle BAC $\tan 45° = \frac{AB}{AC} \left(\tan\theta = \frac{\text{perpendicular}}{\text{base}}\right)$

$$1 = \frac{AB}{AC} \Rightarrow AB = AC$$

In triangle BAC, $\tan 30° = \frac{AB}{AD}$

$$\frac{1}{\sqrt{3}} = \frac{AB}{AC + 2y}$$

$$\sqrt{3}\text{AB} = \text{AB} + 2\text{y}$$

$$\sqrt{3}\text{AB} - \text{AB} = 2\text{y} (\text{as AB=AC})$$

$$\text{AB} = \frac{2\text{y}}{\sqrt{3}-1} \times \frac{\sqrt{3}+1}{\sqrt{3}+1}$$

$$AB = \frac{2y}{\sqrt{3}-1} \times \frac{\sqrt{3}+1}{\sqrt{3}+1}$$
$$AB = y(\sqrt{3}+1)$$

Proved

35. PQR is a triangle. S is a point on the side QR of triangle PQR such that $\angle PSR = \angle QPR$. Given $QP = 8\,cm, PR = 6\,cm$ and $SR = 3\,cm.$

(a) Prove that: $\Delta PQR \sim \Delta SPR$

(b) Find the length of QR and PS.

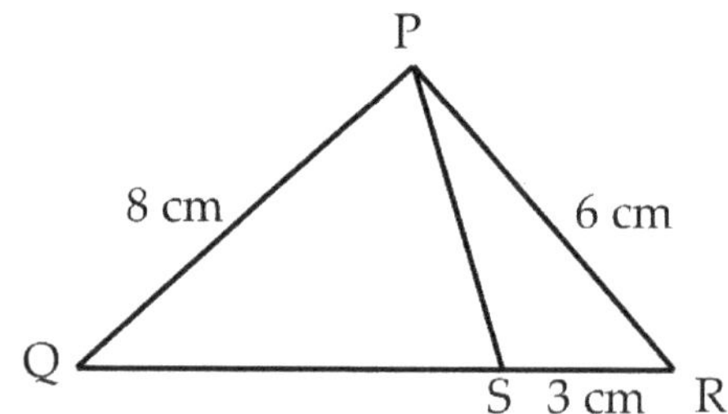

Solution:

In $\Delta\, PQR$ and $\Delta\, SPR$

$\angle QPR = \angle PSR$ (Given)

$\angle QRP = \angle\, PRS$ (common)

So $\Delta\, PQR \sim \Delta\, SPR$ (AA similarity criterion)

$\frac{PQ}{SP} = \frac{QR}{PR} = \frac{PR}{SR}$ (Corresponding sides of similar triangles are proportional)

$$\frac{8}{SP} = \frac{QR}{6} = \frac{6}{3}$$

$$\frac{QR}{6} = \frac{6}{3} \Rightarrow QR = \frac{36}{3} = 12cm$$

$$\frac{8}{SP} = \frac{6}{3} \Rightarrow SP = \frac{24}{6} = 4cm$$

SECTION- E

(3 Case study-based question of 4 (1 + 1 + 2) marks each)

36. Case Study based – 1 (Bank Loan)

Ravish was wishing to buy a new car but he didn't have enough of money. One of his friends suggested he to take a loan from XYZ bank. Influenced by his idea, he decides to take a loan of Rs. 1,18,000 and decides to repay by Rs. 1000 per month. On a further note, he decides to increase the instalment by Rs. 100 every month. Answer the following questions.

(i) What is the amount paid by him in the 30th instalment?

(a) Rs. 3900

(b) Rs. 3800

(c) Rs. 3700

(d) Rs. 3600

Solution:

Option (a) is correct

First term $a = 1000$ and common difference $(d) = 100$

So $t30 = a + 29\,d$

$= 1000 + 29 \times 100$

$= Rs.\,3900$

(ii) What is the total amount paid by him in 30 instalments?

(a) Rs. 74000

(b) Rs. 75000

(c) Rs. 73000

(d) Rs. 73500

Solution:

Option (d) is correct

The total amount paid in 30 instalments is given by $S_n = (a + l)$

$S_{30} = \frac{30}{2}(1000 + 3900)$ $(l = t_{30})$

$= 15 \times 4900$

$=$ Rs. 73500

(iii) What amount is left after 30th instalment?

(a) Rs. 44500

(b) Rs. 45000

(c) Rs. 45500

(d) Rs. 40000

Solution:

Option (a) is correct

Till $30th$ installment Rs.73500 paid, so the remaining balance amount

$= 118000 - 73500 =$ Rs. 44500

(iv) If the total number of instalments is 40, what is the amount paid in the last instalment?

(a) Rs. 4900

(b) Rs. 4800

(c) Rs. 4300

(d) Rs. 4500

Solution:

Option (a) is correct.

Amount paid in the last instalment

$$t_{40} = a + 39d = 1000 + 39 \times 100 = \text{Rs. } 4900$$

37. Case Study based – 2 (Test Tube)

A student performing a test using a test tube in a chemistry lab. The test tube is shown in the above figure.

(i) What shapes are found in a test tube?

(a) Cylinder

(b) Hemi – sphere

(c) Both A and B

(d) None of the above

Solution:

Option (c) is correct.

(ii) What is the volume of the cylinder when the radius is 1 cm, and the total height is 12 cm? (Take $\pi = 3.14$)

(a) 30 cm^3

(b) 31.4 cm^3

(c) 33.81 cm^3

(d) 35 cm^3

Solution:

Option (d) is correct

Radius $r = 1$ cm, height $h = 12$ cm

Volume of cylinder

$$= \pi r^2 h$$

$$= 3.14 \times 1 \times 1 \times 12 = 37.68 \text{ cm}^3.$$

The nearest value is 35 cm^3.

(iii) What is the volume of the hemisphere?

(a) 3 cm^3

(b) 1.4 cm^3

(c) 3.81 cm^3
(d) 2.093 cm^3

Solution:

Option (d) is correct

Radius $r = 1$

Volume of cylinder $= \frac{2}{3}\pi r^2$

$= \frac{2}{3} \times 3.14 \times 1 \times 1 \times 1 = 2.093\text{cm}^3$

(iv) What is the total volume?

(a) 33 cm^3
(b) 39.77 cm^3
(c) 35.21cm^3
(d) 36.4 cm^3

Solution:

Option (ii) is correct

Total Volume of vessel $= 2.093 + 37.68 = 39.77\text{cm}^3$

38. Case Study based – 2 (Heights and distances)

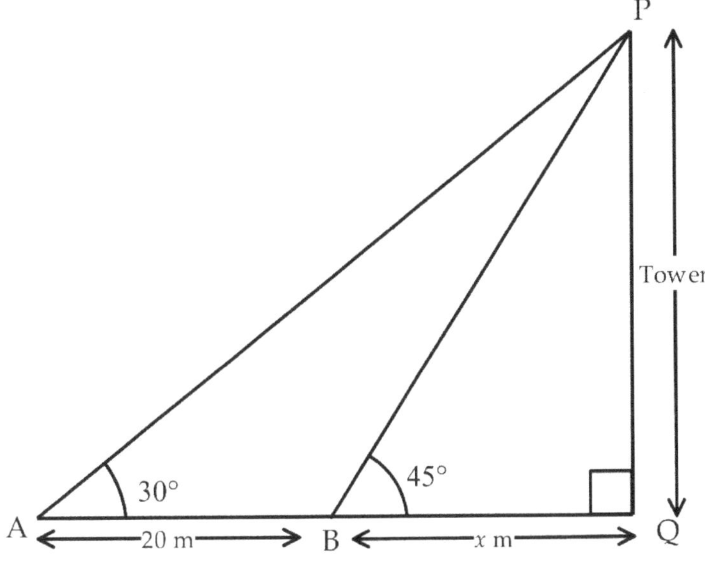

Priya was walking on the road when she saw a high tower in front of her. She observed that when she was standing at point A, the angle of elevation to the top of the tower was 30°. On moving 20 m toward the tower to point B, the angle of elevation changed to 45° as shown in the figure.

(i) What is the height of the tower?

(a) 14.35 m
(b) 16.76 m
(c) 27.32 m
(d) None of these

Solution:

Option (c) is correct

In triangle BQP, $tan\ 45^o = \frac{h}{x}$

$$\tan\theta = \frac{\text{perpendicular}}{\text{base}}$$

$$1s = \frac{h}{x}, \text{so } h = x$$

In triangle AQP, $tan30^0 = \frac{h}{x+20}$

$$\frac{1}{\sqrt{3}} = \frac{h}{h+20} \text{ (as } h = x)$$

$$\sqrt{3h} = h + 20$$

$$\sqrt{3h} - h = 20$$

$$h(\sqrt{3} - 1) = 20$$

$$h = \frac{20}{\sqrt{3}-1} \times \frac{\sqrt{3}+1}{\sqrt{3}-1} = \frac{20(\sqrt{3}+1)}{2} = 10 \times 2.732 = 27.32m$$

(ii) What is the distance Priya when she is standing at point B from the base of the tower?

(a) 14.35 m

(b) 16.76 m

(c) 27.32 m

(d) None of the above

Solution:

Option (c) is correct

As $x = h$ so $x = 27.32\ m$

(iii) What is the value of angle APQ?

(a) 30°

(b) 60°

(c) 90°

(d) 120°

Solution:

Option (b) is correct.

As triangle AQP is a right-angled triangle, so angle APQ $= 180 - (90 + 30) = 60^o$

(iv) What is the value of angle BPQ?

(a) 30°

(b) 45°

(c) 90°

(d) 120°

Solution:

Option (b) is correct

Class- X Session- 2022-23

SAMPLE PAPER-2

Sample Question Paper

Time Allowed: 3 Hrs. **Maximum Marks: 80**

General Instructions:

1. This Question Paper has 5 Sections A-E.
2. Section **A** has 20 MCQs carrying 1 mark each
3. Section **B** has 5 questions carrying 02 marks each.
4. Section **C** has 6 questions carrying 03 marks each.
5. Section **D** has 4 questions carrying 05 marks each.
6. Section **E** has 3 case-based integrated units of assessment (04 marks each) with subparts of the values of 1, 1, and 2 marks each respectively.
7. All Questions are compulsory. However, an internal choice in 2 Qs of 5 marks, 2 Qs of 3 marks, and 2 Questions of 2 marks has been provided. An internal choice has been provided in the 2marks questions of Section E
8. Draw neat figures wherever required. Take π =22/7 wherever required if not stated

SECTION A

(Section A consists of 20 questions of 1 mark each)

1. If d = LCM (36,198) then the value of d is:

(a) 396
(b) 198
(c) 36
(d) 1
Answer. (a)

2. If -4 is a zero of the polynomials$p(x) = x^2 - x - (2 + 2k)$, then find the value of k.

(a) 8
(b) 5
(c) -5
(d) 6
Answer. (b)

3. The value of c for which the pair of equations $cx - y = 2$ and $6x - 2y = 4$ will have infinitely many solutions is

(a) 3
(b) -3
(c) -12
(d) No value
Answer. (a)

4. A quadratic equation can have:
   (a) At most two roots
   (b) At least two roots
   (c) Only one root
   (d) Always two roots
   Answer. (a)

5. If $\triangle$ PQR~ $\triangle$ XYZ, $\angle Q = 50°$ and $\angle R = 70°$, then $\angle X$ is equal to:
   (a) 70°
   (b) 50°
   (c) 120°
   (d) 60°
   Answer. (d)

6. The coordinates of the point where the line $x - y = 5$ cuts the y-axis are:
   (a) $(0, -5)$
   (b) $(5, 0)$
   (c) $(0, 5)$
   (d) $(-5, 0)$
   Answer. (a)

7. If $\tan A + \cot A = 2$, (A is acute) the value of $\tan^2 A + \cot^2 A$ is
   (a) 0
   (b) 1
   (c) 2
   (d) 4
   Answer. (c)

8. The number of tangents to a circle that is parallel to a secant is:
   (a) 1
   (b) 2
   (c) 3
   (d) Infinite
   Answer. (b)

9. XY is drawn parallel to the base BC of an $\triangle$ ABC cutting AB at X and AC at Y. If AB = 4BX and YC = 2cm, then AY =
   (a) 2cm
   (b) 4cm
   (c) 6cm
   (d) 8cm
   Answer. (c)

10. The angle of depression from the top of a tower 24m high, at a point on the ground is 30°. The distance of the point from the top of the tower is:

(a) 24m

(b) 12m

(c) $24\sqrt{3}$m

(d) 48m

Answer. (c)

11. The ratio of the outer and inner circumferences of a circular path is 23: 22. If the path is 5 meters wide, the diameter of the inner circle is:

(a) 55m

(b) 110m

(c) 220m

(d) 230m

Answer. (c)

12. The curved surface area of a right circular cone with a height of 15 cm and a base diameter of 16 cm is:

(a) 60π cm^2

(b) 68π cm^2

(c) 120π cm^2

(d) 136π cm^2

Answer. (d)

13. $\frac{2\tan 30°}{1+\tan^2 30°}$ is equal to

(a) sin60°

(b) cos60°

(c) tan60°

(d) sin30°

Answer. (a)

14. If ΔABC and ΔDEF are similar triangles such that $2AB = DE$ and $BC = 8$ cm, then $EF =$

(a) 16 cm

(b) 12 cm

(c) 8 cm

(d) 4 cm

Answer. (a)

15. If the area of a circle is numerically equal to twice its circumference, then the diameter of the circle is:

(a) 4 units

(b) π units

(c) 8 units

(d) 2 units

Answer. (c)

16. If the median of the data: $24, 25, 26, x + 2, x + 3, 30, 31, 34$ is 27.5, then $x =$

(a) 27

(b) 25

(c) 28

(d) 30

Answer. (b)

17. A pair of coins are tossed simultaneously. Then, the probability of getting exactly one head is:

(a) $\frac{3}{4}$

(b) $\frac{1}{4}$

(c) $\frac{1}{2}$

(d) 1

Answer. (c)

18. The mean of 20 numbers is 13. The new mean if each observation is increased by 5, is:

(a) 13

(b) 18

(c) 65

(d) 8

Answer. (b)

Direction: In the following questions, a statement of Assertion (A) is followed by a statement of Reason (R). Mark the correct choice as:

(a) Both Assertion (A) and Reason (R) are true, and Reason (R) is the correct explanation of Assertion (A).

(b) Both Assertion (A) and Reason (R) are true, but Reason (R) is not the correct explanation of Assertion (A).

(c) Assertion (A) is true, but Reason (R) is false.

(d) Assertion (A) is false, but Reason (R) is true.

19. Assertion: For any two positive integers p and q, $\text{HCF}(p, q) \times \text{LCM}(p, q) = p \times q$

Reason: If the HCF of two numbers is 9 and their product is 1620, then their LCM is 90.

Answer. (c)

We have, $\text{LCM}(p, q) \times \text{HCF}(p, q) = p \times q$

$\text{LCM} \times 9 = 1620$

$\text{LCM} = 1620 / 9 = 180 \neq 90$

Therefore, the Reason is false.

20. Assertion: Let the positive numbers a, b, c be in A.P., then 1/bc, 1/ac, and 1/ab are also in A.P.

Reason: If each term of an A.P. is divided by *abc*, then the resulting sequence is also in A.P.
Answer. (a)

SECTION B

(Section A consists of 5 questions of 2 marks each)

21. Solve the following systems of simultaneous linear equations.

$0.4x + 0.3y = 1.7$ ......(i)

$0.7x - 0.2y = 0.8$ .....(ii)

Answer. $[x = 2, y = 3]$

Solution: Multiply both equations by 10 we get

$$4x + 3y = 17(i)$$
$$7x - 2y = 8(ii)$$

Multiply (i) by 2 and (ii) by 3 and add them

$$8x + 6y = 34$$
$$21x - 6y = 24$$
$$24x = 58$$
$$x = \frac{58}{29} = 2$$

Put x in (i) we get

$$4 \times 2 + 3y = 17$$
$$3y = 17 - 8$$
$$y = \frac{9}{3}$$
$$y = 3$$
$$\therefore x = 2 \text{ and } y = 3$$

22. In the figure, $DE \parallel BC$ and $\frac{AD}{DB} = \frac{3}{5}$ and AC = 4.8cm. Find the value of AE.

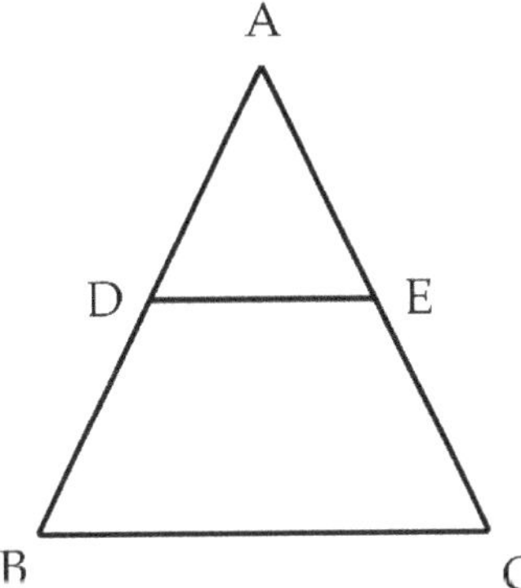

Solution. Let AE = x

$\therefore$ CE = AC − AE = $4.8 - x$[$\because$ AC = 4.8cm, given] since, DE ∥ BC, then by basic proportionality theorem,

$$\frac{AD}{BD} = \frac{AE}{CE}$$
$$\frac{3}{5} = \frac{x}{4.8 - x}$$
$$5x = 3(4.8 - x)$$
$$[\because CE = 4.8 - x]$$

$$5x = 14.4 - 3x$$
$$8x = 14.4$$
$$x = 1.8\text{cm}$$
$$\therefore \quad AE = 1.8\text{cm}$$

23. If $3\tan A - 5\cos B = \sqrt{3}$ and $B = 90°$, find the value of A.

Solution:

If $3\tan A - 5\cos 90° = \sqrt{3}$

$$3\tan A - 5 \times 0 = \sqrt{3}$$
$$3\tan A = \sqrt{3}$$
$$\tan A = \frac{\sqrt{3}}{3}$$
$$= \frac{\sqrt{3}}{3} \times \frac{\sqrt{3}}{\sqrt{3}}$$
$$= \frac{1}{\sqrt{3}} = \tan 30°$$

So $$A = 30°$$

24. Two tangents PA and PB are drawn to a circle with center O, such that $\angle APB = 120°$. Prove that $OP = 2AP$.

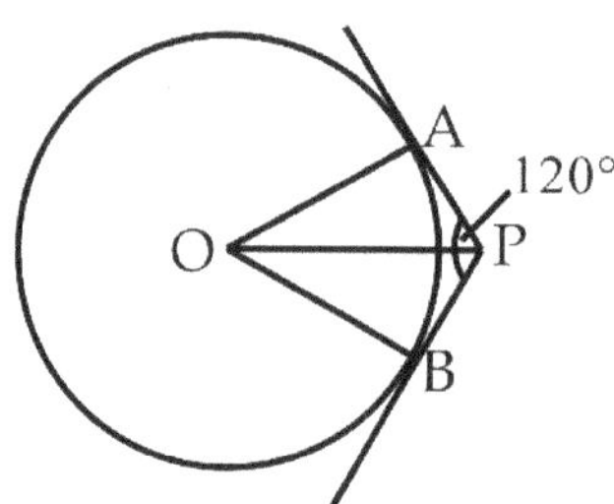

Solution.

Let PA and PB be two tangents to the circle with center O (see figure). Join OA and OB.

$\angle APO = \angle BPO$ [radiuses bisect the angle between tangents]

$$= \frac{1}{2}\angle APB = \frac{1}{2} \times 120^0 = 60^0$$

In the right $\triangle$ OAP,

$$\text{COS } 60^0 = \frac{AP}{OP} \qquad \left[\text{COS } \theta = \frac{\text{perpendicular}}{\text{hypotenuse}}\right]$$
$$\frac{1}{2} = \frac{AP}{OP} \rightarrow OP = 2AP$$

Hence proved

25. The area between two concentric circles is 346.5sq. cm, and the circumference of the inner circle is 88cm. Calculate the radius of the outer circle. (Use $\pi = \frac{22}{7}$)

Solution.

Let the radius of the inner circle be r.

But the circumference of the inner circle = 88cm.

So, $2\pi r = 88$

$$2 \times \frac{22}{7} \times r = 88$$

$$r = \frac{88 \times 7}{2 \times 22} = 14\text{cm}$$

Let the radius of outer circle be R.

Then, $\pi r^2 - \pi r^2 = 346.5$

or $\pi(R^2 - r^2) = 346.5$

or $\frac{22}{7}(R^2 - 14^2) = 346.5$

or $R^2 = \frac{346.5 \times 7}{22} + 196$

or $R^2 = 110.25 + 196$

or $R^2 = 306.25$

$\Rightarrow$ $R = \sqrt{306.25} = 17.5\text{cm}$

SECTION C

(Section C consists of 6 questions of 3 marks each)

26. Check whether 15^n can end with the digit 0 for any natural number n where $n \in N$.

Solution:

To end with the digit 0 a number must contain at least one 2 and one 5 in its prime factorization. Prime factorization of 15 contains 3 and 5 primes in its prime factorization, and according to the fundamental theorem of arithmetic, this factorization is unique apart from the order.

Here 2 are missing. So 15^n can not terminate with a 0 for any value of n.

27. If α and β are the zeroes of the quadratic polynomial $p(s) = 3s^2 - 6s + 4$, then find the value of $\frac{\alpha}{\beta} + \frac{\beta}{\alpha} + 2\left(\frac{1}{\alpha} + \frac{1}{\beta}\right) + 3\alpha\beta$.

Solution.

Since α and β are the zeroes of the quadratic polynomial

$$p(s) = 3s^2 - 6s + 4.$$

$$\therefore \alpha + \beta = -\frac{\text{Coefficient of } x}{\text{Coefficient of } x^2} = \frac{-(-6)}{3} = \frac{6}{3} = 2$$

and $$\alpha\beta = \frac{\text{Constant term}}{\text{Coefficient of } x^2} = \frac{4}{3}$$

We have $\frac{\alpha}{\beta} + \frac{\beta}{\alpha} + 2\left(\frac{1}{\alpha} + \frac{1}{\beta}\right) + 3\alpha\beta$

$$= \frac{\alpha^2 + \beta^2}{\alpha\beta} + 2\left(\frac{\alpha + \beta}{\alpha\beta}\right) + 3\alpha\beta$$

$$= \frac{(\alpha+\beta)^2 - 2\alpha\beta}{\alpha\beta} + 2\left(\frac{\alpha+\beta}{\alpha\beta}\right) + 3\alpha\beta$$

$$= \frac{(2)^2 - 2\left(\frac{4}{3}\right)}{\frac{4}{3}} + 2\left(\frac{2}{\frac{4}{3}}\right) + 3 \times \frac{4}{3}$$

$$= \frac{4 - \frac{8}{3}}{\frac{4}{3}} + 2 \times 2 \times \frac{3}{4} + 4 = \frac{12 - 8}{3} \times \frac{3}{4} + 3 + 4$$

$$= \frac{4}{3} \times \frac{3}{4} + 7 = 1 + 7 = 8$$

28. A two-digit number is obtained by either multiplying the sum of the digits by 8 and then subtracting 5 or by multiplying the difference of the digits by 16 and then adding 3. Find the number.

Solution:

Let the ten's digit be x and the unit's digit be y.

Then the two-digit number $= 10x + y$

ATQ,

$$8(x + y) - 5 = 10x + y$$
$$8x + 8y - 5 = 10x + y$$
$$8x - 10x + 8y - y - 5 = 0$$
$$-2x + 7y - 5 = 0$$

$\therefore$ $2x - 7y = -5$ ....(i)

and

$$16(x - y) + 3 = 10x + y$$

$\Rightarrow$ $16x - 16y + 3 = 10x + y$

$\Rightarrow$ $16x - 10x - 16y - y + 3 = 0$

$\therefore$ $6x - 17y = -3$ ....(ii)

Multiplying (i) by 3, we get

$\therefore$ $6x - 21y = -15$ ....(iii)

$$6x - 21y = -15$$
$$6x - 17y = -3$$
$$- \quad + \qquad +$$
$$-4y = -12$$
$$y = 3$$

$\therefore$ Putting y = 3 in (i), we get

$$2x - 7 \times 3 = -5$$
$$2x - 21 = -5$$
$$2x = 16$$
$$x = 8$$

So, the two-digit number $= 10 \times 8 + 3 = 83$.

29. $(\cot A - \operatorname{cosec} A)^2 = \frac{1-\cos A}{1+\cos A}$

Solution:

LHS

$$= (\cot A - \operatorname{cosec} A)^2$$
$$= \left(\frac{\cos A}{\sin A} - \frac{1}{\sin A}\right)^2$$
$$= \left(\frac{\cos A - 1}{\sin A}\right)^2$$
$$= \frac{(1 - \cos A)^2}{\sin^2 A}$$

$$= \frac{(1 - \cos A)(1 - \cos A)}{1 - \cos^2 A}$$

$$= \frac{(1 - \cos A)(1 - \cos A)}{(1 + \cos A)(1 - \cos A)} \quad [(a - b)^2 = (b - a)^2]$$

$$= \frac{(1 - \cos A)}{(1 + \cos A)} \text{ RHS } [b^2 = (a + b)(a - b)]$$

30. In the diagram, find the radius of the circle.

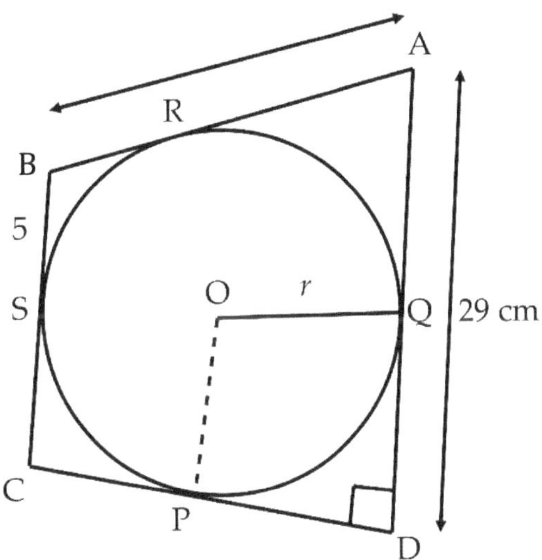

Solution:

Join OP.

BS = BR = 5cm (∵ BR and BS are tangents drawn from external point B)

$AR = AB - BR$

∴ AR = 23 − 5 = 18cm

AQ = AR = 18cm (∵ AQ and AR are tangents drawn from external point A).

QD = AD − AQ

= 29 − 18 = 11 cm

Again

$PD = QD = 11\,m$ [tangents from an external point]

In quadrilateral OQDP

∠D = 90° [Given]

∠Q = 90° [Radius and tangents are perpendicular at point of contact]

∠P = 90° [$OP \perp CD$]

so ∠O = 90°

So quadrilateral OQDP is a rectangle in which QD = PD

So quadrilateral OQDP is a square

and so $OQ = OD = 11\ cm$

So, a radius of circle: $r = 11\ cm$

31. King, queen, and jack of hearts are removed from a pack of 52 playing cards and then the pack is well shuffled. A card is drawn from the remaining cards. Find the probability of getting a card of:

(i) Hearts
(ii) A queen
(iii) Not a king

Solution:

Number of cards remaining after removing three cards = 49

So the total number no. of outcomes = 49

(i) Favourable outcomes for hearts = 10 (as three hearts are removed)

So, $P(E) = \frac{\text{No.of favorable outcomes}}{\text{Total no.of outcomes}} => \frac{10}{49}$

(ii) Favourable outcomes for a queen = 3 (as one queen is removed)

$P(E) = \frac{\text{No.of favorable outcomes}}{\text{Total no.of outcomes}} => \frac{3}{49}$

(iii) Favourable outcomes for not a king = 49 – 3 = 46 (as one king has been already removed)

$P(E) = \frac{\text{No.of favorable outcomes}}{\text{Total no.of outcomes}} => \frac{46}{49}$

SECTION D

(Section D consists of 4 questions of 5 marks each)

32. A wooden article as shown in the figure was made from a cylinder by scooping out a hemisphere from one end and a cone from the other end. Find the total surface area of the article.

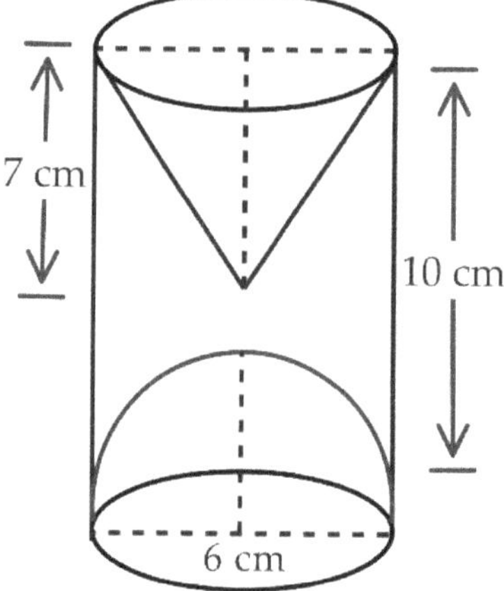

Solution.

Total surface area = curved surface of a cylinder
= Curved surface of a hemisphere
= Curved surface of cone

Now, curved surface area of cylinder = $2\pi rh$

$= 2 \times \pi \times 3 \times 10 = 60\pi cm^2$

Curved surface of hemisphere

$= 2\pi r^2 = 2\pi \times 9 \quad = 18\pi cm^2$

Let slant height of the cone be l.

So, $\quad l^2 = 3^2 + 7^2 = 9 + 49 \Rightarrow l = \sqrt{58}cm$

So, curved surface area of cone

$$= \pi rl = \pi \times 3 \times \sqrt{58} cm^2$$

So, total surface area

$$= (60\pi + 18\pi + 3\pi\sqrt{58}) cm^2$$
$$= (78 + 3\sqrt{58})\pi cm^2$$

33. PQR is a triangle. S is a point on the side QR of triangle PQR such that $\angle PSR = \angle QPR$. Given $QP = 8\ cm, PR = 6\ cm$ and $SR = 3\ cm$.

(i) Prove that: $\Delta PQR \sim \Delta SPR$

(ii) Find the length of QR and PS.

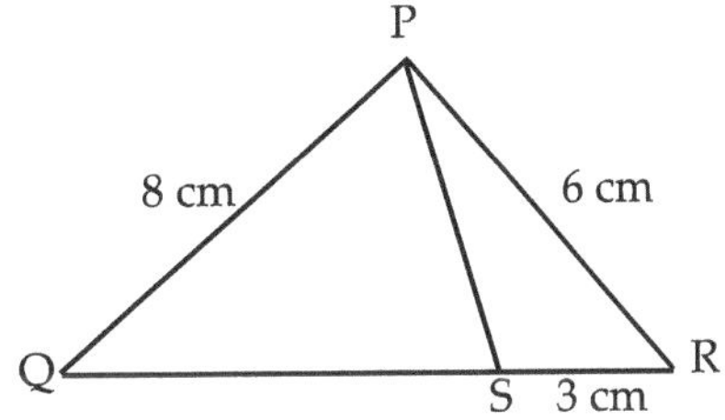

Solution:

(i) In Δ PQR and Δ SPR

$\angle QPR = \angle PSR$ (Given)

$\angle QRP = \angle PRS$ (common)

So $\Delta PQR \sim \Delta SPR$ (AA similarity criterian)

(ii) $\frac{PQ}{SP} = \frac{QR}{PR} = \frac{PR}{SR}$ (Corresponding sides of similar triangles are proportional)

$\frac{8}{SP} = \frac{QR}{6} = \frac{6}{3}$

$\frac{QR}{6} = \frac{6}{3} \Rightarrow QR = \frac{36}{3} = 12$ cm

$\frac{8}{SP} = \frac{6}{3} \Rightarrow SP = \frac{24}{6} = 4$ cm

34. The marks obtained by 120 students in mathematics test is given in the following distribution.

Marks	0 – 20	20 – 40	40 – 60	60 – 80	80 – 100	Total
No. of students	17	$f1$	32	$f2$	19	120

The mean of the following distribution is 50 and the sum of the frequencies is 120. Find the missing frequencies f_1 and f_2.

Solution:

Marks	No. of students (f)	class mark (x)	fx
0 – 20	17	10	170
20 – 40	$f1$	30	$30f1$
40 – 60	32	50	1600
60 – 80	$f2$	70	$70f2$
80 – 90	19	90	1710

$$f = 68 + f1 + f2 \qquad fx = 3480 + 30f1 + 70f2$$

Mean $= \frac{\Sigma fx}{\Sigma f}$

$$50 = \frac{3480 + 30f1 + 70f2}{120}$$

$$3480 + 30f1 + 70f2 = 6000$$
$$30f1 + 72f2 = 2520$$
$$3f1 + 7f2 = 252$$
$$68 + f1 + f2 = 120$$
$$f1 + f2 = 52 \qquad \text{(ii)}$$

substitute $f1 = 52 - f2$ in equation (i) we get

$$3(52 - f2) + 7f2 = 252$$
$$156 - 3f2 + 7f2 = 252$$
$$4f2 = 252 - 156$$
$$4f2 = 96$$
$$f2 = 24$$

substitute f2 in equation (ii) we get $f1 + 24 = 52$

$$f1 = 28$$

Answer. f1 = 28, f2 = 24

35. In a two-digit number, the ten's digit is bigger. The product of the digits is 27 and the difference between the two digits is 6, find the number.

Solution:

Let unit digit is 'x' so ten's digit is $(x + 6)$, as given ten's digit is bigger.

So number is $10(x + 6) + x = 11x + 60$

According to question: $x(x + 6) = 27$

$$x2 + 6x = 27$$
$$x2 + 6x - 27 = 0$$
$$x2 + 9x - 3x - 27 = 0$$
$$x(x + 9) - 3(x + 9) = 0$$
$$(x + 9)(x - 3) = 0$$
$$x = 3 \text{ or } -9$$

but the number is positive so number $11 \times 3 + 60 = 93$

SECTION E

(3 Case study-based question of 4 (1 + 1 + 2) marks each)

36. Case Study based - 1 (Sanchi Stupa)

The Great Stupa at Sanchi is one of the oldest stone structures in India and an important monument of Indian Architecture. It was originally commissioned by the emperor Ashoka in the 3rd century BC. Its nucleus was a simple hemispherical brick structure built over the relics of the Buddha. It is a perfect example of a combination of solid figures. A big hemispherical dome with a cuboidal structure mounted on it. (Take$\pi = \frac{22}{7}$)

(i) Calculate the volume of the hemispherical dome if the height of the dome is 21 m.

(a) 19404 m^3

(b) 20000 m^3

(c) 15000 m^3

(d) 19000 m^3

Solution:

Option (a) is correct

Height can be taken as radius of the tomb, so

$$r = 21\,m$$

Volume of hemisphere $= \frac{2}{3}\pi r^3$

$$= \frac{2}{3} \times \frac{22}{7} \times 21 \times 21 \times 21$$

$$= 19404 \text{ m}^3$$

(ii) The formula to find the Volume of Sphere is-

(a) $\frac{2}{3}\pi r^3$

(b) $\frac{4}{3}\pi r^3$

(c) $4\pi r^3$

(d) $\frac{4}{3}\pi r^2$

Solution:

Option (c) is correct

(iii) The cloth requires to cover the hemispherical dome if the radius of its base is 14m is

(a) 1222 m^2

(b) 1232 m^2

(c) 1200m^2

(d) 1400 m^2

Solution:

Option (b) is correct

Radius $r = 14\,m$

Cloth required to cover its curved surface area $= 2\pi r^2$

$$= 2 \times \frac{22}{7} \times 14 \times 14 = 1232m^2$$

(iv) The total surface area of the combined figure i.e., hemispherical dome with radius of 14m and cuboidal-shaped top with dimensions 8m $\times$ 6m $\times$ 4m is:

(a) 1200 m^2

(b) 1232 m^2

(c) 1392 m^2
(d) 1932m^2
Solution:
Option (c) is correct

$$\begin{aligned}\text{Total required area} &= \text{CSA of dome + lateral surface area of cuboid + area of the roof}\\ &= 1232 + (2(8+6) \times 4) + 8 \times 6\\ &= 1392\ m^2\end{aligned}$$

37. Case Study based – 2(Sports Day)

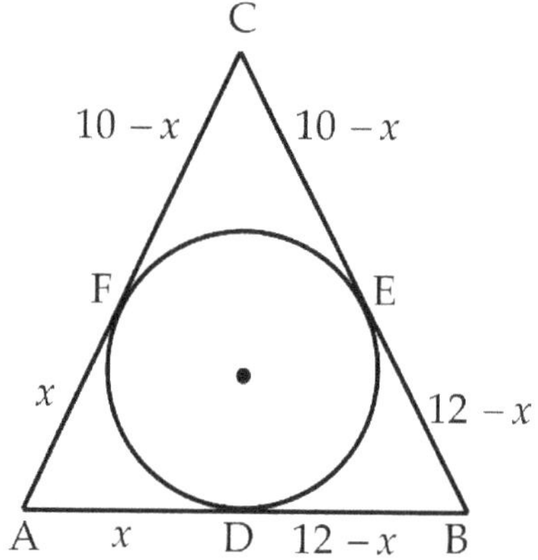

Varun has been selected by his School to design a logo for Sports Day T-shirts for students and staff. The logo design is as given in the figure, and he is working on the fonts and different colors according to the theme. In the given figure, a circle with center O is inscribed in a ΔABC, such that it touches the sides AB, BC, and CA at points D, E, and F respectively. The lengths of sides AB, BC, and CA are 12 cm, 8 cm, and 10 cm respectively.

(i) Find the length of AD:
(a) 7 cm
(b) 8 cm
(c) 5 cm
(d) 9 cm
Solution:
Option (a) is correct

$$AB = 12\ cm, BC = 8\ cm \text{ and } CA = 10\ cm$$

Let $$AD = AF = x\ cm$$

(tangents from external point are equal)

$$BD = BE = 12 - x\ cm,$$
$$AD = AF = x\ cm$$

and

$$CF = CE = 10 - x\ cm$$

So $$BC = BE + CE$$
$$8 = 12 - x + 10 - x$$
$$2x = 22 - 8 = 14$$
$$x = 7\ cm$$

(ii) Find the length of BE:

(a) 8 cm

(b) 5 cm

(c) 2 cm

(d) 9 cm

Solution:

Option (b) is correct

$BE = 12 - x = 12 - 7 = 5\,cm$

(iii) Find the length of CF:

(a) 9 cm

(b) 5 cm

(c) 2 cm

(d) 3 cm

Solution:

Option (d) is correct

$CF = 10 - x = 10 - 7 = 3$ cm

(iv) If radius of the circle is 4 cm, find the area of triangle AOB.

(a) 20 cm^2

(b) 36 cm^2

(c) 24 cm^2

(d) 48 cm^2

Solution:

Base $AB = 12\,cm$, drop perpendicular OP on AB i.e., radius = $4\,cm$

So, area of triangle = $\frac{1}{2} \times \text{base} \times \text{height}$

Area of triangle $= \frac{1}{2} \times 12 \times 4 = 24cm^2$

(v) Find the area of triangle ABC:

(a) 50 cm^2

(b) 60 cm^2

(c) 100cm^2

(d) 90 cm^2

Solution:

Option (b) is correct

area of triangle ABC = area of $\triangle AOB$ + area of $\triangle BOC$ + area of $\triangle AOC$

$$= 24 + \frac{1}{2} \times 8 \times 4 + \frac{1}{2} \times 10 \times 4$$

$$= 24 + 16 + 20 = 60 \text{ cm}^2$$

38. Case Study based – 1 (Upstream and Downstream)

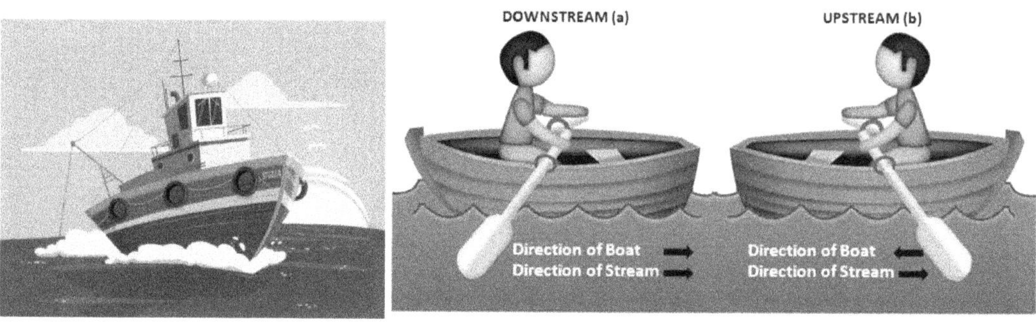

The speed of a motorboat is 20 km/hr. A boat goes 15 km upstream and returns to the original point. For covering the distance of 15 km the boat took 1 hour extra for upstream than downstream.

(i) Let the speed of the stream be x km/hr. then the speed of the motorboat in upstream shall be:

(a) $20 - x$ km/hr
(b) $x - 20$ km/hr
(c) $20 + x$ km/hr
(d) 20 km/hr

Solution:

Option (a) is correct

As in the upstream boat has to go to the opposite to stream.

(ii) What is the relationship between speed, distance, and time?

(a) Speed = distance × time
(b) Distance = speed / time
(c) Speed = time / distance
(d) None of these

Solution:

Option (d) is correct

(iii) What is the right quadratic equation for the speed of the stream?

(a) $x^2 + 30x - 200 = 0$
(b) $x^2 + 20x - 400 = 0$
(c) $x^2 + 30x - 400 = 0$
(d) $x^2 - 20x - 400 = 0$

Solution:

Option (iii) is correct

Upstream speed = $(20 - x)\ km/hr$

Downstream speed = $(20 + x)\ km/hr$

Time to go 15 km upstream $= \frac{15}{20-x}$ hr $\left(\text{Time} = \frac{\text{distance}}{\text{speed}}\right)$

Time to go 15 km downstream $= \frac{15}{20+x} hx$

$$\frac{15}{20-x} - \frac{15}{20+x} = 1$$

$$\frac{300+15x-300+15x}{(20-x)(20+x)} = 1$$

$$30x = 400 - x2$$

$$x^2 + 30x - 400 = 0$$

(iv) What is the speed of the stream?

(a) 20 km/hour

(b) 10 km/hour

(c) 15 km/hour

(d) 25 km/hour

Solution:

Option (b) is correct

On solving equation obtained in (c) part

$$x2 + 40x - 10x - 400 = 0$$

$$x(x + 40) - 10(x + 40) = 0$$

$$(x + 40)(x - 10) = 0$$

$x = -40, 10$, since speed can not be negative, so speed of stream = $10\ km/hr$.

UNSOLVED SAMPLE PAPER

Class- X Session- 2022-23

SAMPLE PAPER-1

Sample Question Paper

Time Allowed: 3 Hrs. **Maximum Marks: 80**

General Instructions:

1. This Question Paper has 5 Sections A-E.
2. Section **A** has 20 MCQs carrying 1 mark each
3. Section **B** has 5 questions carrying 02 marks each.
4. Section **C** has 6 questions carrying 03 marks each.
5. Section **D** has 4 questions carrying 05 marks each.
6. Section **E** has 3 case-based integrated units of assessment (04 marks each) with subparts of the values of 1, 1, and 2 marks each respectively.
7. All Questions are compulsory. However, an internal choice in 2 Qs of 5 marks, 2 Qs of 3 marks, and 2 Questions of 2 marks has been provided. An internal choice has been provided in the 2marks questions of Section E
8. Draw neat figures wherever required. Take π =22/7 wherever required if not stated

SECTION A

(Section A consists of 20 questions of 1 mark each)

1. If two positive integers a and b are written as $a = x^5y^2$ and $b = x^2y^3$(x and y are prime numbers) then HCF(a, b) is

(a) xy

(b) x^5y^3

(c) x^3y^3

(d) x^2y^2

Answer. (d)

2. If the sum of the squares of zeroes of the quadratic polynomial $f(x) = x^2 - 4x + k$ is 20, then find the value of k.

(a) 2

(b) −3

(c) −2

(d) 4

Answer. (c)

3. The value of k for which the pair of linear equations $4x - 6y - 1 = 0$ and $2x + ky - 7 = 0$ represents parallel lines is

(a) k = −3

(b) k = 2

(c) k = 4

(d) k = −2

Answer. (a)

4. If $\frac{1}{2}$ is a root of the equation $x^2 + kx - \frac{5}{4} = 0$, then the value of k is:

(a) $\frac{1}{2}$

(b) -2

(c) $\frac{1}{4}$

(d) 2

Answer. (d)

5. In triangles, ABC and DEF, $\angle B = \angle E, \angle C, = \angle F$, and $AB = 3DE$. Then, the two triangles are

(a) Congruent but not similar

(b) Neither congruent nor similar

(c) Similar but not congruent

(d) Congruent as well as similar

Answer. (c)

6. The value of $(\sin A + \cos A)^2 + (\sin A - \cos A)^2$ is:

(a) 2

(b) 1

(c) 4

(d) -2

Answer. (a)

7. If abscissa of a point is zero, then it lies on:

(a) x-axis

(b) y-axis

(c) I Quadrant

(d) III Quadrant

Answer. (b)

8. A tangent is perpendicular to the radius at the

(a) Point of contact

(b) Centre

(c) Infinity

(d) Chord

Answer. (a)

9. The perimeter of a quadrant of a circle of radius ' r ' is:

(a) $\frac{\pi r}{2}$

(b) $2\pi r$

(c) $\frac{r}{2}[\pi + 4]$

(d) $2\pi r + \frac{r}{2}$

Answer. (c)

10. If the angles of elevation of the top of a tower 200m high from two points A and B on the ground on either side of the tower are 45° and 30° respectively, then the distance between points A and Bis:

(a) $200\left(1+\frac{1}{\sqrt{3}}\right)$ m

(b) $200(1+\sqrt{3})$m

(c) 300m

(d) 400m

Answer. (b)

11. The ratio of the total surface area of a solid hemisphere to the square of its radius is:

(a) $2\pi: 1$

(b) $3\pi: 1$

(c) $4\pi: 1$

(d) $1: 4\pi$

Answer. (b)

12. In $\triangle$ ABC, a line XY parallel to BC cuts AB at X and AC at Y. If BY bisects $\angle$XYC, then

(a) $BC = CY$

(b) $BC = BY$

(c) $BC \neq CY$

(d) $BC \neq BY$

Answer. (a)

13. If $x \tan 45° \cos 60° = \sin 60° \cot 60°$, then x is equal to

(a) 1

(b) $\sqrt{3}$

(c) $\frac{1}{2}$

(d) $\frac{1}{\sqrt{2}}$

Answer. (a)

14. If the mode of the data: $64,60,48,x,43,48,43,34$ is 43, then $x + 3 =$

(a) 44

(b) 45

(c) 46

(d) 48

Answer. (c)

15. If the circumference of a circle increases from 2π to 4π, then its area is:

(a) Halved

(b) Doubled

(c) Tripled

(d) Four times

Answer. (d)

16. A card is drawn from a well-shuffled deck of 52 playing cards. The probability of drawing a red face card is:

(a) $\frac{1}{26}$

(b) $\frac{3}{26}$

(c) $\frac{4}{26}$

(d) $\frac{1}{13}$

Answer. (b)

17. If f $\Sigma f_i = 12, \Sigma f_i x_i = 2p + 52$, and the mean of a distribution is 7, then the value of p

(a) 14

(b) 15

(c) 12

(d) 16

Answer. (d)

18. In the given figure DE || AC, which of the following is true?

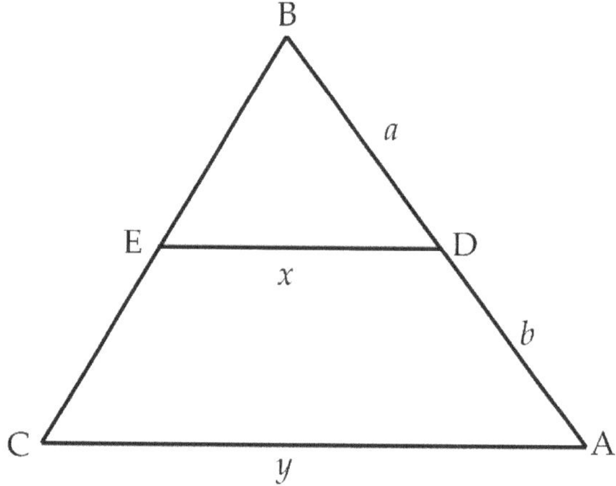

(a) $x = \frac{a+b}{xy}$

(b) $y = \frac{ax}{a+b}$

(c) $x = \frac{ay}{a+b}$

(d) $\frac{x}{y} = \frac{a}{b}$

Answer. (c)

Direction: In the following questions, a statement of Assertion (A) is followed by a statement of Reason (R). Mark the correct choice as:

(a) Both Assertion (A) and Reason (R) are true, and Reason (R) is the correct explanation of Assertion (A).

(b) Both Assertion (A) and Reason (R) are true, but Reason (R) is not the correct explanation of Assertion (A).
(c) Assertion (A) is true, but Reason (R) is false.
(d) Assertion (A) is false, but Reason (R) is true.

19. Assertion: If Sn is the sum of the first n terms of an A.P., then its nth term a_n is given by $a_n = S_n - S_{n-1}$.
Reason: The 10th term of the A.P. 5, 8, 11, 14, ... is 35.
Answer. (c)

20. Assertion: The sum of the series with the nth term, $T_n = (9 - 5n)$ is (465), when no. of terms n = 15.
Reason: Given series is in A.P. and sum of n terms of an A.P. is: $\frac{n}{2}[2a + (n-1)d]$
Answer. (d)

SECTION B

(Section B consists of 5 questions of 2 marks each)

21. Solve the following systems of simultaneous linear equations.
$\frac{x+y}{xy} = 2, \frac{x-y}{xy} = 6$

22. The given figure shows a parallelogramABCD. E is a point in AD and CE produced meets BA produced at point F. If AE = 4 cm, AF = 8 cm, and AB = 12 cm, find the perimeter of the parallelogram ABCD.

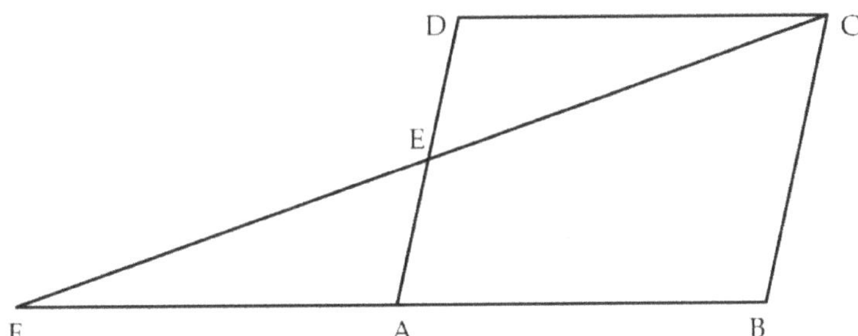

23. Ifsin (A + B) = cos (A – B) = $\frac{\sqrt{3}}{2}$, then find the values of A and B where A and B are acute angles.

24. If in the given diagram PT is tangent to a circle with center O and TM ⊥ OP, prove that △ POT and △ PTM have their corresponding angles equal.

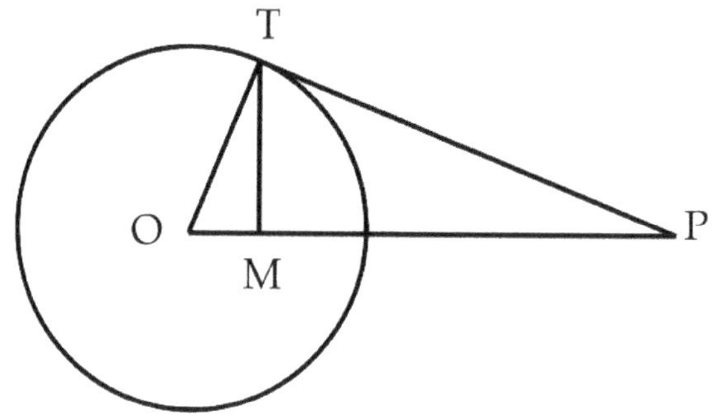

25. What will be the increase in the area of a circle, if its radius is increased by 40%?

SECTION -C

(Section C consists of 6 questions of 3 marks each)

26. What is the smallest number which when divided by 144,180 and 192 leaves the remainder 3 in each case?

27. If $4\cos^2 x^\circ - 1 = 0$ and $0 \leq x^\circ \leq 90^\circ$, find:

(i) x^o

(ii) $\sin^2 x^\circ + \cos^2 x^\circ$

(iii) $\frac{1}{\cos^2 x^\circ} - \tan^2 x^\circ$

28. If α and β are the zeroes of the quadratic polynomial, such that $\alpha + \beta = 24$ and $\alpha - \beta = 8$, then find the quadratic polynomial having α and β as its zeroes.

29. A fraction is such that if the numerator is multiplied by 3 and the denominator reduced by 3, we get $\frac{18}{11}$, but if the numerator is increased by 8 and the denominator is doubled, we get $\frac{2}{5}$. Find the fraction.

30. In the figure, the sides AB, BC, and CA of triangle ABC touch a circle with center O and radius r at P, Q and R respectively.

Prove that:

(i) $AB + CQ = AC + BQ$

(ii) Area $(\triangle ABC) = \frac{1}{2}($ Perimeter of $\triangle ABC) \times r$

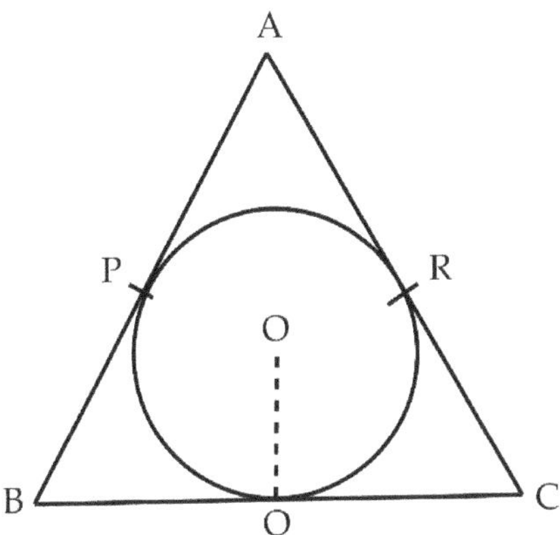

31. A bag contains 18 balls out of which x balls are red.

(i) If one ball is drawn at random from the bag, what is the probability that it is a red ball (in terms of x)?

(ii) If 2 more red balls are put in the bag, the probability of drawing a red ball will be $\frac{9}{8}$ times that of the probability of the red ball coming in part (i)Find x.

SECTION D

(Section D consists of 4 questions of 5 marks each)

32. A take 3 days longer than B to finish work. But if they work together, then work is completed in 2 days. How long would each take to do it separately?

33. PQR is a triangle right angled at P and M is a point on QR, such that. Show that: $PM^2 = QM \times MR.$

34. A cylindrical pillar of a temple is shown in the figure, which is conical at the top. There are 14 such pillars, in the temple. Find the cost of polishing their curved surface area at the rate of Rs. 1.50 per m^2.$\left(\text{Use } \pi = \frac{22}{7}\right)$

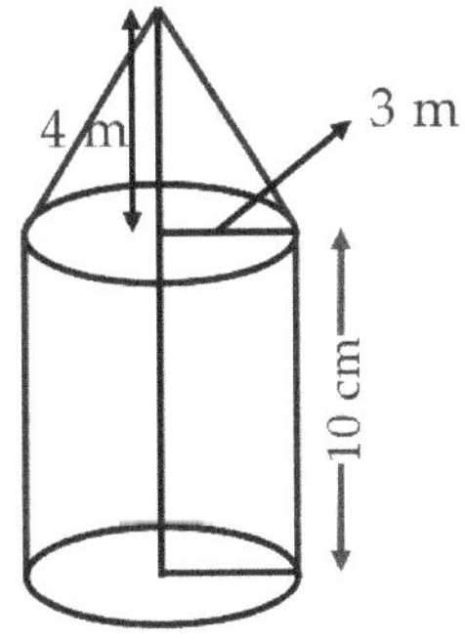

35. The arithmetic mean of the following distribution is 25. Determine the value of p

Class	0 - 10	10 − 20	20 - 30	30 − 40	40 - 50
Frequency	5	18	15	p	6

SECTION E

(3 Case study-based question of 4 (1 + 1 + 2) marks each)

36. Case Study based – 2 (T.V. Manufacturing Company) (not taken)

During the summer of 2003, Manisha thought of starting a business of her own and lent some money from her father and started a TV manufacturing company. After some years, she was known as one of the leading manufacturers in her area and kept expanding her limit year by year. Assuming that the production increases uniformly year by year, the number of tv sets produced by her in the third year was 600 units and in the seventh year, it was 700.

(i) What was the gradual increase in manufacturing per year?

(a) 20 units
(b) 25 units
(c) 30 units
(d) 45 units

(ii) What was the production in the first year?

(a) 550 units
(b) 555 units
(c) 560 units
(d) 545 units

(iii) What was the production in the tenth year?

(a) 770 units
(b) 775 units
(c) 780 units
(d) 785 units

(iv) What is the total production till seven years?

(a) 4365 units
(b) 4370 units
(c) 4375 units
(d) 4380 units

37. The class X students' school in Krishnagar has been allotted a rectangular plot of land for their gardening activity. Saplings of Gul Mohar are planted on the boundary at a distance of 1 m from each other. There is a triangular grassy lawn in the plot as shown in the figure. The students are to sow seeds of flowering plants on the remaining area of the plot.

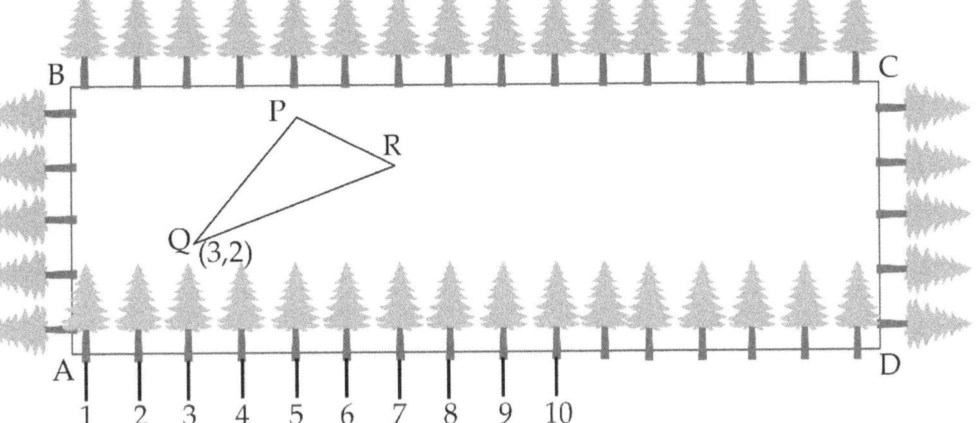

(i) Taking A as the origin, find the coordinates of P

(a) (4,6)
(b) (6,4)
(c) (0,6)
(d) (4,0)

(ii) What will be the coordinates of R, if C is the origin?

(a) (8,6)
(b) (3,10)
(c) (10,3)
(d) (0,6)

(iii) What will be the coordinates of Q, if C is the origin?

(a) (6,13)
(b) (−6,13)
(c) (−13,6)
(d) (13,6)

(iv) Which type of triangle is PQR, if the origin is C?

(a) Scalene triangle
(b) Isosceles triangle
(c) Equilateral triangle
(d) Right-angled triangle

38. To enhance the reading skills of grade X students, the school nominates you and two of your friends to set up a class library. There are two sections- section A and section B of grade X. There are 36 students in section A and 45 students in section B.

(i) What is the minimum number of books you will acquire for the class library so that they can be distributed equally among students of Section A or Section B?

(a) 150

(b) 180

(c) 280

(d) 300

(ii) If the product of two positive integers is equal to the product of their HCF and LCM is true then, the HCF (36, 45) is

(a) 4

(b) 5

(c) 9

(d) 6

(iii) 45 can be expressed as a product of its primes as

(a) $3^3 \times 5$

(b) $3^2 \times 5$

(c) $2^3 \times 5$

(d) $2^2 \times 5$

(iv) If p and q are positive integers such that $p = x^2y^3$and $q = x^3y^2$, where a, b are prime numbers, then the LCM (p, q) is

(a) x^2y^3

(b) x^3y^2

(c) x^3y^3

(d) x^2y^2

Answers:

Section B
21. $[x = -\frac{1}{2}, y = 1/4]$
22. 44 cm
23. A = 45° and B= 15^0
25. 96%
Section C
26. 2883
27. (i)60^0 (ii) 1 (iii)1
28. $x^2 - 24x + 128$
29. $\frac{12}{25}$
31. (i) $\frac{x}{18}$ (ii) $x = 8$
Section D
32. A: 6 days, B: 3 days
34. 4950
35. P = 16
Section E
36. (a) 25 units (b) 550 units (c) 775 units (d) 4375 units
37. (a) (4,6) (b) (10,3) (c) (13,6) (d) Scalene triangle
38. (a) 180 (b) 9 (c) $3^2 \times 5$ (d) x^3y^3

Class- X Session- 2022-23

SAMPLE PAPER-2

Sample Question Paper

Time Allowed: 3 Hrs. **Maximum Marks: 80**

General Instructions:

1. This Question Paper has 5 Sections A-E.
2. Section **A** has 20 MCQs carrying 1 mark each
3. Section **B** has 5 questions carrying 02 marks each.
4. Section **C** has 6 questions carrying 03 marks each.
5. Section **D** has 4 questions carrying 05 marks each.
6. Section **E** has 3 case-based integrated units of assessment (04 marks each) with subparts of the values of 1, 1, and 2 marks each respectively.
7. All Questions are compulsory. However, an internal choice in 2 Qs of 5 marks, 2 Qs of 3 marks, and 2 Questions of 2 marks has been provided. An internal choice has been provided in the 2marks questions of Section E
8. Draw neat figures wherever required. Take π =22/7 wherever required if not stated

SECTION A

(Section A consists of 20 questions of 1 mark each)

1.There are 576 boys and 448 girls in a school that is to be divided into equal sections of either boys or girls alone. The total number of sections thus formed is:

(a) 22
(b) 16
(c) 36
(d) 42
Answer. (b)

2.If one zero of $2x^2 - 3x + k$ is reciprocal to the other, then find the value of k.

(a) 1
(b) -1
(c) -2
(d) 2
Answer. (d)

3.The pair of equations $x = 2$ and $y = 3$ graphically represent lines which are:

(a) Coincident
(b) Parallel
(c) Intersecting at (3,2)
(d) Intersecting at (2,3)
Answer. (d)

4. If $x = 1$ is a common root of the equations $ax^2 + ax + 3 = 0$ and $x^2 + x + b = 0$, then the value of ab is:

(a) 3

(b) 3.5

(c) 6

(d) -3

Answer. (a)

5. In the given figure, if $\angle ADE = \angle ABC$, then CE is equal to:

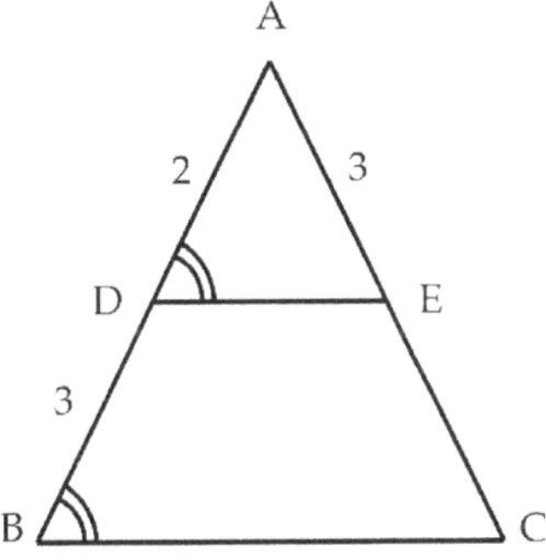

(a) 2

(b) 5

(c) 4.5

(d) 3

Answer. (c)

6. If the altitude of the sun is at 30°, then the height of the vertical tower that will cast a shadow of length 30m on the ground is:

(a) $10\sqrt{3}$m

(b) 10m

(c) $30\sqrt{3}$m

(d) 30m

Answer. (a)

7. The mid-point of line segment AB is the point $(0, 4)$. If the coordinates of B are $(-2, 3)$, then the coordinates of Aare:

(a) (2,5)

(b) $(-2, -5)$

(c) (2,9)

(d) $(-2,11)$

Answer. (a)

8. A line that intersects a circle at two distinct points is called:

(a) Tangent

(b) Secant

(c) Point
(d) Decimal
Answer. (b)

9. If the diameter of a semi-circular protractor is 14cm, then the perimeter of the protractor is :
(a) 26cm
(b) 14cm
(c) 28cm
(d) 36cm
Answer. (d)

10. If θ is an acute angle and $\sin\theta - \cos\theta = 0$, then the value of $2\cot^2\theta - \sin^2\theta + 1$ is
(a) 23
(b) 52
(c) 25
(d) 43
Answer. (b)

11. The radius of a sphere is r cm. It is divided into two equal parts. The whole surface area of the two parts will be:
(a) 8.2 cm^2
(b) 6.2 cm^2
(c) 4.2 cm^2
(d) 3.2 cm^2
Answer. (b)

12. The median class of the following data:

C.I.	10 – 20	20 – 30	30 – 40	40 – 50	50 – 60	60 – 70
Frequency	12	6	10	8	11	13

(a) 20 – 30
(b) 30 – 40
(c) 40 – 50
(d) 50 – 60
Answer. (c)

13. In $\triangle ABC, D$ and E are points on side AB and AC respectively such that $DE \parallel BC$ and $AD:DB = 3:1$. If $EA = 3.3$cm, then $AC =$
(a) 1.1cm
(b) 4cm
(c) 4.4cm
(d) 5.5cm
Answer. (c)

14. The radius of a circle whose circumference is equal to the sum of the circumferences of two circles of diameters 36cm and 20cm is:

(a) 56cm
(b) 42cm
(c) 28cm
(d) 16cm
Answer. (c)

15. If the mode of the data: 16,15,17,16,15, x, 19,17,14 is 15, then $x + 2 =$

(a) 15
(b) 16
(c) 17
(d) 19
Answer. (c)

16. The value of $\sec A(1 - \sin A)(\sec A + \tan A)$ is:

(a) 2
(b) 1
(c) -1
(d) -2
Answer. (b)

17. If the probability of an event is 0.65, then the probability of not happening that event is:

(a) 0.35
(b) 0.035
(c) 1.25
(d) 3
Answer. (a)

18. Two equilateral triangles are similar by:

(a) AAA similarity
(b) SSS similarity
(c) SAS similarity
(d) All
Answer. (d)

Direction: In the following questions, a statement of Assertion (A) is followed by a statement of Reason (R). Mark the correct choice as:

(a) Both Assertion (A) and Reason (R) are true, and Reason (R) is the correct explanation of Assertion (A).

(b) Both Assertion (A) and Reason (R) are true, but Reason (R) is not the correct explanation of Assertion (A).

(c) Assertion (A) is true, but Reason (R) is false.

(d) Assertion (A) is false, but Reason (R) is true.

19. Assertion: If one root of the quadratic equation $6x^2 - x - k = 0$ is $\frac{2}{3}$, then the value of k is 2.

Reason: The quadratic equation $ax^2 + bx + c = 0$, $a \neq 0$ has almost two roots.

Answer. (b)

20. Assertion: $(2x - 1)^2 - 4x^2 + 5 = 0$ is not a quadratic equation.

Reason: An equation of the form $\mathrm{a}x^2 + \mathrm{b}x + \mathrm{c} = 0, \mathrm{a} \neq 0$, where $\mathrm{a, b, c} \in \mathrm{R}$ is called a quadratic equation.

Answer. (a)

SECTION B

(Section B consists of 5 questions of 2 marks each)

21. Solve the following systems of simultaneous linear equations.

$41x + 53y = 135$

$53x + 41y = 147$

22. In the right-angled triangle QPR, PM is an altitude.

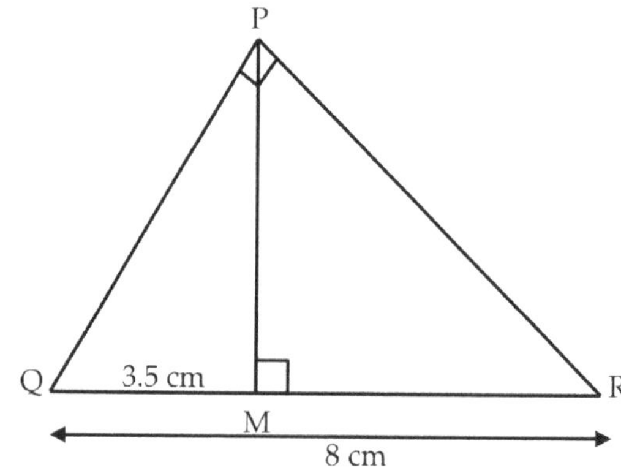

Given that QR = 8cm and MQ = 3.5cm, calculate the value of PR.

23. Solve for x:$cos\left(\frac{x}{2} + 10°\right) = \frac{\sqrt{3}}{2}$

OR

Prove the identity: $(\mathrm{cosec}^2 \mathrm{A} - 1)(\sec \mathrm{A} + 1)(\sec \mathrm{A} - 1) = 1$

24. PA and PB are two tangents drawn from. an external point P to a circle with center O. If AP = 16cm, find the perimeter of $\triangle$ PCD.

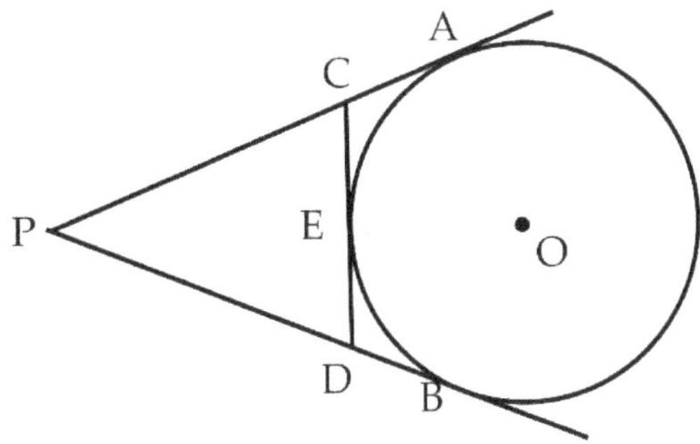

25. In the figure given alongside, a circular track is in the form of a ring whose inner circumference is 88 cm and outer circumference is 132cm. Find its width.

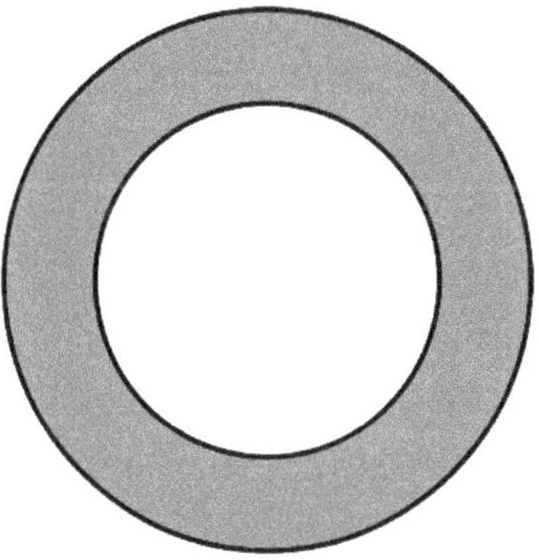

SECTION C

(Section C consists of 6 questions of 3 marks each)

26. In a morning walk, three persons step off together, their steps measuring80cm, 85cm, and 90cm respectively. What is the minimum distance each should walk so that he can cover the distance in complete steps?

27. Use the information given to find the length of AB.

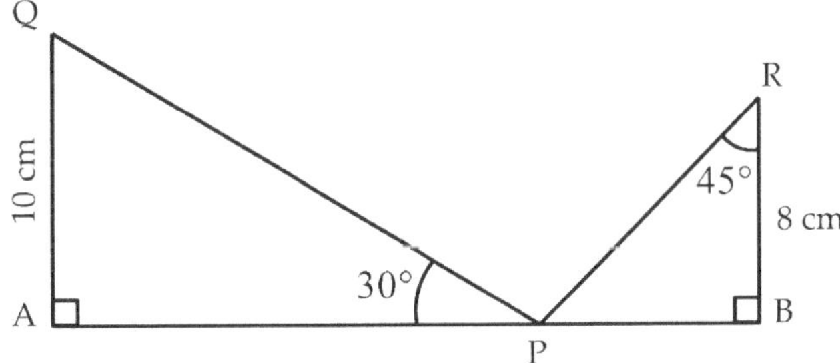

28. If α and β are zeroes of the polynomial $21y^2 - y - 2$, then find a quadratic polynomial, whose zeroes are 2α and 2β.

29. Two years ago, Salim was thrice as old as her daughter and six years later, he will be four years older than twice her age. How old are they now?

30. From the given figure, prove that:

$AP + BQ + CR = BP + CQ + AR$.

Also, show that:

$AP + BQ + CR = \frac{1}{2} \times$ Perimeter of $\triangle ABC$

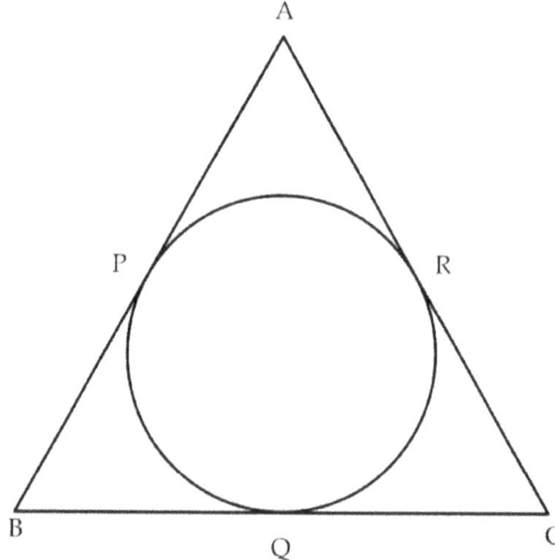

31. A box contains 90 discs which are numbered from 5 to 94. If one disc is drawn at random from the box, find the probability that it bears:

(i) A perfect square numbers

(ii) A two-digit number

(iii) A number divisible by 7

(iv) A number that is divisible by 10.

SECTION D

(Section D consists of 4 questions of 5 marks each)

32. The length of a rectangle exceeds its breadth by 5m. If the breadth were doubled and the length reduced by 9m, the area of the rectangle would have increased by $140m^2$. Find its dimensions.

33. In the given figure PA, QB and RC are perpendicular to AC. Prove that.

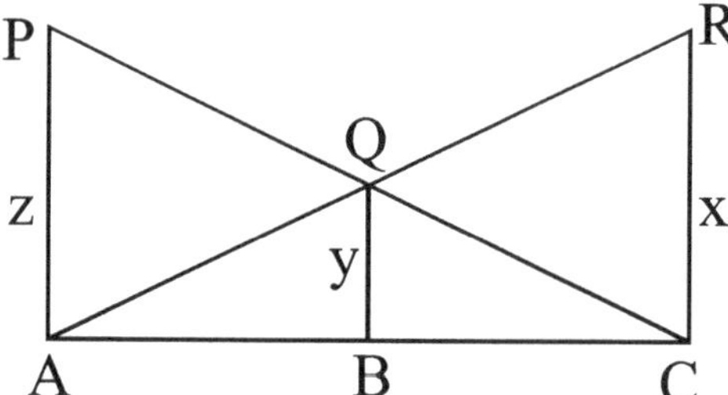

34. A circus tent is made of canvas and is in the form of a right circular cylinder and a right circular cone above it. The diameter and the height of the cylindrical part of the tent are 21 meters and 4 meters respectively. The slant height of the conical part is 12.5m. Find the area of the canvas used for making the tent. Also, find the total cost of the tent if the canvas used costs Rs. 12 per sq. meter.

35. Find the median of the following data:

Profit (in lakhs of rupees)	**Number of shops**
More than or equal to 5	30
More than or equal to 10	28
More than or equal to 15	16
More than or equal to 20	14
More than or equal to 25	10
More than or equal to 30	7
More than or equal to 35	3

Section E

3 Case study-based question of 4 (1 + 1 + 2) marks each

36. Case Study based – 1 (Rubix Cube)

A teacher in his class brought a Rubix cube as shown in the figure. He wanted to explain the surfaces and volumes of the Rubix cube. He explained that the Rubix cube is a combination of smaller cubes. It contains cubes in $3 \times 3 \times 3$manner. Each small cube has a $2 \times$ cm $\times$ 2cm $\times$ 2cm dimension.

(i) What is the total surface area of the Rubix cube?

(a) 216 cm^2
(b) 108 cm^2
(c) 132 cm^2
(d) 5127.07 cm^2

(ii) What is the volume of the Rubix cube?

(a) 127 cm^3

(b) 216 cm^3

(c) 324 cm^3

(d) 108 cm^3

(iii) What is the lateral surface area of each cube?

(a) 32 cm^3

(b) 28 cm^3

(c) 24 cm^3

(d) 48 cm^3

(iv) What is the total surface area when four Rubix cubes are joined in a row?

(a) 1200 cm^2

(b) 648 cm^2

(c) 642 cm^2

(d) 600 cm^2

37. Case Study based – 2 (Ice Cream)

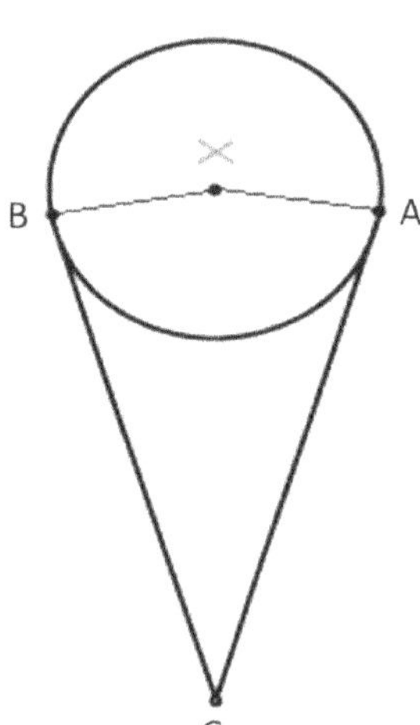

Chris was eating ice cream on the way back home from the shop. When he observed the shape of ice cream, he found it as a circle with 2 tangents.

(i) What is the value of $\angle CAX$

(a) 80°

(b) 90°

(c) 95°

(d) 100°

(ii) Which are the two tangents in the figure?

(a) AX and BX

(b) AX *and* AC

(c) BX and BC

(d) AC and BC

(iii) If $\angle AXB = 130^{o}$ then find the$\angle AXB$

(a) 30°
(b) 50°
(c) 70°
(d) None of these

(iv) If AC $=$ 45 cm and BC $= 15x$, then find the value of x.

(a) 2
(b) 4
(c) 3
(d) 1

38. Rahul and Ravi planned to play Business (a board game) in which they were supposed to use two dice.

(i) Ravi got the first chance to roll the dice. What is the probability that he got the sum of the two numbers appearing on the top face of the dice is more than 9?

(a) $\frac{1}{5}$
(b) $\frac{1}{6}$
(c) $\frac{5}{6}$
(d) $\frac{2}{5}$

(ii) Rahul got the next chance. What is the probability that he got the sum of the two numbers appearing on the top face of the dice is a doublet of prime numbers?

(a) $\frac{1}{3}$
(b) $\frac{1}{6}$
(c) $\frac{1}{9}$
(d) $\frac{1}{12}$

(iii) Now it was Ravi's turn. He rolled the dice. What is the probability that he got the sum of the two numbers appearing on the top face of the dice is less than 12?

(a) $\frac{35}{36}$

(b) 1

(c) $\frac{23}{36}$

(d) $\frac{31}{36}$

(iv) Rahul got the next chance. What is the probability that the difference of the numbers on the top of dice is 2?

(a) $\frac{5}{9}$

(b) $\frac{5}{7}$

(c) $\frac{1}{9}$

(d) $\frac{2}{9}$

Answers:

Section B
21. $[x = 2, y = 1]$,
22. 6 cm
23. 40°
24. 32 cm
25. 7 cm
Section C
26. 122 m 40 cm
27. 25.32 cm
28. $y^2 - \frac{2y}{21} - \frac{8}{21}$
29. Salim = 38 years, daughter = 14 years.
31. (i) $\frac{7}{90}$ (ii) $\frac{17}{18}$ (iii) $\frac{13}{90}$ (iv) $\frac{1}{10}$
Section D
32. Length = 25 m and breadth = 20 m
34. 676.5 m^2, Rs. 8118.0
35. 17.5
Section E
36.(i) 216 cm^2 (ii) 216 cm^3 (iii) 24 cm^3 (iv) 648 cm^2
37.(i) 90° (ii) AC and BC (iii) 50° (iv) 3
38. (i) $\frac{1}{6}$ (ii) $\frac{1}{12}$ (iii) $\frac{35}{36}$ (iv) $\frac{2}{9}$

Class- X Session- 2022-23

SAMPLE PAPER-3

Sample Question Paper

Time Allowed: 3 Hrs. **Maximum Marks: 80**

General Instructions:

1. This Question Paper has 5 Sections A-E.
2. Section **A** has 20 MCQs carrying 1 mark each
3. Section **B** has 5 questions carrying 02 marks each.
4. Section **C** has 6 questions carrying 03 marks each.
5. Section **D** has 4 questions carrying 05 marks each.
6. Section **E** has 3 case-based integrated units of assessment (04 marks each) with subparts of the values of 1, 1, and 2 marks each respectively.
7. All Questions are compulsory. However, an internal choice in 2 Qs of 5 marks, 2 Qs of 3 marks, and 2 Questions of 2 marks has been provided. An internal choice has been provided in the 2marks questions of Section E
8. Draw neat figures wherever required. Take π =22/7 wherever required if not stated

SECTION A

(Section A consists of 20 questions of 1 mark each)

1. If p, q are two prime numbers, then LCM (p, q) is

(a) 1
(b) p
(c) q
(d) pq
Answer: (d)

2. If α and β are the zeroes of the polynomial $2y^2 + 7y + 5$, then find the value of $\alpha + \beta + \alpha\beta$

(a) 1
(b) 2
(c) -1
(d) -2
Answer: (c)

3. The pair of equations $ax + 2y = 7$ and $3x + by = 16$ represent parallel lines if:

(a) $a = b$
(b) $3a = 2b$
(c) $2a = 3b$
(d) $ab = 6$
Answer: (d)

4. For a quadratic equation $ax^2 + bx + c = 0$, if the roots are real and equal, then discriminant ' D ' is:
(a) > 0
(b) < 0
(c) $= 0$
(d) ≥ 0
Answer: (c)

5. In Fig. 6.220, $ABCD$ is a trapezium in which $AB \parallel EF \parallel DC$. The length of AE is:

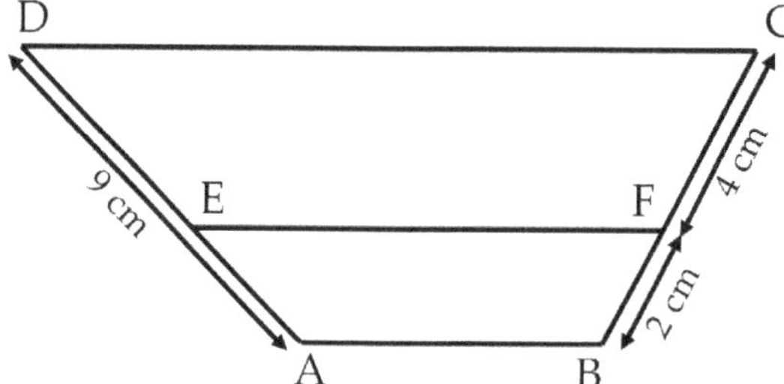

(a) 2cm
(b) 3cm
(c) 4cm
(d) 7cm
Answer: (b)

6. The angles of elevation of the top of two towers at a point on the ground and at equal distances from the base of each tower are 45° and 60°. What will be the ratio of their heights?
(a) $1:\sqrt{3}$
(b) $1:2$
(c) $1:2\sqrt{3}$
(d) $1:3$
Answer: (a)

7. To locate a point P on AB such that $PB = \frac{1}{4}AB$, line segment AB should be divided in the ratio:
(a) $3:1$
(b) $1:3$
(c) $1:4$
(d) $3:5$
Answer: (a)

8. The distance between two parallel tangents of a circle of radius 3cmis:
(a) 6cm
(b) 3cm
(c) 4.5cm
(d) 12cm
Answer: (a)

9. In triangles ABC and $DEF, \angle A = \angle E = 40°, AB: ED = AC: EF$ and $\angle F = 65°$, then $\angle B =$

(a) 35°

(b) 65°

(c) 75°

(d) 85°

Answer: (c)

10. The diameter of a circle whose area is equal to the sum of the areas of the two circles of radii 40cm and 9cm is:

(a) 41cm

(b) 49cm

(c) 82cm

(d) 62cm

Answer: (c)

11. Value of $\sec^2 A + \text{cosec}^2 A$ is equal to:

(a) $\cos^2 A$

(b) $\sin^2 A$

(c) $\sec^2 A \times \text{cosec}^2 A$

(d) $\tan A$

Answer: (c)

12. The radius of the largest right circular cone that can be cut out from a cube of the edge of 4.2cm is:

(a) 4.2cm

(b) 8.4cm

(c) 1.05cm

(d) 2.1cm

Answer: (d)

13. The mean of 1,3,4,5,7,4 is m. The numbers 3,2,2,4,3,3, p have mean $m - 1$ and median q. Then, $p + q =$

(a) 4

(b) 5

(c) 6

(d) 7

Answer: (d)

14. If $\sqrt{3} \tan \theta = 1$, then the value of $\sin^2 \theta - \cos^2 \theta$

(a) $\frac{1}{2}$

(b) 2

(c) $\frac{3}{2}$

(d) $-\frac{1}{2}$

Answer: (d)

15. In the given figure $PQ \parallel BC$, then by using the condition of similarity:

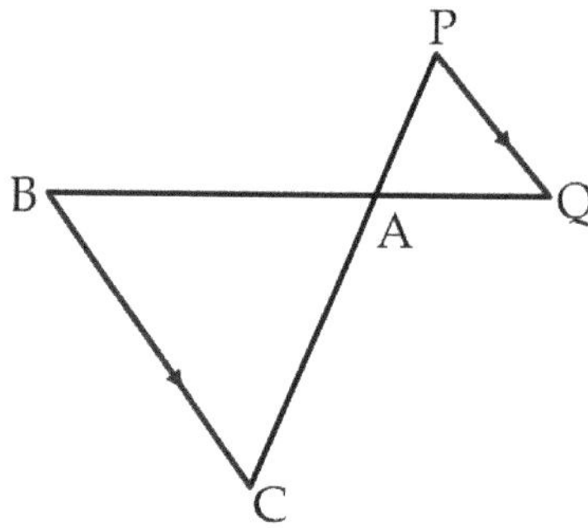

(a) $\frac{PQ}{CB} = \frac{AP}{AB} = \frac{AQ}{AC}$
(b) $\frac{PQ}{CB} = \frac{AP}{AC} = \frac{AQ}{AB}$
(c) $\frac{PQ}{CB} = \frac{AC}{AP} = \frac{AQ}{AC}$
(d) $\frac{PQ}{CB} = \frac{AP}{AC} = \frac{AB}{AQ}$
Answer: (b)

16. The outer and inner diameters of a circular ring are 34cm and 32cm respectively. The area (incm^2) of the ring is:
(a) 66π
(b) 60π
(c) 33π
(d) 29π
Answer: (c)

17. The modal class of the following data:

Class intervals	10 – 20	20 – 30	30 – 40	40 – 50	50 – 60	60 – 70
Frequency	12	6	13	8	11	10

(a) 20 – 30
(b) 30 – 40
(c) 40 – 50
(d) 50 – 60
Answer: (b)

18. If $p(A)$ denotes the probability of an event A, then
(a) $p(\mathrm{A}) < 0$
(b) $p(\mathrm{A}) > 1$
(c) $0 \le p(\mathrm{A}) \le 1$
(d) $-1 \le p(\mathrm{A}) \le 1$
Answer: (c)

Direction: In the following questions, a statement of Assertion (A) is followed by a statement of Reason (R). Mark the correct choice as:

(a) Both Assertion (A) and Reason (R) are true, and Reason (R) is the correct explanation of Assertion (A).

(b) Both Assertion (A) and Reason (R) are true, but Reason (R) is not the correct explanation of Assertion (A).

(c) Assertion (A) is true, but Reason (R) is false.

(d) Assertion (A) is false, but Reason (R) is true

19. Assertion: The roots of the quadratic equation $x^2 + 2x + 2 = 0$ are imaginary

Reason: If discriminant D $= b^2 - 4ac < 0$ then the roots of the quadratic equation $ax^2 + bx + c = 0$ are imaginary.

Answer. (a)

20. Assertion: In a circle of radius 6 cm, the angle of a sector is 60°. Then the area of the sector is $132/7$ cm^2.

Reason: The area of the circle with radius r is πr^2.

Answer. (b)

SECTION B

(Section B consists of 5 questions of 2 marks each)

21. Solve the following systems of simultaneous linear equations.

$$\frac{3}{x+y} + \frac{2}{x-y} = 3 \text{ and } \frac{2}{x+y} + \frac{3}{x-y} = \frac{11}{3}$$

22. In the given figure, QR is parallel to AB and DR is parallel to QB.

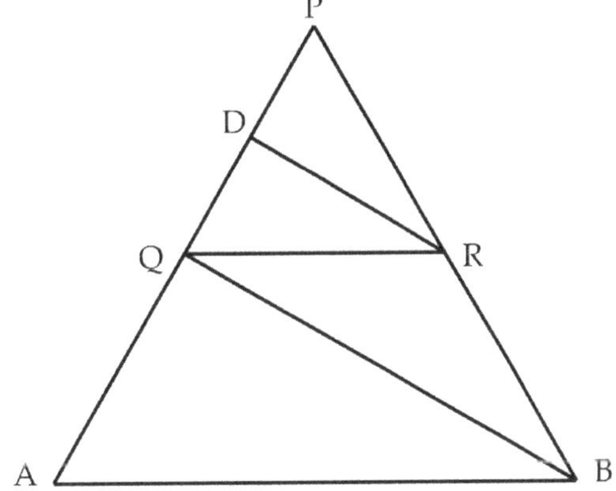

Prove that: $PQ^2 = PD \times PA$.

23. $4\cos^2 x = 3$ and x is an acute angle; find the value of:

(i) x

(ii) $\cos^2 x + \cot^2 x$

(iii) $\cos 3x$

(iv) $\sin 2x$

24. TP is a tangent to the circle with centre O. If $\angle TOQ = 120°$, find the diameter of the circle, when $OT = 10cm$.

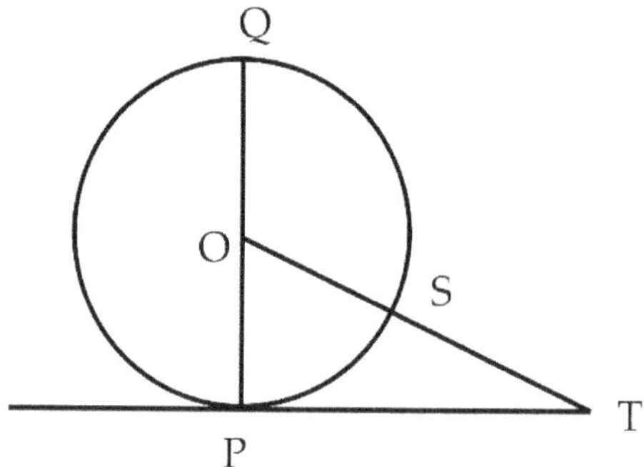

25. A bicycle wheel of radius 35cm is making 25 revolutions in 10 seconds. At what speed in km/h is the bicycle moving?

SECTION C

(Section C consists of 6 questions of 3 marks each)

26. Check whether $5 \times 7 \times 11 + 7$ is a composite number.

27. Prove the identity: $\frac{\sin A}{1+\cot A} - \frac{\cos A}{1+\tan A} = \sin A - \cos A$

28. If α and β are the zeroes of the quadratic polynomial $f(x) = x^2 - 5x + k$, such that $\alpha - \beta = 1$, then find the value of k.

29. The area of a rectangle gets reduced by $8m^2$, when its length is reduced by 5m and its breadth is increased by 3m. If we increase the length by 3 m and breadth by 2m, the area is increased by $74m^2$. Find the length and breadth of the rectangle.

30. ABC is a right-angled triangle with AB = 12cm and AC = 13cm. A circle, with a centre O, has been inscribed inside the triangle. Calculate the value of x, the radius of the inscribed circle.

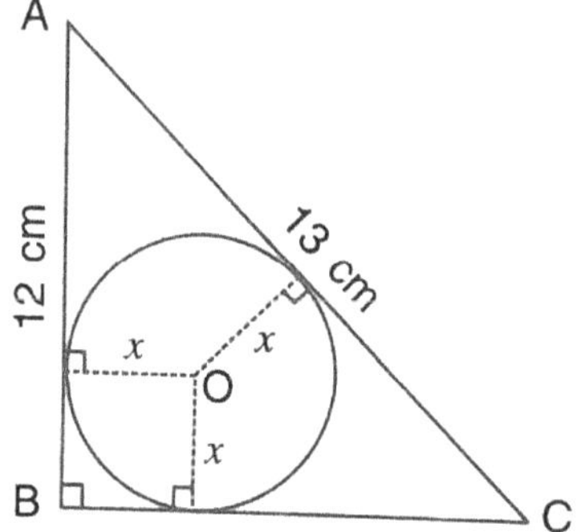

31. From the numbers 1, 2, 3, one number x is selected and from the numbers 1, 4, and 9, the second number y is selected. Find the probability that the:

(i) Product of two numbers is less than 9.

(ii) Product of two numbers is more than 13.

(iii) Sum of two numbers is 12.

SECTION D

(Section D consists of 4 questions of 5 marks each)

32. Two water taps together can fill a tank in $9\frac{3}{8}$ hours. The tap of larger diameter takes 10 hours less than the smaller one to fill the tank separately. Find the time in which each tap can separately fill the tank.

33. Prove: "The line segment joining midpoints of any two sides of a triangle is parallel to the third side and is equal to half of it."

34. Water running in a cylindrical pipe of an inner diameter of 7cm, is collected in a container at the rate of 192.5 liters per minute. Find the rate of flow of water in the pipe in km/h. $\left(\text{Use } \pi = \frac{22}{7}\right)$

35. Given below is a cumulative frequency distribution showing the marks secured by 50 students in a class.

Marks	Below 20	Below 40	Below 60	Below 80	Below 100
Number of students	17	22	29	37	50

Find the median marks.

SECTION E

(3 Case study-based question of 4 (1 + 1 + 2) marks each)

36. Case Study based – 1 (Football)

Ritu packed a football as a gift for her brother's birthday in a cuboidal box whose diameter is the same as that of the length of the base of the box having length, breadth and height respectively 23 cm, 23 cm, and 28 cm. (Take nearest possible answer)

(i) The volume of the football is:

(a) 3581 cm^3

(b) 6373.19 cm^3

(c) 6451 cm^3

(d) 9807 cm^3

(ii) Ritu covers the box with a wrapping sheet. The area of the wrapping sheet that covers the box exactly is:

(a) 3634 cm^2

(b) 2533 cm^2

(c) 2584 cm^2

(d) 3813 cm^2

(iii) The volume of the box is:

(a) 25733 cm^3

(b) 18573 cm^3

(c) 14812 cm^3

(d) 77536 cm^3

(iv) Half of the remaining volume of the box is filled with thermocol balls. Find the volume of the thermocol balls used.

(a) 36150.9 cm^3

(b) 4219.405 cm^3

(c) 2764 cm^3

(d) 4048.05 cm^3

37. Case Study based – 2 (Race)

In a 100 m race a stopwatch was used to find the time that it took a group of students to run 100 m.

Time in seconds	0 – 20	20 – 40	40 – 60	60 – 80	80 – 100
Number of students	8	10	13	6	3

(i) Estimate the mean time taken by a student to finish the race.

(a) 54
(b) 63
(c) 43
(d) 50

(ii) What will be the upper limit of the modal class?
(a) 20
(b) 40
(c) 60
(d) 80

(iii) The construction of a cumulative frequency table is useful in determining the:
(a) Mean
(b) Median
(c) Mode
(d) All of the above

(iv) The sum of a lower limit of the median class and modal class is:
(a) 60
(b) 100
(c) 80
(d) 140

38. Case Study based – 3

The discus throw is a track and field event in which an athlete attempts to throw a heavy disc further than his or her competitors. The athlete spins anticlockwise around one and a half times through a circle, then releases the throw.

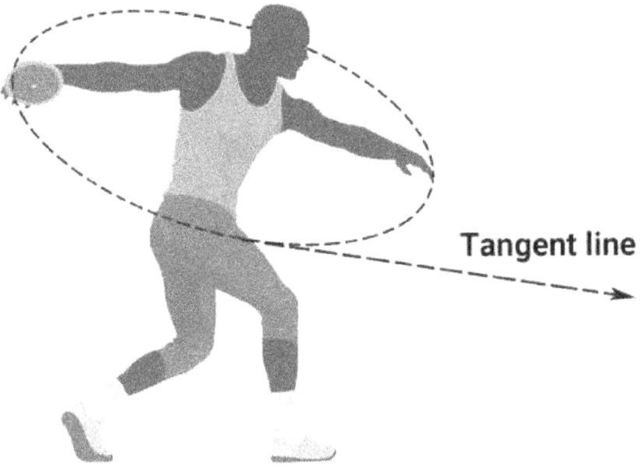

(i) When he releases the disk, it travels a path that is ____________ to the circular spin-orbit.
(a) Tangent
(b) Perpendicular

(ii) If a line or line segment is tangent to a circle, it is _____ to the diameter drawn to the point of contact

(a) Parallel
(b) Perpendicular
(c) Both (i) and (ii)
(d) None of the above

(iii) The length of the tangent from a point at a distance 10 cm from the center of the circle is 8 cm. Find the diameter of the circle.

(a) 5 cm
(b) 10 cm
(c) 12 cm
(d) 18 cm

(iv) From a point inside the circle how many tangents can be drawn to another circle?

(a) 2
(b) 0
(c) 1
(d) 3

Answers:

Section B
21. $[x = 2, y = 1]$
23. (i) 30° (ii) $3\frac{3}{4}$ (iii) 0 (iv) $\frac{\sqrt{3}}{2}$
24. 10 cm
25. 19.8 km/hr
Section C
28. $K = 6$ 29. Length = 19 m and breadth = 10 m
30. 2 cm
31. (i) $\frac{5}{9}$ (ii) $\frac{2}{9}$ (iii) $\frac{1}{9}$
Section D
32. Larger = 15 hrs, smaller = 25 hrs
34. 3 km/hr 35. 48.57
Section E
36. (a) 6373.19 cm^3 (b) 3634 cm^2 (c) 14812 cm^3 (d) 4219.405 cm^3
37. (a) 43 (b) 60 (c) Median (d) 80

38. (a) Tangent (b) Perpendicular (c) 12 cm (d) 2

Class- X Session- 2022-23

SAMPLE PAPER-4

Sample Question Paper

Time Allowed: 3 Hrs. **Maximum Marks: 80**

General Instructions:

1. This Question Paper has 5 Sections A-E.
2. Section **A** has 20 MCQs carrying 1 mark each
3. Section **B** has 5 questions carrying 02 marks each.
4. Section **C** has 6 questions carrying 03 marks each.
5. Section **D** has 4 questions carrying 05 marks each.
6. Section **E** has 3 case-based integrated units of assessment (04 marks each) with subparts of the values of 1, 1, and 2 marks each respectively.
7. All Questions are compulsory. However, an internal choice in 2 Qs of 5 marks, 2 Qs of 3 marks, and 2 Questions of 2 marks has been provided. An internal choice has been provided in the 2marks questions of Section E
8. Draw neat figures wherever required. Take π =22/7 wherever required if not stated

SECTION A

(Section A consists of 20 questions of 1 mark each)

1. The largest number which divides 125 and 70, leaving remainders 8 and 5 respectively, is
(a) 1750
(b) 850
(c) 65
(d) 13
Answer: (d)

2. If α and β be two zeroes of the quadratic polynomial $f(x) = 2x^2 - 3x + 7$, then evaluate $\frac{1}{\alpha} + \frac{1}{\beta}$
(a) $\frac{7}{3}$
(b) $\frac{3}{7}$
(c) $-\frac{7}{3}$
(d) $\frac{4}{7}$
Answer: (b)

3. If $x = a, y = b$ is the solution of the equations $x - y = 2$ and $x + y = 4$, then the values of a and b are, respectively
(a) 3 and 1
(b) 5 and 3
(c) 3 and 5
(d) -1 and -3

Answer: (a)

4. The value(s) of p for which the quadratic equation $2x^2 + 3x + p = 0$ has no real roots is :
(a) $p > \frac{9}{8}$
(b) $p < \frac{9}{8}$
(c) $p = \frac{9}{8}$
(d) $p \leq \frac{9}{8}$
Answer: (a)

5. In $\triangle XYZ$ and $\triangle PQR$ if $\frac{XZ}{PQ} = \frac{YX}{RQ} = \frac{YZ}{PR}$
(a) $\triangle YXZ \sim \triangle PQR$
(b) $\triangle XYZ \sim \triangle RQP$
(c) $\triangle YXZ \sim \triangle RQP$
(d) $\triangle ZYX \sim \triangle PQR$
Answer: (c)

6. Quadrilateral ABCD circumscribes a circle as shown in the figure. The side of the quadrilateral which is equal to AP + BR is:

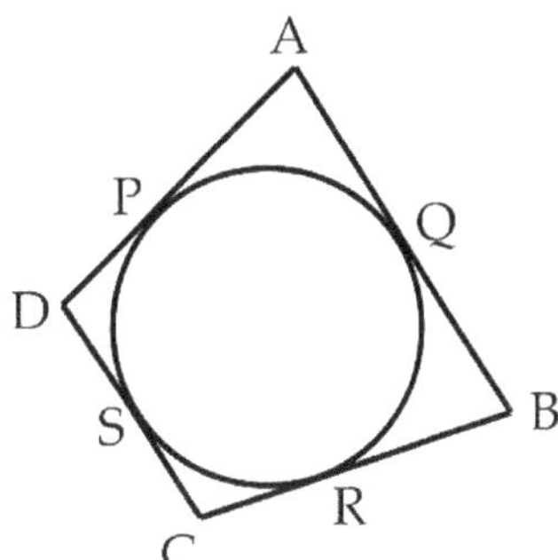

(a) AD
(b) AC
(c) AB
(d) BC
Answer: (c)

7. The length of the shadow on the ground of a pole of height 6m when the angle of elevation θ of the sun is such that $\tan\theta = \frac{3}{4}$ is:
(a) 4.5m
(b) 8m
(c) $8\sqrt{3}$m
(d) 9m
Answer: (b)

8. If in $\triangle ABC$ and $\triangle DEF, \frac{AB}{DE} = \frac{BC}{FD}$, then $\triangle ABC \sim \triangle DEF$ when

(a) $\angle A = \angle F$

(b) $\angle A = \angle D$

(c) $\angle B = \angle D$

(d) $\angle B = \angle E$

Answer: (c)

9. If the points $(7,-2), (5,1)$, and $(3, k)$ are collinear, then the value of k is :

(a) 4

(b) 10

(c) -4

(d) 0

Answer: (a)

10. If the circumference of a circle of radius ' r ' and the perimeter of a square of side ' a ' are equal, then the ratio of the area of the circle to that of the square is :

(a) $4:\pi$

(b) $\pi:4$

(c) $\pi^2:16$

(d) $\pi^2:4$

Answer: (a)

11. If the height and length of the shadow of a man are the same, then the angle of elevation of the sun is:

(a) 30°

(b) 60°

(c) 45^0

(d) 15^0

Answer: (c)

12. If the circumference of a circle is 44cm and the sum of two sides of a square is 22cm, then

(a) Area of the circle = Area of the square

(b) Area of the circle > Area of the square

(c) Area of the circle < Area of the square

(d) Area of circle = 2 Area of square

Answer: (b)

13. In the following figure, if AB || CD, find the value of x.

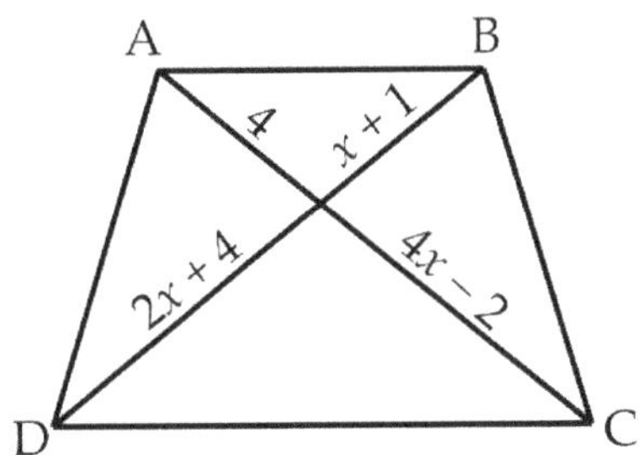

(a) 5 cm
(b) 3 cm
(c) 4 cm
(d) 4.5 cm
Answer: (b)

14. If the surface areas of two spheres are in the ratio 16: 9, then their volumes will be in the ratio :
(a) 27: 64
(b) 64: 27
(c) 4: 3
(d) 3: 4
Answer: (b)

15. The most frequently occurring observation of data is called:
(a) Mean
(b) Median
(c) Mode
(d) Lower Quartile
Answer: (c)

16. Find the value of θ for $2 \sin 3\theta = \sqrt{3}$, where θ is an acute angle
(a) 20°
(b) 60°
(c) 30°
(d) 10°
Answer: (a)

17. If the mean of a frequency distribution is 8.1 and $\Sigma f_i x_i = 132 + 5k, \Sigma f_i = 20$, then $k =$
(a) 3
(b) 4
(c) 5
(d) 6
Answer: (d)

18. The probability of guessing the correct answer to a certain question is $\frac{p}{12}$. If the probability of not guessing the correct answer to the same question is $\frac{3}{4}$, the value of p is:

(a) 3

(b) 4

(c) 2

(d) 1

Answer: (a)

Direction: In the following questions, a statement of Assertion (A) is followed by a statement of Reason (R). Mark the correct choice as:

(a) Both Assertion (A) and Reason (R) are true, and Reason (R) is the correct explanation of Assertion (A).

(b) Both Assertion (A) and Reason (R) are true, but Reason (R) is not the correct explanation of Assertion (A).

(c) Assertion (A) is true, but Reason (R) is false.

(d) Assertion (A) is false, but Reason (R) is true.

19. Assertion: The point $(-1, 6)$ divides the line segment joining the points $(-3, 10)$ and $(6, -8)$ in the ratio 2: 7 internally.

Reason: Given three points, i.e., A, B, and C form an equilateral triangle, then $\text{AB} = \text{BC} = \text{AC}$.

Answer. (b)

20. Assertion: Mid-point of a line segment divides the line in the ratio 1: 1.

Reason: The ratio in which the point $(-3, \text{k})$ divides the line segment joining the points $(-5, 4)$ and $(-2, 3)$ is 1: 2.

Answer. (c)

SECTION B

(Section B consists of 5 questions of 2 marks each)

21. For what value of 'k' following system of the linear equation has a unique solution:
$2x + 3y = 5$ and $kx - 6y = 8$

22. In the figure, given below, straight lines AB and cd intersect at p; and ac//bd. Prove that:

(i) $\triangle$ APC and $\triangle$ BPD are similar.

(ii) if BD = 2.4 cm, AC = 3.6 cm, PD = 4.0 cm and PB = 3.2 cm; find the lengths of PA and PC.

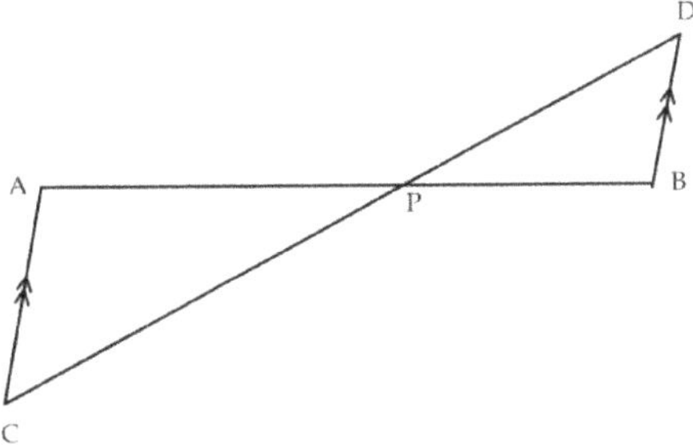

23. Use the given figure to find:

(i) $\tan \theta^o$

(ii) θ^o

(iii) $\sin^2\theta - \cos^2\theta$

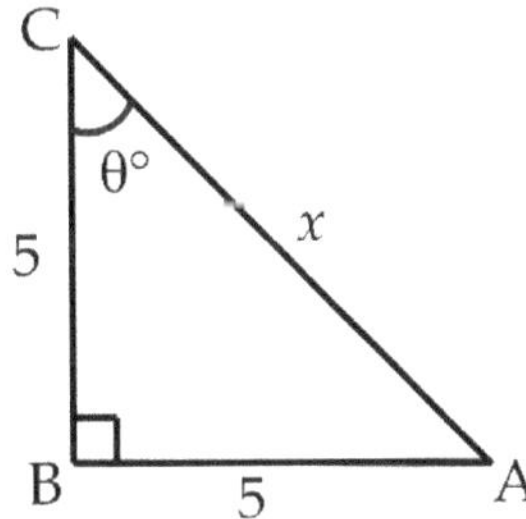

24. PA and TB are two tangents to the circle with centre O at A and B respectively. If OP = 5cm, AP = 4cm and BT = 6cm, find OP

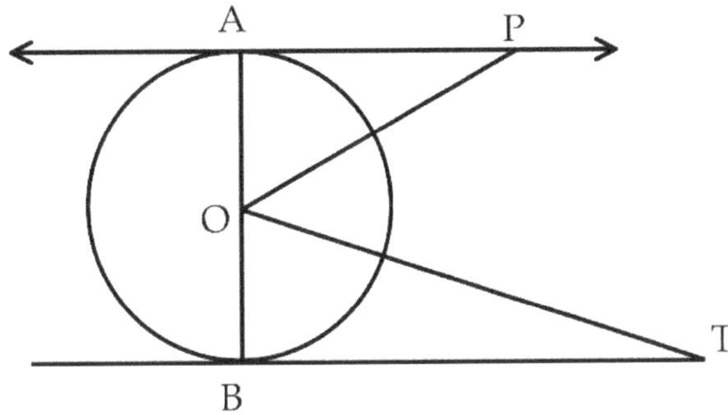

25. A wire when bent in the form of a square encloses an area of 121sq. cm. If the wire were bent in the form of a circle, find the area enclosed by the circle (Use = 22/7).

SECTION C

(Section C consists of 6 questions of 3 marks each)

26. The HCF of two numbers is 23 and their LCM is 1449. If one of the numbers is 161, find the other.

27. If α and β are the zeroes of the quadratic polynomial $p(x) = 4x^2 - 5x - 1$, then find the value of $\alpha^2\beta + \beta^2\alpha$.

28. Prove the identity: $\frac{\sin^3 A - \cos^3 A}{\sin A - \cos A} - \sin A . \cos A = 1$

29. Some amount is distributed equally among students. If there are 8 students, everyone will get Rs. 10 more. If there are 16 students more, everyone will get Rs. 10 less. What is the number of students and how much does each get? What is the total amount distributed?

30. In Fig. two circles touch each other externally at C. Prove that the common tangent at C bisects the other two common tangents.

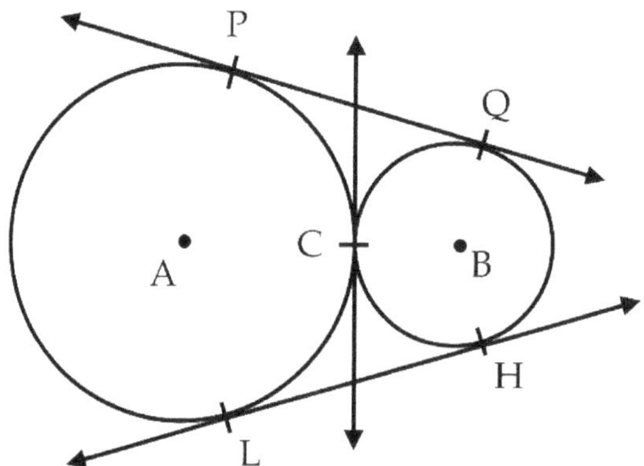

31. Cards marked with numbers 5 to 50, are placed in a box and mixed thoroughly. A card is drawn from the box at random. Find the probability that the number on the card taken out is:

(i) A prime number less than 20

(ii) A perfect square numbers

(iii) A multiple of 5 or 6.

SECTION D

(Section D consists of 4 questions of 5 marks each)

32. A student scored a total of 32 marks in class tests in Mathematics and English. Had he scored 2 marks less in English and 4 marks more in Mathematics, the product of his marks would have been 253. Find his marks in two subjects.

OR

The roots of the quadratic equation $(a^2 + b^2)x^2 - 2(ac + bd)x + (c^2 + d^2) = 0$ are equal. Prove that $\frac{a}{b} = \frac{c}{d}$

33. In the given figure, D and E are points lying on side AB such that $AD = BE$. If $DP || BC$ and EQ || AC, then prove that PQ || AB.

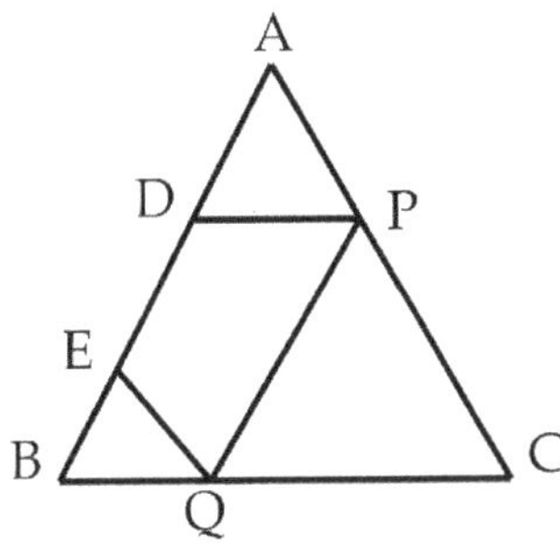

34. Water is flows through a cylindrical pipe of an internal diameter of 2cm into a cylindrical tank of base radius of 40cm, at the rate of 0.4m/s. Determine the rise in the level of water in the tank in half an hour.

35. The following distribution shows the height of students of a certain class in a certain city:

Height (in cm)	160 – 162	163 – 165	166 – 168	169 – 171	172 – 174
No. of students	15	118	142	127	18

Find the modal height of students.

SECTION E

(3 Case study-based question of 4 (1 + 1 + 2) marks each)

36. Case Study based – 1 (Circle)

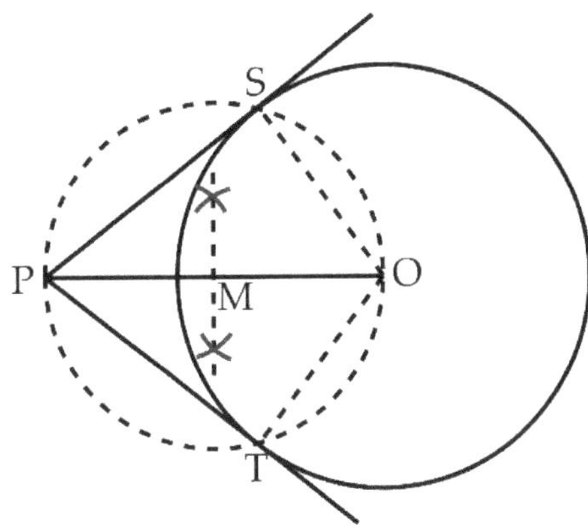

Madhuri has drawn a circle of radius 6 cm. From a point 10 cm away from its center, she constructed the pair of tangents to the circle. A few questions came to her mind while drawing the tangents. Give answers to her questions by looking at the figure:

(i) What is the pair of tangents that are drawn?

(a) PS and PT

(b) PO and PT

(c) PS and PO

(d) None of these

(ii) What is the length of the tangents PS?

(a) 6 cm

(b) 7 cm
(c) 8 cm
(d) 9 cm

(iii) What is the length of the tangent PT?
(a) 6 cm
(b) 7 cm
(c) 8 cm
(d) 9 cm

(iv) What is the measurement of angle PSO?
(a) 30°
(b) 60°
(c) 180°
(d) 90°

37. Case Study based – 2

Aman got his name registered for a sprint race. The race is scheduled for a month later than the time he registered for the race. He started practicing for the race. His current run time is 51 sec for the distance to be covered in the race. He wants to reduce his time to 31 seconds. Answer the following questions

(i) What would be a suitable A.P. for the above situation?
(a) 51, 53, 55, and so on.
(b) 51, 49, 47, and so on.
(c) – 51, – 53, – 55, and so on.
(d) None of these.

(ii) Would he be able to achieve his target in one month?
(a) Yes
(b) No

(iii) If Aman is able to achieve his target, then in how many days will be able to achieve it?
(a) 10 days
(b) 11 days

(c) 12 days
(d) 13 days

(iv) Which of the following is not a term of the A.P. found in part (a)?
(a) 30
(b) 41
(c) 37
(d) 39

38. A teacher in her class placed different shapes on his table. He is teaching her students by making a combination of these objects.

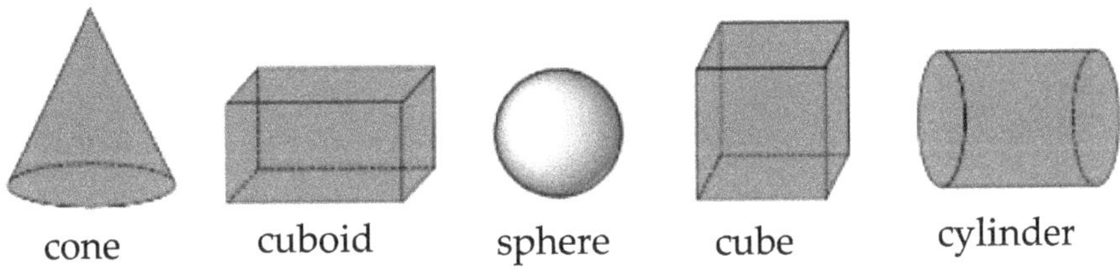

(i) He placed the cube on the cuboid. Cube is 1cm × 1cm × 1cm and cuboid is 6cm × 4cm × 1cm. What is the total surface of the combination?
(a) 68 cm^2
(b) 74 cm^2
(c) 72 cm^2
(d) 670 cm^2

(ii) He placed cube on a sphere which has 3.5 cm diameter. What is the total surface area of the combination?
(a) 55 cm^2
(b) 68.5 cm^2
(c) 38.5 cm^2
(d) 44.5 cm^2

(iii) What is the total volume of combination obtained in part (a)?
(a) 45 cm^3
(b) 35 cm^3
(c) 25 cm^3
(d) 35.5 cm^3

(iv) If he placed the cube on a solid hemisphere of radius 3.5 cm. What is total surface area of the resultant combination?
(a) 115 cm^2
(b) 121 cm^2
(c) 131 cm^2
(d) 125 cm^2

Answers:

Section B
21. $k \neq -4$
22. PA = 4.8 cm, PC = 6 cm
23. (i) 1, (ii) 45°, (iii) 0
24. $3\sqrt{5}$ cm
25. 154 cm^2
Section C
26. 207
27. $-\frac{5}{16}$
29. 32, Rs. 30, Rs. 960
31. (i) $\frac{3}{23}$, (ii) $\frac{5}{46}$, (iii) $\frac{17}{46}$
Section D
32. Mathematics: 7 or 19; English: 25 or 13
34. $\frac{225}{4}$ cm
35. 167.35 cm
Section E
36. (a) PS and PT, (b) 8 cm, (c) 8 cm, (d) 90°
37. (a) 51, 49, 47, . . ., (b) yes, (c) 11 days, (d) 30
38. (a) 72 cm^2, (b) 44.5 cm^2, (c) 25 cm^3, (d) 121 cm^2

Class- X Session- 2022-23

SAMPLE PAPER-5

Sample Question Paper

Time Allowed: 3 Hrs. **Maximum Marks: 80**

General Instructions:

1. This Question Paper has 5 Sections A-E.
2. Section **A** has 20 MCQs carrying 1 mark each
3. Section **B** has 5 questions carrying 02 marks each.
4. Section **C** has 6 questions carrying 03 marks each.
5. Section **D** has 4 questions carrying 05 marks each.
6. Section **E** has 3 case-based integrated units of assessment (04 marks each) with subparts of the values of 1, 1, and 2 marks each respectively.
7. All Questions are compulsory. However, an internal choice in 2 Qs of 5 marks, 2 Qs of 3 marks, and 2 Questions of 2 marks has been provided. An internal choice has been provided in the 2marks questions of Section E
8. Draw neat figures wherever required. Take π =22/7 wherever required if not stated

SECTION A

(Section A consists of 20 questions of 1 mark each)

1. The reciprocal of an irrational number is

(a) An integer

(b) Rational

(c) A natural number

(d) Irrational

Answer:(d)

2. Graph of a quadratic polynomial can meet the x-axis at most

(a) 1

(b) 3

(c) 4

(d) 2

Answer:(d)

3. The lines represented by the equations $a_1x + b_1y + c_1 = 0$ and $a_2x + b_2y + c_2 = 0$ are coincident if

(a) $\frac{a_1}{a_2} \neq \frac{b_1}{b_2}$

(b) $\frac{a_1}{a_2} = \frac{b_1}{b_2} = \frac{c_1}{c_2}$

(c) $\frac{a_1}{a_2} = \frac{b_1}{b_2} \neq \frac{c_1}{c_2}$

(d) $\frac{a_1}{a_2} \neq \frac{b_1}{b_2} \neq \frac{c_1}{c_2}$

Answer:(b)

4. If the equation $x^2 - 4x + k = 0$ has equal roots, then the value of ' k ' is :
(a) 2
(b) -2
(c) 4
(d) -4
Answer: (c)

5. PQ is drawn parallel to base BC of a $\triangle ABC$ cutting AB at P and AC at Q. If $AB = 4BP$ and $CQ =$ 2cm, then AQ is equal to
(a) 2cm
(b) 4cm
(c) 6cm
(d) 8cm
Answer:(c)

6. If A $(2, 2)$, B$(-4, -4)$, and C$(5, -8)$ are the vertices of a triangle, then the length of the median through vertex C is
(a) $\sqrt{65}$
(b) $\sqrt{117}$
(c) $\sqrt{85}$
(d) $\sqrt{113}$
Answer:(c)

7. If $\cot A = \frac{7}{8}$, then the value of $\frac{(1+\sin A)(1-\sin A)}{(1+\cos A)(1-\cos A)}$:
(a) $\frac{64}{49}$
(b) $\frac{49}{64}$
(c) $\frac{49}{25}$
(d) $\frac{49}{36}$
Answer:(b)

8. Triangle ABC is isosceles with $AB = AC$. A circle touches all sides of the triangle, then which of the following is true?
(a) $AB = BC$
(b) $BQ = QC$
(c) $BP = AP$
(d) $AR = RC$
Answer:(b)

9. If the radius of the base of a right circular cylinder is halved, keeping the height the same, the ratio of the volume of the reduced cylinder to that of the original cylinder is:

(a) $2:3$

(b) $3:4$

(c) $1:4$

(d) $4:1$

Answer: (c)

10. The given figure shows the observation of point C from point A. The angle of depression from A is:

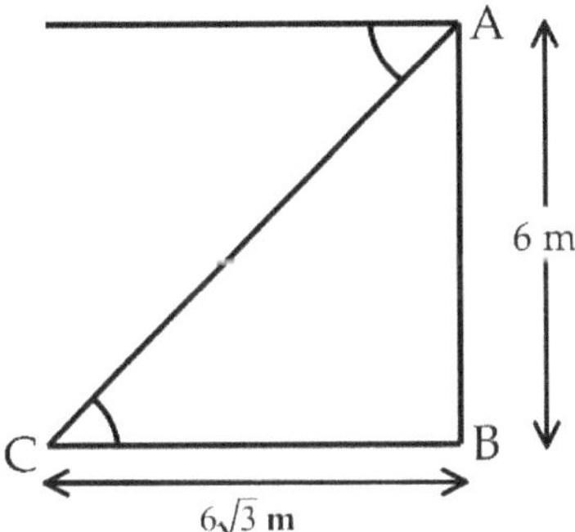

(a) 60°

(b) 30°

(c) 45°

(d) 90°

Answer:(b)

11. Two parallel lines touch the circle at points A and B separately. If the area of the circle is $25\pi \text{cm}^2$, then AB is equal to

(a) 8cm

(b) 5cm

(c) 10cm

(d) 25cm

Answer:(c)

12. If in two triangles ABC and DEF, $\frac{AB}{DE} = \frac{BC}{FE} = \frac{CA}{FD}$, then

(a) $\triangle FDE \sim \triangle CAB$

(b) $\triangle FDE \sim \triangle ABC$

(c) $\triangle CBA \sim \triangle FDE$

(d) $\triangle BCA \sim \triangle FDE$

Answer:(a)

13. Value of $\frac{sin^3\theta - cos^3\theta}{\sin\theta - \cos\theta} - \sin\theta.\cos\theta$

(a) 2

(b) 1

(c) 0
(d) -1
Answer:(b)

14. If the mean of $6, 7, x, 8, y, 14$ is 9, then
(a) $x + y = 21$
(b) $x + y = 19$
(c) $x - y = 19$
(d) $x - y = 21$
Answer:(b)

15. If π is taken as $\frac{22}{7}$, the distance (in meters) covered by a wheel of a diameter of 35cm, in one revolution, is:
(a) 2 .2
(b) 1.1
(c) 9.625
(d) 96.25
Answer:(b)

16. If $p - 1, p + 3, 3p - 1$ are in A.P., then p is equal to:
(a) 4
(b) -4
(c) 2
(d) -2
Answer:(a)

17. The graphical representation of cumulative frequency distribution is called
(a) Median
(b) Ogive
(c) Histogram
(d) Frequency curve
Answer:(b)

18. In a throw of a pair of dice, the probability of getting a doublet is :
(a) $\frac{1}{2}$
(b) $\frac{1}{3}$
(c) $\frac{1}{6}$
(d) $\frac{5}{6}$
Answer:(c)

Direction: In the following questions, a statement of Assertion (A) is followed by a statement of Reason (R). Mark the correct choice as:

(a) Both Assertion (A) and Reason (R) are true, and Reason (R) is the correct explanation of Assertion (A).

(b) Both Assertion (A) and Reason (R) are true, but Reason (R) is not the correct explanation of Assertion (A).

(c) Assertion (A) is true, but Reason (R) is false.

(d) Assertion (A) is false, but Reason (R) is true.

19. Assertion: If the sum of the zeroes of the quadratic polynomial $x^2 - 2\text{k}x + 8$ is 2 then value of k is 1.

Reason: Sum of zeroes of a quadratic polynomial $ax^2 + \text{b}x + \text{c}$ is $-\frac{\text{b}}{\text{a}}$

Answer. (a)

20. Assertion: If a pair of linear equations is consistent, then the lines are intersecting or coincident

Reason: Because the two lines have a solution.

Answer. (a)

SECTION B

(Section B consists of 5 questions of 2 marks each)

21. Solve the following systems of simultaneous linear equations.

$$2bx + ay = 2ab \text{ and } bx - ay = 4ab$$

22. In the given figure, PQ||ab; CQ = 4.8cm, QB = 3.6cm and AB = 6.3 cm. Find:

(i) $\frac{\text{CP}}{\text{PA}}$

(ii) PQ

(iii) if AP = x, then the value of AC in terms of x.

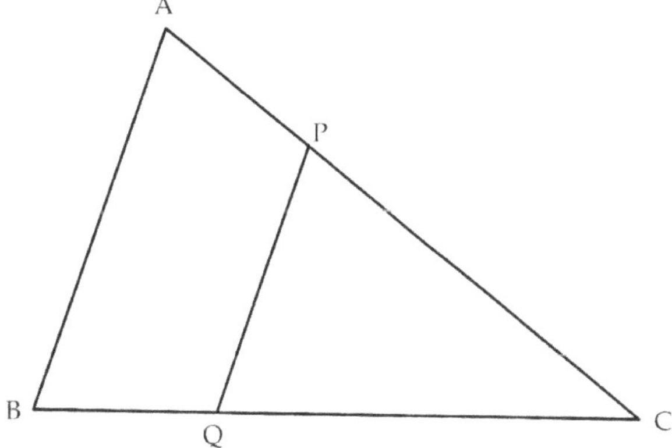

23. If 2cos (A + B) = 2sin (A – B) = 1; find the values of A and B.

24. Prove that the tangents to a circle from an external point are equal.

25. A circular footpath of a width of 2 meters is constructed at the rate of Rs. 20 per square meter, around a circular park of radius 1500 m. Find the total cost of construction of the footpath. (Take = 3.14)

SECTION C

(Section C consists of 6 questions of 3 marks each)

26. Find the greatest number which on dividing 1657 and 2037 leaves remainders 6 and 5, respectively.

27. Prove the identity: $(\sin A + \cos A)(\tan A + \cot A) = \sec A + \text{cosec } A$

28. If α and β are the zeroes of the quadratic polynomial $f(x) = x^2 - 2x + 1$, then find a quadratic polynomial whose zeroes are $\frac{2\alpha}{\beta}$ and $\frac{2\beta}{\alpha}$.

29. A shopkeeper sold a saree and a sweater together for Rs. 1050, thereby making a profit of 10% on the saree and 25% on the sweater. If he had taken a profit of 25% on the saree and 10% on the sweater, he would have got Rs. 15 more. Find the cost price of each.

30. In Fig, AB, and CD are two common tangents of two circles with centres P and Q. These circles touch each other at M. If the common tangent at M meets AB and CD at X and Y respectively, prove that $XY = \frac{1}{2}(AB + CD)$.

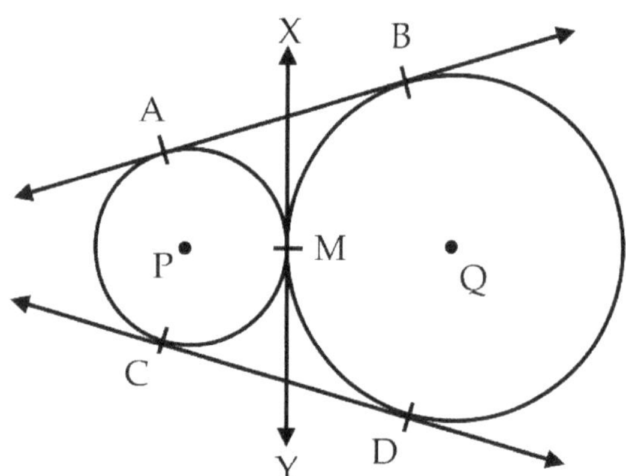

31. Five cards-the ten, jack, queen, king, and ace of diamonds, are well shuffled with their face downwards. One card is picked up at random:
   (i) What is the probability that the card is the queen?
   (ii) If the queen is drawn and put aside, what is the probability that the second card picked up is:
      (a) An ace
      (b) Queen.

SECTION D

(Section D consists of 4 questions of 5 marks each)

32. Five years ago, a woman's age was square of her son's age. Ten years hence her age will be twice that of her son's age. Find: -

(i) The age of son five years ago

(ii) The present age of the woman.

33. In the given figure, $PQ \parallel BA$ and $PR \parallel CA$. If $PD = 12$ cm, then find $BD \times CD$.

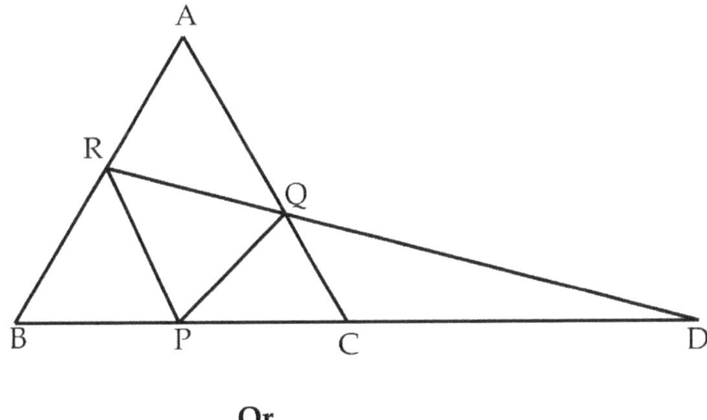

Or

PQR is a triangle. S is a point on the side QR of triangle PQR such that $\angle PSR = \angle QPR$. Given $QP = 8\ cm, PR = 6\ cm$ and $SR = 3\ cm$.

(i) Prove that: $\Delta PQR \sim \Delta SPR$

(ii) Find the length of QR and PS.

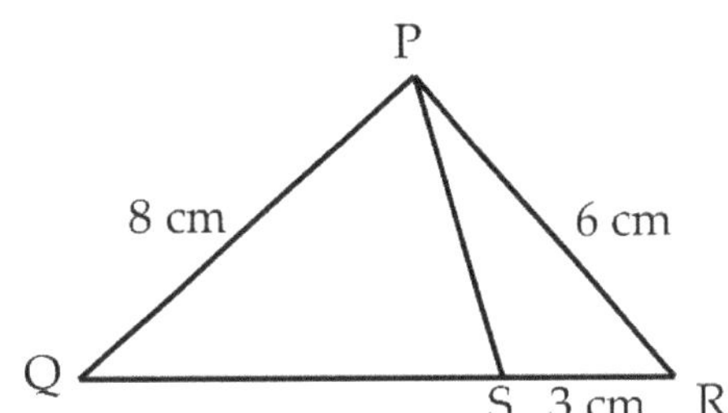

34. Water in a canal 30m wide and 12m deep is flowing at a speed of 20km/h. How much area will it irrigate in 30 minutes, if 9cm of standing water is desired?

35. The mode of the following distribution is 65. Find the value of x and y, if the sum of the frequency is 50.

Class intervals	0 – 20	20 – 40	40 – 60	60 – 80	80 – 100	100 – 120	120 – 140
Frequency	6	8	x	12	6	y	3

SECTION E

(3 Case study-based question of 4 (1 + 1 + 2) marks each)

36. Case Study based – 1 (Eiffel Tower)

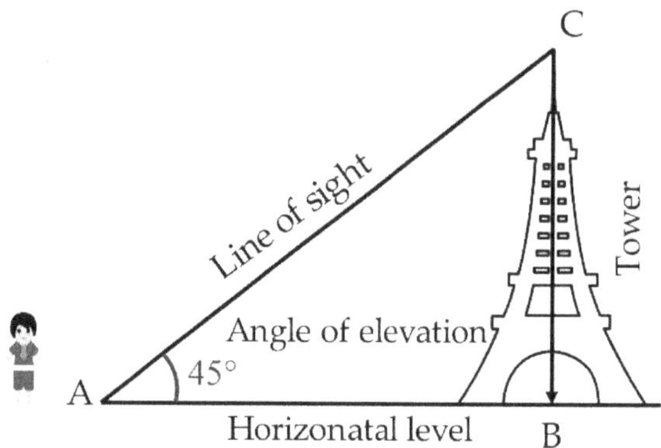

Mr. Henry visited the Eiffel tower. He was standing at a place from where the angle of elevation to the top of the tower was 45°. The height of the tower was 300m.

(i) At what distance was Mr. Henry standing from the tower?

(a) 100 m

(b) 200 m

(c) 300 m

(d) 400 m

(ii) What would be the angle of elevation of the midpoint of the tower as seen by Mr. Henry (Take the nearest possible value)?

(a) 26.5°

(b) 45°

(c) 67.5°

(d) 90°

(iii) What is the length of the line of sight?

(a) $100\sqrt{2}$

(b) $200\sqrt{2}$

(c) $300\sqrt{2}$

(d) $400\sqrt{2}$

(iv) What is the value of angle ACB?

(a) 22.5°

(b) 45°

(c) 67.5°

(d) 90°

37. Case Study based – 2 (Bheeshma and Arjun)

The angry Arjun carried some arrows for fighting with Bheeshm. With half the arrows, he cut down the arrows thrown by Bheeshm on him, and with six other arrows, he killed the rath driver of Bheeshm. With one arrow each, he knocked down respectively the rath, flag and the bow of Bheeshm. Finally, with one more than four times the square root of total arrows he laid Bheeshm unconscious on an arrow bed. Find the total number of arrows Arjun had. Answer the following questions, based on this information.

(i) What is the total number of arrows Arjun had?

(a) 80
(b) 100
(c) 120
(d) 140

(ii) What is the number of arrows used by Arjun to cut down the arrows thrown by Bheeshm?

(a) 50
(b) 40
(c) 70
(d) 60

(iii) What will be an equation for the number of arrows left before killing Bheeshm (in terms of x)?

(a) $\frac{x}{2} - 9$
(b) $\frac{x}{2} + 9$

(c) $\frac{2}{x} - 9$
(d) $\frac{x}{3} + 9$

(iv) What is the number of arrows to kill Bheeshm?
(a) 43
(b) 34
(c) 41
(d) 51

38. Seema being a plant lover came up with the idea of opening a nursery during the lockdown and she bought a few plants with pots. She wants to place pots in such a way that a number of pots in row one is 5, pots in row second is 8 and in the third is 11, and so on.

(i) What is the difference in the number of pots increasing per row?
(a) 3
(b) 4
(c) 1
(d) 2

(ii) What will be the number of pots in row 8
(a) 30
(b) 34
(c) 26
(d) 22

(iii) If Seema wants to place 220 pots, how many rows will it require?
(a) 12
(b) 11
(c) 15
(d) 13

(iv) Find the difference between the number of pots of 5th and 8th row
(a) 7

(b) 10
(c) 9
(d) 12

Answer:

Section B
21. [$x = 2a; y = 2b$]
22. (i) 4: 6 (ii) 3.6 cm (iii) $\frac{7}{3}x$
23. $A = 45°, B = 15°$
25. Rs. 377051.20
Section C
26. 127
28. $x^2 - 4x + 4$
29. Saree = Rs. 500 and Sweater = Rs. 400
31. (i) $\frac{1}{5}$ (ii) (a) $\frac{1}{4}$ (b) $\frac{0}{4} = 0$
Section D
32. Son = 5yrs, Women = 30yrs
33. 144(ii) QR = 12 cm, PS = 4 cm
34. 4,00,00,000 m^2
35. $x = 10, y = 5$
Section E
36. (a) 300 m (b) 26.56o (c) $300\sqrt{2}$m (d) 45^0
37. (a) 100 (b) 50 (c) $\frac{x}{2} + 9$(d) 41
38. (a) 3 (b) 26 (c) 11 (d) 9

PREVIOUS YEAR PAPER

Class- X Session- 2022-23
PREVIOUS YEAR PAPER-2019
Sample Question Paper

Time Allowed: 3 Hrs. **Maximum Marks: 80**

General Instructions:

1. This Question Paper has 5 Sections A-E.
2. Section **A** has 20 MCQs carrying 1 mark each
3. Section **B** has 5 questions carrying 02 marks each.
4. Section **C** has 6 questions carrying 03 marks each.
5. Section **D** has 4 questions carrying 05 marks each.
6. Section **E** has 3 case-based integrated units of assessment (04 marks each) with subparts of the values of 1, 1, and 2 marks each respectively.
7. All Questions are compulsory. However, an internal choice in 2 Qs of 5 marks, 2 Qs of 3 marks, and 2 Questions of 2 marks has been provided. An internal choice has been provided in the 2marks questions of Section E
8. Draw neat figures wherever required. Take π =22/7 wherever required if not stated

SECTION A
(Question numbers1 up to 6 carry 1 mark each.)

1. Find the coordinates of a point A, where AB is the diameter of a circle whose centre is $(2,-3)$, and B is the point $(1,4)$.

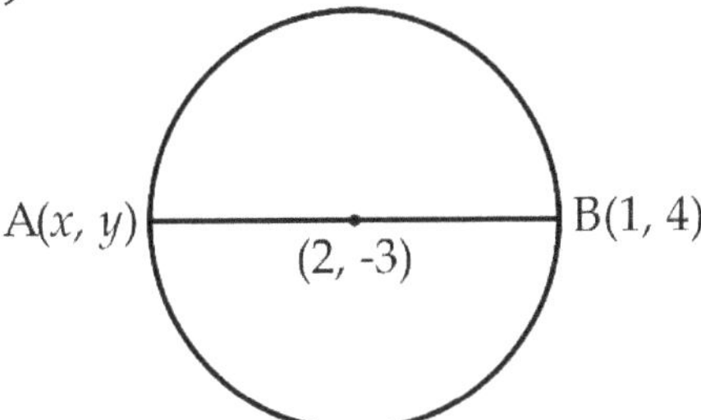

Solution.

Let the coordinates of A be (x,y)

Since $(2,-3)$ is the center, it is also the midpoint of AB

$\therefore \dfrac{x+1}{2} = 2 \Rightarrow x+1 = 4 \Rightarrow x = 3$

Similarly,

$\dfrac{y+4}{2} = -3 \Rightarrow y+4 = -6 \Rightarrow y = -10$

So, coordinates of A$(3,-10)$

2. For what value of k, the roots of the equation $x^2 + 4x + k = 0$ are real?

OR

Find the value of k, for which the roots of equation $3x^2 - 10x + k = 0$ are reciprocal of each other.

Solution.

Given $x^2 + 4x + k = 0$

For roots to be real, $b^2 - 4ac \geq 0 \Rightarrow 4^2 - 4(1)(k) \geq 0$

$\Rightarrow -4k \geq -16$ [Multiply by -1 on both side]

$\Rightarrow 4k \leq 16$

$\Rightarrow k \leq 4$

OR

Given $3x^2 - 10x + \mathrm{k} = 0 \Rightarrow \mathrm{a} = 3, \mathrm{b} = -10, c = k$

Let roots are α and $\frac{1}{\alpha}$ [since roots are reciprocal of each other]

Product of zeroes $= \alpha \times \frac{1}{\alpha}$

$\frac{c}{a} = 1 \rightarrow \frac{k}{3} = 1 \rightarrow k = 3$

3. Find A if tan $2\mathrm{A} = \cot(\mathrm{A} - 24^\circ)$

OR

Find the value of $(\sin^2 33^\circ + \sin^2 57^\circ)$

Solution. Out of Syllabus

4. How many two digits numbers are divisible by 3?

Solution.

Numbers divisible by 3 are $3, 6, 9, 12, \cdots$

The smallest $2-$digit number divisible by 3 is 12

The largest 2-digit number divisible by 3 is 99

So, the series starts with 12 and ends with 99

The difference between the numbers is 3

So, the AP will be $12, 15, 18, \cdots, 99$

We need to find n

$\therefore a = 12, a_n = 99, d = 3$

Now $a_n = a + (n-1)d$

$\Rightarrow 99 = 12 + (n-1)(3)$

$\Rightarrow 99 = 9 + 3n$

$\Rightarrow 90 = 3n$

$\Rightarrow n = 30$

Therefore, there are 30 two-digit numbers divisible by 3

5. In Fig.1, $DE \parallel BC, AD = 1\text{cm}$, and $BD = 2\text{cm}$. What is the ratio of the ar $(\triangle ABC)$ to the ar $(\triangle ADE)$?

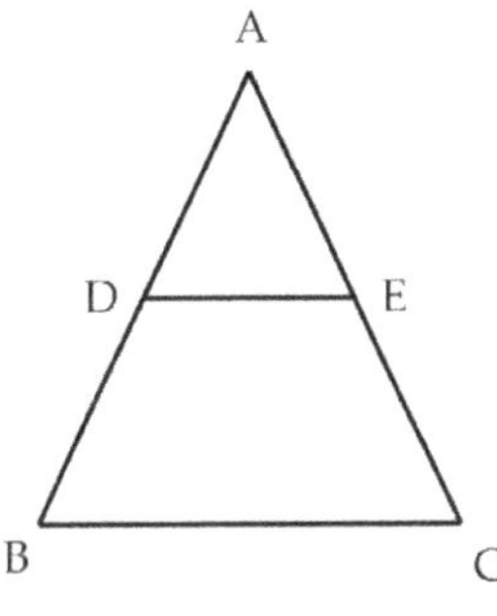

Fig. 1

Solution. Out of syllabus

6. Find a rational number between $\sqrt{2}$ and $\sqrt{3}$.

Solution.

We know $\sqrt{2} = 1.412$ and $\sqrt{3} = 1.732$

Therefore 1.5 is between $\sqrt{2}$ and $\sqrt{3}$

$\Rightarrow 1.5 = \frac{15}{10} = \frac{3}{2}$

Hence $\frac{3}{2}$ is between $\sqrt{2}$ and $\sqrt{3}$

SECTION B

(Question numbers7 up to 12 carry 2 marks each.)

7. Find the HCF of 1260 and 7344 using Euclid's algorithm.

OR

Show that every positive odd integer is of the form $(4q + 1)$ or $(4q + 3)$, where q is some integer.

Solution. Out of syllabus

8. Which term of AP $3, 15, 27, 39, \cdots$ will be 120 more than its 21st term?

OR

If S_n, the sum of the first n terms of an AP is given by $S_n = 3n^2 - 4n$, find the nth term.

Solution.

Given AP is $3, 15, 27, 39, \cdots$

Here $a = 3, d = 15 - 3 = 12$

Therefore 21th the term is given by

$$T_{21} = a + (21 - 1)d = 3 + 20 \times 12 = 243$$

Required term $= 243 + 120 = 363$

Let it be the nth term, then

$$T_n = 363$$

$$\Rightarrow \quad a + (n - 1)d = 363$$

$$\Rightarrow 3 + (n - 1) \times 12 = 363$$

$$\Rightarrow \quad 12n = 372$$

$\Rightarrow \qquad n = 31$

Hence 31st the term is the required term.

OR

Given $\quad S_n = 3n^2 - 4n$

Put, $n = 1, S_1 = 3(1)^2 - 4(1) = -1$

$n = 2, S_2 = 3(2)^2 - 4(2) = 12 - 8 = 4$

$n = 3, S_3 = 3(3)^2 - 4(3) = 27 - 12 = 15$

$S_1 = -1 \Rightarrow a = -1$

$T_2 = S_2 - S_1 = 4 - (-1) = 5 \qquad [T_n = S_n - S_{n-1}]$

Hence the common difference is $\quad d = 5 - (-1) = 6$

Therefore n^{th} term $t_n = a + (n-1)d = -1 + (n-1)6$

$\Rightarrow t_n = 6n - 7$

9. Find the ratio in which the segment joining the points $(1, -3)$ and $(4, 5)$ is divided by x-axis. Also, find the coordinates of this point on x-axis.

Solution.

Given Points $A(1, -3)$ and $B(4, 5)$

Let the point $P(x, 0)$ be the point that divides the segment joining A and B in the ratio $m_1 : m_2$

Using the section formula, we get

$$(x, y) = \left(\frac{m_1x_2 + m_2x_1}{m_1 + m_2}, \frac{m_1y_2 + m_2y_1}{m_1 + m_2}\right)$$

$$0 = \left(\frac{m_1 \times 5 + m_2 \times (-3)}{m_1 + m_2}\right)$$

$$\Rightarrow 0 = \frac{5m_1 - 3m_2}{m_1 + m_2}$$

$$5m_1 - 3m_2 = 0$$

$$5m_1 = 3m_2$$

$$\frac{m_1}{m_2} = \frac{3}{5}$$

Therefore P divides $(1, -3)$ and $(4, 5)$ in the ratio $3 : 5$

$$\therefore x = \frac{3 \times 4 + 5 \times 1}{3 + 5}$$

$$= \frac{12 + 5}{8} = \frac{17}{8}$$

Therefore, the point is $\left(\frac{17}{8}, 0\right)$

10. A game consists of tossing a coin three times and noting the outcome each time. If getting the same result in all the tosses is a success, find the probability of losing the game.

Solution.

The possible outcome of tossing a coin three times is $2 \times 2 \times 2 = 8$

All possible events $= \{HHH, HHT, HTH, HTT, THH, THT, TTH, TTT\}$

i.e. Total number of events $= 8$

The favourable events are HHH and TTT

So, no. of favourable events $= 2$

Therefore Probability of success is given by P(E) $= \frac{\text{No.of favorale outcomes}}{\text{Total no.of outcomes}}$

$= \frac{2}{8} => \frac{1}{4}$

Hence the probability of losing is $1 - \frac{1}{4} = \frac{3}{4}$

11. A die is thrown once. Find the probability of getting a number which
(i) Is a prime number
(ii) Lies between 2 and 6.

Solution.
The possible outcomes when dice are thrown are $1, 2, 3, 4, 5, 6$
Therefore Total No. of events $= 6$
No of prime events $= 3(2, 3, 5$ are prime numbers $)$
No of events when the number lies between 2 and 6 $= 3$ [i.e. $3, 4, 5$]
$\text{P(E)} = \frac{\text{No.of favorale outcomes}}{\text{Total no.of outcomes}}$
(i) Probability (is a prime number) $= \frac{3}{6} = \frac{1}{2}$
(ii) Probability (number lies between 2 and 6) $= \frac{3}{6} = \frac{1}{2}$

12. Find c if the system of equations $cx + 3y + (3 - c) = 0; 12x + cy - c = 0$ has infinitely many solutions.

Solution.
Given: $cx + 3y + (3 - c) = 0$ and $12x + cy - c = 0$
If the system of equations is $a_1\text{x} + b_1y + c_1 = 0$ and $a_2\text{x} + b_2y + c_2 = 0$ and they have infinitely many solutions, then it satisfies the following:

$$\frac{a_1}{a_2} = \frac{b_1}{b_2} = \frac{c_1}{c_2}$$

From the given system

$$a_1 = c, b_1 = 3, c_1 = 3 - c$$
$$a_2 = 12, b_2 = c, c_2 = -c$$

Therefore

$$\frac{c}{12} = \frac{3}{c} = \frac{3 - c}{-c}$$

Taking the first two

$$c^2 = 36 \Rightarrow c = \pm 6 \quad \text{..........(i)}$$

Taking the last two

$$-3c = 3c - c^2 \Rightarrow c^2 = 6c \Rightarrow c = 0, 6 \quad \text{.......(ii)}$$

From(i)and (ii) we get $c = 6$

SECTION C

(Question numbers13 to 22 carries 3 marks each.)

13. Prove that $\sqrt{2}$ is an irrational number.

Solution.

Let us assume that $\sqrt{2}$ is rational.

So, $\sqrt{2} = \frac{a}{b}$, [where a and b are co-primes as they do not have any common factor except 1 and $b \neq 0$.]

$\Rightarrow b\sqrt{2} = a$

$\Rightarrow 2b^2 = a^2$ [squaring both sides]

$\Rightarrow$ 2 divides a^2

$\Rightarrow$ 2 divides a [$\because$ 2 is a prime and divides a^2]

So 2 is a factor of a ....(i)

Let $a = 2c$

Putting $a = 2c$ in (i) we get

$2b^2 = 4c^2$

$\Rightarrow b^2 = 2c^2$

$\Rightarrow$ 2 divides b^2

$\Rightarrow$ 2 divides b[$\because$ 2 is a prime and divides b^2]

So 2 is a factor of b ....(ii)

Thus (i) and (ii) a and b have a common factor 2.

This contradicts the fact that a and b have no common factor other than 1.

This contradiction has arisen because of our incorrect assumption that $\sqrt{2}$ is rational.

Hence, $\sqrt{2}$ is an irrational number.

14. Find the value of k such that the polynomial $x^2 - (k+6)x + 2(2k-1)$ has a sum of its zeros equal to half of their products.

Solution.

Polynomial is $p(x) = x^2 - (k+6)x + 2(2k-1)$

Let α and β be the zeros of the polynomial

In comparison with $ax^2 + bx + c = 0$ we get

$$a = 1, b = -(k+6)c = 2(2k-1)$$

Therefore $\alpha + \beta = -\frac{b}{a} = \frac{k+6}{1}$

$\Rightarrow \alpha + \beta = k + 6$ ....(i)

$$\alpha.\beta = \frac{c}{a} = \frac{2(2k-1)}{1}$$

$\Rightarrow \alpha.\beta = 4k - 2$ ....(ii)

Given $\alpha + \beta = \frac{1}{2}\alpha \cdot \beta$

$\Rightarrow$ $$k + 6 = \frac{1}{2}(4k - 2)$$

$\Rightarrow$ $k + 6 = 2k - 1$

$\Rightarrow$ $k = 7$

15. A father's age is three times the sum of the ages of his two children. After 5 years his age will be two times the sum of their ages. Find the present age of the father.

OR

A fraction becomes $\frac{1}{3}$ when 2 is subtracted from the numerator and it becomes $\frac{1}{2}$ when 1 is subtracted from the denominator. Find the fraction.

Solution.

Let the ages of sons be x and y

Given that father's age is 3 times the ages of his two sons

Therefore present age of father $= 3(x + y)$ ....(i)

Given 5 years hence, the father's age will be twice the sum of the ages of his sons

Father's age after 5 years $= 3(x + y) + 5$

Ages of his sons 5 years hence $= (x + 5)$ and $(y + 5)$

$$\therefore 3(x + y) + 5 = 2[(x + 5) + (y + 5)]$$
$$\Rightarrow 3x + 3y + 5 = 2x + 10 + 2y + 10$$
$$\Rightarrow \quad x + y = 15 \qquad \text{.........(ii)}$$

Using (i) and (ii) we get that the present age of the father is $3(15) = 45$ years.

OR

Let the fraction be $\frac{x}{y}$

$$\therefore \quad \frac{x-2}{y} = \frac{1}{3}$$
$$\Rightarrow \quad 3x - 6 = y$$
$$\Rightarrow \quad 3x - y = 6 \qquad \text{...........(i)}$$

Also, $$\frac{x}{y-1} = \frac{1}{2}$$
$$\Rightarrow \quad 2x = y - 1$$
$$\Rightarrow \quad 2x - y = -1 \qquad \text{...........(ii)}$$

Subtracting (ii) from (i) we get $x = 7$

From (ii)

$$y = 2x + 1$$
$$= 2(7) + 1$$
$$= 15$$

Hence the fraction is $\frac{7}{15}$

16. Find the point on y-axis which is equidistant from the point $(5, -2)$ and $(-3,2)$.

OR

The line segment joining the points $A(2,1)$ and $B(5,-8)$ is trisected at points P and Q such that P is nearer to A. If P also lies on the line given by $2x - y + k = 0$, find the value of k.

Solution.

Let $P(0, y)$ is a point of the y – axis which equidistant from $A(5, -2)$ and $B(-3, 2)$

$$\therefore AP = \sqrt{(5-0)^2 + (-2-y)^2} = \sqrt{25 + (-2-y)^2}$$
$$BP = \sqrt{(-3-0)^2 + (2-y)^2} = \sqrt{9 + (2-y)^2}$$

Since $$AP = BP$$
$$\Rightarrow \quad AP^2 = BP^2$$

$\therefore \quad 25 + (-2 - y)^2 = 9 + (2 - y)^2$

$\Rightarrow \quad 25 + 4 + y^2 + 4y = 9 + 4 + y^2 - 4y[(a + b)^2 = (-a - b)^2)]$

$\Rightarrow \quad 29 + 8y = 13$

$\Rightarrow \quad 8y = -16$

$\Rightarrow \quad y = -2$

Hence the point is $(0, -2)$

OR

1 : 1 : 1

A(2,1) B(5,-8)

AB is trisected at P and Q so AP = PQ = QB

$$\frac{AP}{PB} = \frac{1}{2}$$

Applying section formula

$$\text{P}(x, \text{y}) = \left(\frac{m_1x_2 + m_2x_1}{m_1 + m_2}, \frac{m_1y_2 + m_2y_1}{m_1 + m_2}\right)$$

$$P = \left(\frac{1 \times 5 + 2 \times 2}{1 + 2}, \frac{1 \times (-8) + 2 \times (1)}{1 + 2}\right)$$

$$\Rightarrow \quad P = \left(\frac{5 + 4}{3}, \frac{-8 + 2}{3}\right)$$

$$\Rightarrow \quad P = (3, -2)$$

Since $P(3, -2)$ lies on $2x - y + k = 0$

$$\therefore 2(3) - (-2) + k = 0$$

$$\Rightarrow \quad 6 + 2 + k = 0$$

$$\Rightarrow \quad k = -8$$

17. Prove that $(\sin\,\theta + \text{cosec}\,\theta)^2 + (\cos\,\theta + \sin\,\theta)^2 = 7 + \tan^2\,\theta + \cot^2\,\theta.$

OR

$(1 + \cot\,A - \text{cosec}\,A)(1 + \tan\,A + \sec\,A) = 2$

Solution.

To Prove: $(\sin\,\theta + \text{cosec}\,\theta)^2 + (\cos\,\theta + \sec\,\theta)^2 = 7 + \tan^2\,\theta + \cot^2\,\theta$

LHS:

$(\sin\,\theta + \text{cosec}\,\theta)^2 + (\cos\,\theta + \sec\,\theta)^2$

$= \sin^2\,\theta + 2\sin\,\theta\text{cosec}\,\theta + \text{cosec}^2\,\theta + \cos^2\,\theta + \sec^2\,\theta + 2\cos\,\theta\sec\,\theta$

$= 1 + 2 + 2 + \text{cosec}^2\,\theta + \sec^2\,\theta$

$[\sin^2\theta + \cos^2\theta = 1$

$\sin\theta\,\text{cosec}\,\theta = 1$

$\cos\theta\sec\theta = 1]$

$= 5 + (1 + \cot^2\,\theta) + (1 + \tan^2\,\theta)$

$= 7 + \tan^2\,\theta + \cot^2\,\theta$

= RHS. Hence proved.

OR

To Prove: $(1+\cot A-\operatorname{cosec} A)(1+\tan A+\sec A)=2$

LHS:

$(1+\cot A-\operatorname{cosec} A)(1+\tan A+\sec A)$

$$=\left(1+\frac{\cos A}{\sin A}-\frac{1}{\sin A}\right)\left(1+\frac{\sin A}{\cos A}+\frac{1}{\cos A}\right)$$

$$=\left(\frac{\sin A+\cos A-1}{\sin A}\right)\left(\frac{\cos A+\sin A+1}{\cos A}\right)$$

$$=\frac{(\sin A+\cos A)^2-1}{\sin A\cos A} \qquad [a^2-b^2=(a+b)(a-b)]$$

$$=\frac{\sin^2 A+\cos^2 A+2\sin A\cos A-1}{\sin A\cos A} \qquad [\sin^2\theta+\cos^2\theta=1]$$

$$=\frac{2\sin A\cos A}{\sin A\cos A}$$

$$=2$$

RHS. Hence proved

18. In Fig. 2, PQ is a chord of length 8cm of a circle of radius 5cm and center O. The tangent at P and Q intersect at point T. Find the length of TP.

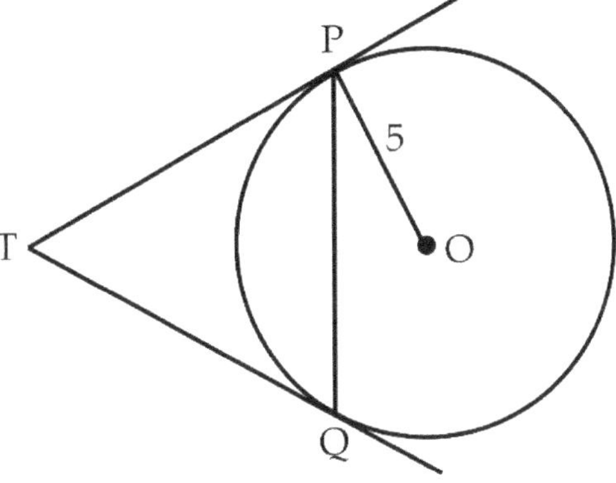

Solution.

Join OT

$TP=TQ$ (Length of the tangents from an external point to a circle are equal)

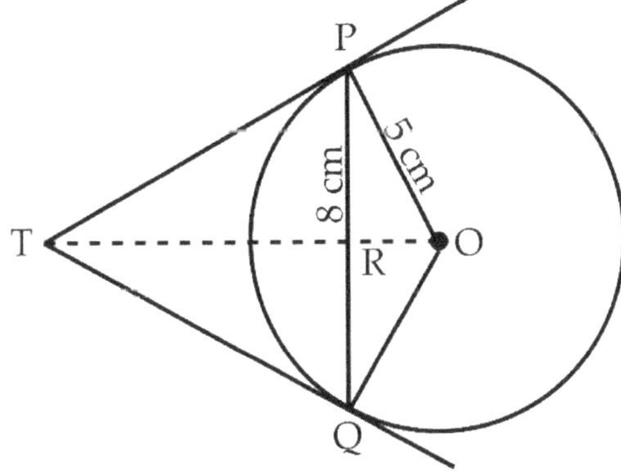

In $\triangle TPQ$: $TP=TQ$

OT is the bisector of $\angle PTQ$

$\therefore OT \perp PQ$ [diagonals of a kite are perpendicular]

Since $OT \perp PQ$

$PR = RQ$ (perpendicular from center to a chord bisects the chord)

$\therefore \; PR = QR = \frac{1}{2}PQ = 4\text{cm}$

In the Right triangle ORP

$OP^2 = OR^2 + PR^2$

$\Rightarrow \; 5^2 = OR^2 + 4^2$

$\Rightarrow OR^2 = 25 - 16 = 9$

$\Rightarrow \; OR = 3\text{cm}$

Now in ΔTPO and ΔPRO

$\angle TPO = \angle PRO$ [90° each]

$\angle O$ is common

$\therefore \Delta TPO \sim \Delta PRO$ [AA criterian]

$\frac{TP}{PR} = \frac{PO}{RO} = \frac{TO}{PO}$ [Corresponding sides of similar triangles are proportioal]

$\frac{TP}{4} = \frac{5}{3}$

Hence TP is $\frac{20}{3}$ cm

19. In Fig. 3, $\angle ACB = 90°$ and $CD \perp AB$, prove that $CD^2 = BD \times AD$

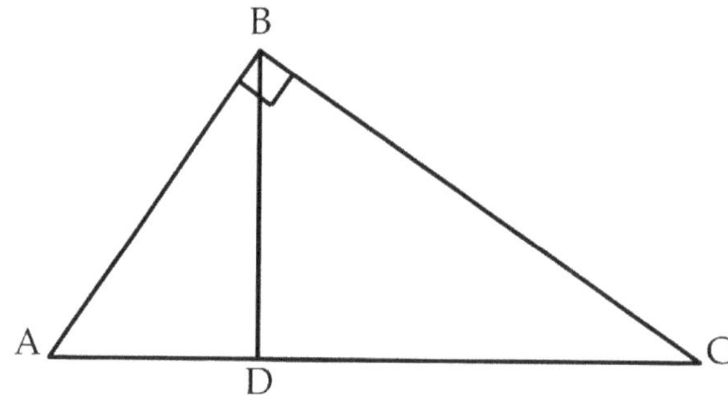

OR

If P and Q are a point of sides CA and CB respectively, of $\triangle ABC$, right-angled at C, prove that $(AQ^2 + BP^2) = (AB^2 + PQ^2)$ [Out of syllabus]

Solution.

Let $\angle C = x$ then $\angle A = 90° - x$ [complimentary angles of a right-angled triangle]

And $\angle CBD = 90° - x$ [as BD is perpendicular so $\angle BDC = 90°$]

Now in ΔADC and ΔCDB

$\angle ADC = \angle BDC$ [90° each]

$\angle CAD = \angle DBC$ [$90° - x$]

$\therefore \Delta ADC \sim \Delta BDC$ [AA criterian]

$\frac{AD}{CD} = \frac{DC}{DB}$ [Corresponding sides of similar triangles are proportioal]

$\Rightarrow \; CD^2 = DB.AD.$ Hence proved.

20. Find the area of the shaded region in Fig. 4, if $ABCD$ is a rectangle with sides 8cm and 6 cm and O is the center of the circle. (Take $\pi = 3.14$)

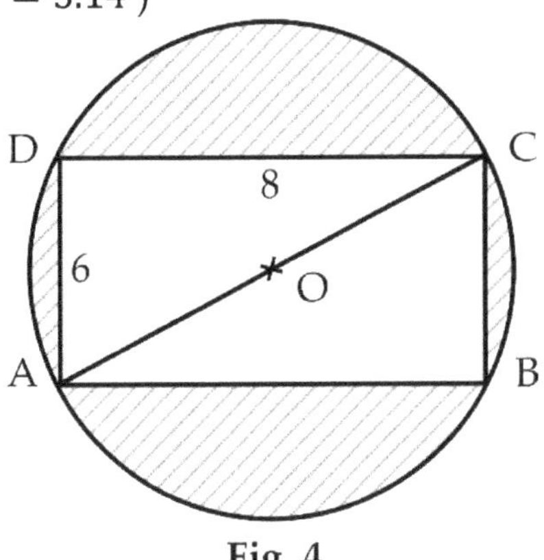

Fig. 4

Solution.

$\angle ADC = 90°$ [as ABCE is a rectanglee]

$AC = \sqrt{8^2 + 6^2} = 10\text{cm}$ [Pythagoras theorem]

Therefore, the radius of the circle = 5cm

Area of the circle = $\pi(5)^2 = 25\pi$

Area of $ABCD$ = $6 \times 8 = 48\text{cm}^2$

Hence the shaded area

$$= 25\pi - 48 = 25 \times 3.14 - 48 = 30.50 \text{ cm}^2$$

21. Water in a canal, 6m wide and 1.5m deep, is flowing at the speed of 10km/ hour. How much area will it irrigate in 30 minutes, if 8cm of standing water is needed?

Solution.

Speed of water = $\frac{10\text{km}}{hr}$

Volume of water flows in the canal in 1 hr. = area of cross-section × rate of flow of water

$= 6 \times 1.5 \times 10 \times 1000\text{m}^3 = 90000 \text{ m}^3$

Therefore, the volume of water in 30mins = $\frac{1}{2} \times 90000\text{m}^3 = 45000\text{m}^3$

Let Area of irrigation = x

$$\therefore x \times \frac{8}{100} = 45000$$

$$x = \frac{45000 \times 100}{8} m^2 = 562500\text{m}^2$$

22. Find the mode of the following frequency distribution

Class	0 – 10	10 – 20	20 – 30	30 – 40	40 – 50	50 – 60	60 – 70
Frequency	8	10	10	16	12	6	7

Solution.

Here the maximum frequency is 16 and the corresponding modal class is 30 – 40

$\therefore$ 30 – 40 is the modal class

$\therefore \quad l = 30, h = 10, f_1 = 16, f_0 = 10, f_2 = 12$

$$\text{Mode } = l + \frac{f_1 - f_0}{2f_1 - f_0 - f_2} \times h$$

$$= 30 + \frac{16-10}{2\times16-10-12} \times 10$$

$$= 30 + \frac{6}{10} \times 10 = 30 + 6 = 36$$

SECTION - D

(Question numbers23 to 30 carry 4 marks each.)

23. Two water taps can together fill in a tank in $1\frac{7}{8}$ hours. The tap with a longer diameter takes 2 hours less than the tap with the smaller one to fill the tank separately. Find the time in which each tap can fill the tank separately.

OR

A boat goes 30km upstream and 44km downstream in 10 hours. In 13 hours, it can go 40km upstream and 55km downstream. Determine the speed of the stream and that of the boat in still water.

Solution.

Let the time taken by the smaller tap to fill up the tank completely = x hours

So, the volume of a tank filled by the smaller tap in 1 hour $= \frac{1}{x}$

Also, it is given that the time taken by the larger tap is 2 hours less

Time is taken by a larger tap to fill the tank completely $= x - 2$

So, the volume of a tank filled by the larger tap in 1 hour $= \frac{1}{x-2}$

Given that both the taps fill the tank in $1\frac{7}{8}$ hours $= \frac{15}{8}$ hours

Tank filled by a smaller tap in $\frac{15}{8}$ hours $= \frac{15}{8x}$

Similarly, a tank filled with a larger tap in $\frac{15}{8}$ hours $= \frac{15}{8(x-2)}$

Therefore $\frac{15}{8x} + \frac{15}{8(x-2)} = 1$

$$15[8(x-2)] + 15[8x] = 8x[8(x-2)]$$

$$120x - 240 + 120x = 64x^2 - 16x$$

$$240x - 240 = 64x^2 - 16x$$

$$64x^2 - 256x + 240 = 0$$

$$4x^2 - 16x + 15 = 0$$

$$x = \frac{16 \pm \sqrt{16^2 - 4 \times 4 \times 15}}{8} = \frac{16 \pm 4}{8}$$

$\therefore x = 2.5$ hours or 1.5 hours

x cannot be 1.5 hours as the larger tap takes 2 hours less.

Hence $x = 2.5$ hours

Therefore, small tap will fill the tank in 2.5 hours and a larger tap will fill the tank in 0.5 hours.

OR

Let the speed of the boat in still water = $x$km/hr
Let the speed of the stream = $y$km/hr
Speed of the boat downstream = $(x + y)$km/hr
Sped of the boat upstream= $(x - y)$km/hr
A boat goes 30km upstream and 44km downstream in 10 hours

$$\Rightarrow \frac{30}{x-y} + \frac{44}{x+y} = 10 \quad \text{.......(i)}$$

Boat goes 40km upstream and 55km downstream in 13 hours

$$\Rightarrow \frac{40}{x-y} + \frac{55}{x+y} = 13 \quad \text{.........(ii)}$$

Let $\frac{1}{x-y} = m$ and $\frac{1}{x+y} = n$
Substituting in (i) and (ii)

$$30m + 44n = 10 \quad \text{........(iii)}$$
$$40m + 55n = 13 \quad \text{........(iv)}$$

From (iii) we get $m = \frac{10-44n}{30}$
Substituting in (iv) we get

$$40\left(\frac{10-44n}{30}\right) + 55n = 13$$
$$\Rightarrow \quad 40 - 176n + 165n = 39$$
$$\Rightarrow \quad 11n = 1$$
$$\Rightarrow \quad n = \frac{1}{11}$$

Substituting in (iii) we get

$$30m + 44\left(\frac{1}{11}\right) = 10$$
$$\Rightarrow \quad 30m + 4 = 10$$
$$\Rightarrow \quad m = \frac{6}{30} = \frac{1}{5}$$

Now solving for x and y

$$\frac{1}{x-y} = \frac{1}{5} \Rightarrow x - y = 5 \quad \text{........(v)}$$
$$\frac{1}{x+y} = \frac{1}{11} \Rightarrow x + y = 11 \quad \text{......(vi)}$$

Adding (v) and (vi) we get $2x = 16 \Rightarrow x = 8$km/hr
From (vi) $y = 11 - 8 = 3$km/hr
Therefore, speed a boat in still water is 8km/hr and speed of a stream is 3km/hr

24. If the sum of the first four terms of an AP is 40 and that of the first 14 terms is 280. Find the sum of the first n terms.

Solution.

$$S_n = \text{ sum of n terms of an A.P.}$$
$$= \frac{n}{2}[2a + (n-1)d]$$

$$S_4 \Rightarrow \quad 40 = \frac{4}{2}[2a + 3d] = 2a + 3d = 20 \quad \text{......(i)}$$
$$S_{14} \Rightarrow \quad 280 = \frac{14}{2}[2a + 13d] = 2a + 13d = 40 \quad \text{......(ii)}$$

solving (i) and (ii)

gives $a = 7$ and $d = 2$

so $S_n = \frac{n}{2}[2(7) + (n-1)2] = 7n + n^2 - n = n^2 + 6n$

25. Prove that

$$\frac{\sin A - \cos A + 1}{\sin A + \cos A + 1} = \frac{1}{\sec A - \tan A}$$

Solution.

LHS:

$$= \frac{(\sin A - \cos A + 1) \div \cos A}{(\sin A + \cos A - 1) \div \cos A}$$ [Divide by cos A in numerator and denominator]

$$= \frac{(\tan A - 1 + \sec A)}{(\tan A + 1 - \sec A)}$$

$$= \frac{\tan A + \sec A - 1}{\tan A + 1 - \sec A}$$

$$= \frac{\tan A + \sec A - (\sec^2 A - \tan^2 A)}{\tan A + 1 - \sec A}$$ $[1 + \tan^2 A = \sec^2 A]$

$$= \frac{(\sec A + \tan A)(1 - \sec A + \tan A)}{\tan A + 1 - \sec A}$$

$$= \sec A + \tan A$$

$$= (\sec A + \tan A) \times \left(\frac{\sec A - \tan A}{\sec A - \tan A}\right)$$

$$= \frac{\sec^2 A - \tan^2 A}{\sec A - \tan A}$$

$$= \frac{1}{\sec A - \tan A}$$ $[1 + \tan^2 A = \sec^2 A]$

= RHS ,Hence proved

26. A man in a boat is rowing away from the lighthouse at 100m high takes 2 minutes to change the angle of elevation of the top of the lighthouse from 60° to 30°. Find the speed of the boat in meters per minute. [Use $\sqrt{3} = 1.732$]

OR

Two poles of equal height are standing opposite each other on either side of the road, which is 80m wide. From a point between them on the road, the angle of elevation of the top of the poles are 60° respectively. Find the height of the poles and the distance of the point from the poles.

Solution.

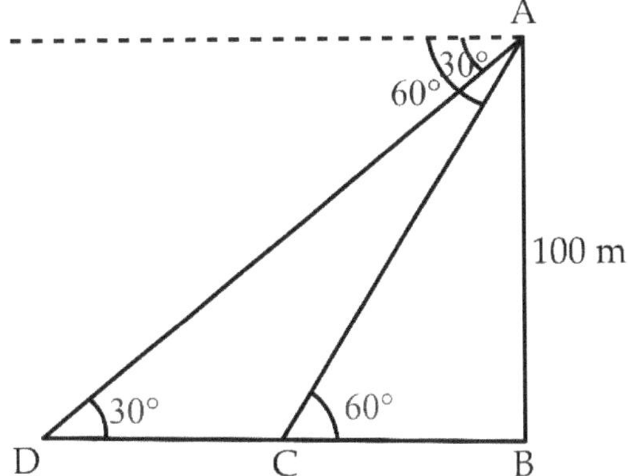

In Δ ABC $\quad \tan 60^\circ = \frac{AB}{BC} = \sqrt{3}$

$$\therefore BC = \frac{AB}{\sqrt{3}} = \frac{100}{\sqrt{3}}$$

In ΔABD $\quad \tan 30^\circ = \frac{AB}{DB} = \frac{1}{\sqrt{3}}$

$$\therefore DB = \sqrt{3}AB = 100\sqrt{3}$$

$$\therefore CD = DB - BC = 100\sqrt{3} - \frac{100}{\sqrt{3}} = \frac{200}{\sqrt{3}} \times \frac{\sqrt{3}}{\sqrt{3}} = \frac{200\sqrt{3}}{3}\text{m}$$

Therefore Speed $= \frac{\text{distance}}{\text{time}} = \frac{200\sqrt{3}}{3\times2\times60} = \frac{5\sqrt{3}}{9}\text{ m/sec}$

OR

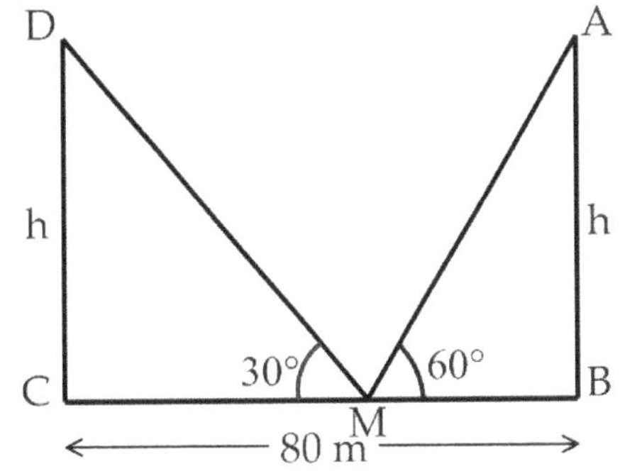

In ΔABM $\tan 60^\circ = \frac{h}{MB} \rightarrow MB = \frac{h}{\sqrt{3}}$

In ΔDCM $\tan 30^\circ = \frac{h}{CM} \Rightarrow \frac{1}{\sqrt{3}} = \frac{h}{CM} \Rightarrow CM = \sqrt{3}h$

Given $\quad CM + BM = 80$

$$h\sqrt{3} + \frac{h}{\sqrt{3}} = 80$$

$$3h + \text{h} = 80\sqrt{3}$$

$$h = \frac{80\sqrt{3}}{4} = 20\sqrt{3}\text{m}$$

$\therefore \quad CM = \sqrt{3}(20\sqrt{3}) = 60\text{m}$

Hence $\quad MB = 80 - 60 = 20\text{m}$

27. Construct a $\triangle ABC$ in which CA is 6cm, $AB = 5$cm, and $\angle BAC = 45°$. They construct a triangle whose sides are $\frac{3}{5}$ of the corresponding sides of $\triangle ABC$.

Solution. Out of syllabus

28. A bucket open at the top is in the form of a frustum of a cone with a capacity of 12308.08cm^3. The radii of the top and bottom of the circular ends of the bucket and 20cm and 12cm respectively. Find the height of the bucket, and also the area of the metal sheet used in making it. (Use $\pi =$ 3.14)

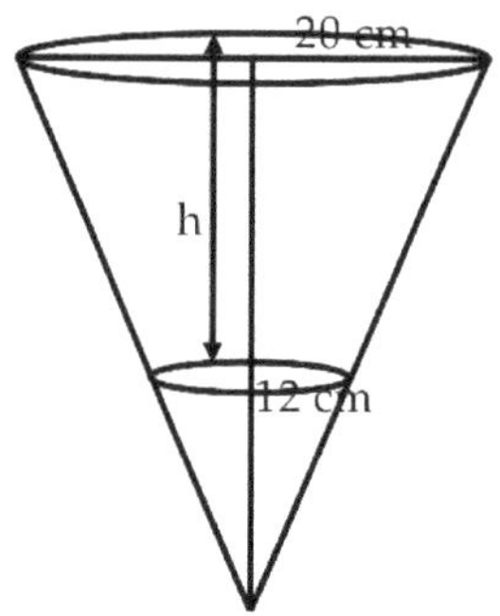

Solution. Out of syllabus

29. Prove that in a right-angle triangle, the square of the hypotenuse is equal to the sum of the square of the other two sides.

Solution. Out of syllabus

30. If the median of the following frequency distribution is 32.5, find the values of f_1 and f_2.

Class	0 – 10	10 – 20	20 – 30	30 – 40	40 – 50	50 – 60	60 – 70	Total
Frequency	f_1	5	9	12	f_2	3	2	40

OR

The marks obtained by 100 students in a class in an examination are given below.

Marks	No. of Students
0 – 5	2
5 – 10	5
10 – 15	6
15 – 20	8
20 – 25	10
25 – 30	25
30 – 35	20
35 – 40	18
40 – 45	4
45 – 50	2

Solution.

Class Interval	Frequency	Cumulative Frequency
$0-10$	f_1	f_1
$10-20$	5	f_1+5
$20-30$	9	f_1+14
$30-40$	12	f_1+26
$40-50$	f_2	f_1+f_2+26
$50-60$	3	f_1+f_2+29
$60-70$	2	f_1+f_2+31
	$N=40$	

Given, Median $= 32.5$

The median class $= 30-40$

$$L=30, h=40-30=10, f=12, F=14+f_1$$

Median $$= l+\frac{\frac{N}{2}-F}{f}\times h$$

$$\Rightarrow \quad 32.5 = 30+\frac{20-(14+f_1)}{12}\times 10$$

$$\Rightarrow \quad 32.5-30 = \frac{20-(14+f_1)}{12}\times 10$$

$$\Rightarrow \quad 2.5 = \frac{6-f_1}{12}\times 10$$

$$\Rightarrow \quad 2.5 = \frac{6-f_1}{6}\times 5$$

$$\Rightarrow \quad 2.5\times 6 = (6-f_1)\times 5$$

$$\Rightarrow \quad 3 = 6-f_1$$

$$\Rightarrow \quad f_1 = 3$$

Given the sum of frequencies $= 40$

$$f_1+f_2+31 = 40$$

$$f_2+34 = 40$$

$$f_2 = 6$$

Hence $f_1 = 3$ and $f_2 = 6$

OR

Marks	CI	No. of Students
Less than 5	0 – 5	2
Less than 10	5 – 10	7
Less than 15	10 – 15	13
Less than 20	15 – 20	21
Less than 25	20 – 25	31
Less than 30	25 – 30	56
Less than 35	30 – 35	76

Less than 40	35 – 40	94
Less than 45	40 – 45	98
Less than 50	45 – 50	100

$N = 100$ (even)

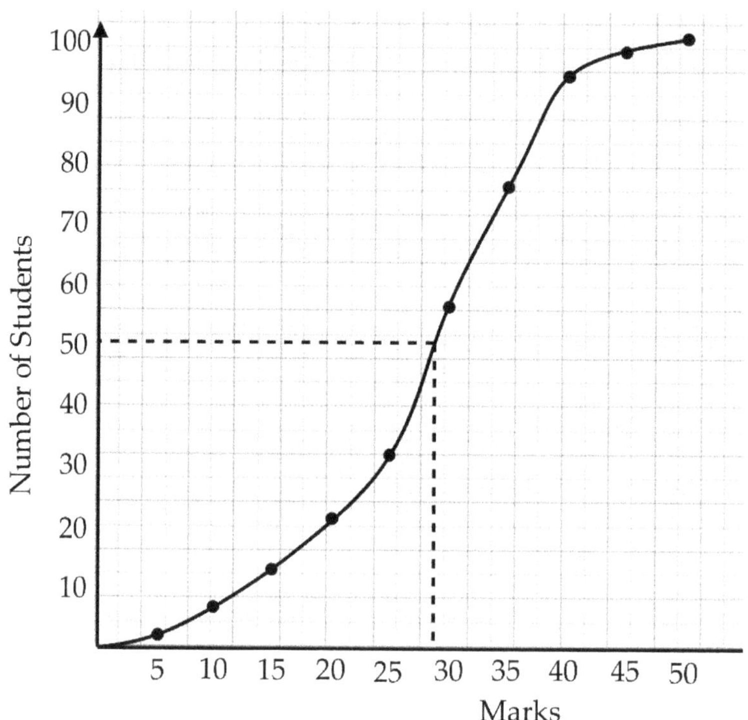

So median = $\left(\frac{N}{2}\right)^{th}$ term

$= \left(\frac{100}{2}\right)^{th}$ term

$= 50^{th}$ term

For graph median = 29(appr.)

Class- X Session- 2022-23

PREVIOUS YEAR PAPER-2020

Sample Question Paper

Time Allowed: 3 Hrs. **Maximum Marks: 80**

General Instructions:

1. This Question Paper has 5 Sections A-E.
2. Section **A** has 20 MCQs carrying 1 mark each
3. Section **B** has 5 questions carrying 02 marks each.
4. Section **C** has 6 questions carrying 03 marks each.
5. Section **D** has 4 questions carrying 05 marks each.
6. Section **E** has 3 case-based integrated units of assessment (04 marks each) with subparts of the values of 1, 1 and 2 marks each respectively.
7. All Questions are compulsory. However, an internal choice in 2 Qs of 5 marks, 2 Qs of 3 marks and 2 Questions of 2 marks has been provided. An internal choice has been provided in the 2marks questions of Section E
8. Draw neat figures wherever required. Take π =22/7 wherever required if not stated

SECTION A

(Question numbers 1 to 10 are multiple choice questions of 1 mark each.)
(Select the correct option.)

1. The sum of exponents of prime factors in the prime factorization of 196 is

(a) 3
(b) 4
(c) 5
(d) 2

Answer: (b)

$196 = 2 \times 2 \times 7 \times 7 = 2^2 \times 7^2$

Therefore, the sum of exponents of prime factors in the prime factorization of 196 is $= 2 + 2 = 4$

2. Euclid's division Lemma states that for two positive integers a and b there exists unique integers q and r satisfying a = bq + r and

Answer. Out of syllabus

3. The zeros of the polynomial $x^2 - 3x - m(m + 3)$ are

(a) $m, m + 3$
(b) $-m, m + 3$
(c) $m, -(m + 3)$
(d) $-m_1 - (m + 3$

Answer. (b)

$$x^2 - 3x - m(m + 3) = 0$$
$$\Rightarrow \quad x^2 - m^2 - 3x - 3m = 0$$
$$\Rightarrow (x - m)(x + m) - 3(x + m) = 0$$

$\Rightarrow \qquad (x+m)[x-m-3]=0$

Therefore, zeros are $-m, (m+3)$

4. The value of k for which the system of linear equations $x + 2y = 3$ and $5x + ky + 7 = 0$ is inconsistent is

(a) $-\frac{14}{3}$

(b) $\frac{2}{5}$

(c) 5

(d) 10

Answer. (d)

For $x + 2y = 3 \Rightarrow a_1 = 1, b_1 = 2$ and $c_1 = -3$

For $5x + ky + 7 = 0 \Rightarrow a_2 \;= 5, b_2 = k$ and $c_2 = 7$

For a unique solution, $\frac{a_1}{a_2} = \frac{b_1}{b_2} \neq \frac{c_1}{c_2}$

$$\frac{1}{5} = \frac{2}{k} \neq \frac{-3}{7}$$

Hence for $k = 10$, the given equations will be inconsistent.

5. The roots of the quadratic equation $x^2 - 0.04 = 0$ are

(a) ± 0.2

(b) ± 0.02

(c) 0.4

(d) 2

Answer. (a)

$x^2 - 0.04 = 0 \Rightarrow (x - 0.2)(x + 0.2) = 0$

$\therefore \qquad x = \pm 0.2$

6. The common difference of the AP $\frac{1}{p}, \frac{1-p}{p}, \frac{1-2p}{p} \ldots$ is

(a) 1

(b) $\frac{1}{p}$

(c) -1

(d) $-\frac{1}{p}$

Answer. (c)

First term $(a) = \frac{1}{p}$

Common difference $(d) = \frac{1-p}{p} - \frac{1}{p} = \frac{1-p-1}{p} = -1$

7. The nth term of the A.P. $a, 3a, 5a, \cdots$, is

(a) na

(b) $(2n - 1)a$

(c) $(2n + 1)a$

(d) 2na

Answer. (b)
First term $(a) = a$
Common difference $(d) = 3a - a = 2a$
Therefore n^{th} term $= a + (n-1)d = a + (n-1)(2a) = (2n-1)a$

8. The point P on the x-axis equidistant from points A(−1,0) and B(5,0) is
(a) (2,0)
(b) (0,2)
(c) (3,0)
(d) (2,2)
Answer. (a)
Since P is on the x-axis, the coordinate of P would be $(x, 0)$
Since P is equidistant from A and B we get

$$x = \frac{-1+5}{2} = 2$$

Therefore, a coordinate of P is (2,0)

9. The coordinate of the point which is the reflection of the point (−3,5) in the x-axis is
(a) $(3, 5)$
(b) $(3, -5)$
(c) $(-3, -5)$
(d) $(-3, 5)$
Answer. (c)
Because if the reflection is in x-axis, the y coordinate will change.

10. If the point P(6,2) divides the line segment joining A(6,5) and B(4, y) in the ratio of 3: 1, then the value of y is
(a) 4
(b) 3
(c) 2
(d) 1
Answer (d)
Using the section formula, we get

$$2 = \frac{3y+5}{3+1}$$
$$= 3y = 3$$
$$= y = 1$$

SECTION B

(In Questions Nos. 11 to 15, Fill in the blanks.)
(Each question carries 1 mark.)

11. In Fig, MN || BC and AM: MB = 1: 2, then

$$\frac{ar\,(\triangle AMN)}{ar\,(\triangle ABC)} = \_\_\_\_\_\_\_$$

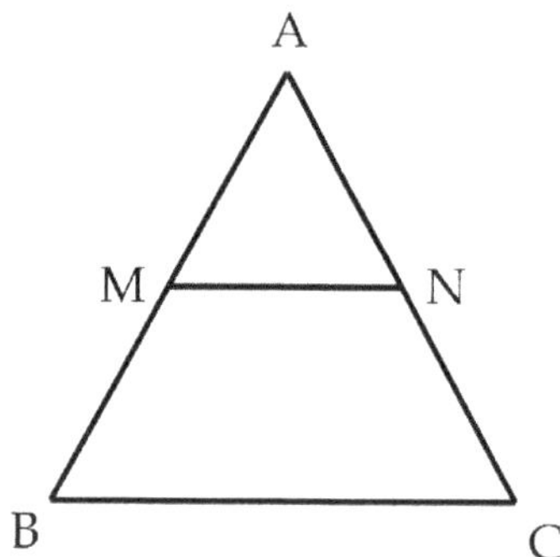

Solution. Out of syllabus

12. In given Fig. 2, the length PB = _____cm.

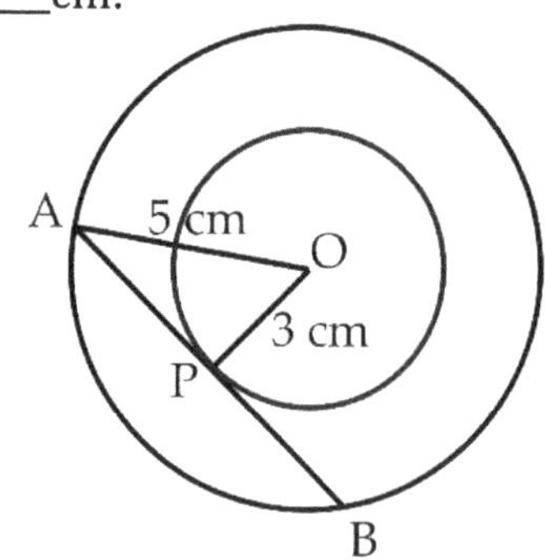

Solution. PB = 4cm

$$\angle APO = 90^\circ$$

$\therefore \triangle$ AOP is a right-angled triangle, Using Pythagoras $AP = \sqrt{AP^2 - OP^2}$

$\therefore$ $$AP = \sqrt{5^2 - 3^2} = \sqrt{16} = 4cm$$

Since $OP \perp AB, AP = PB$ [Perpendicular from center to chord bisect the chord]

Hence PB = 4cm

13. In $\triangle$ ABC, $AB = 6\sqrt{3}$cm, AC = 12cm and BC = 6cm, then $\angle B =$_______

OR

Two triangles are similar if their corresponding sides are

Solution. $\angle B = 90^\circ$

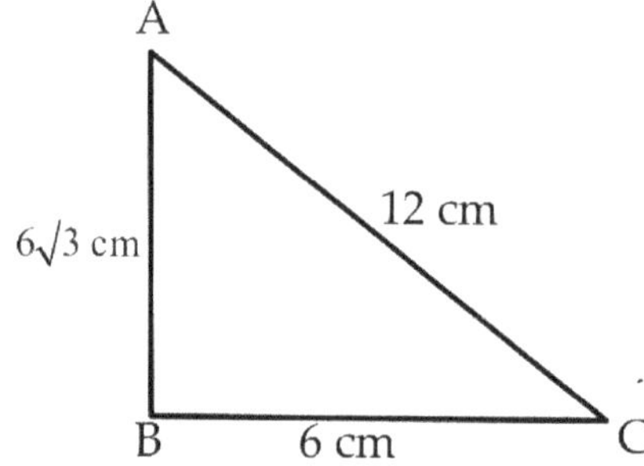

We have to first check if the $\triangle$ ABC is a right-angled triangle.

If it is a right-angled triangle, then Pythagoras' theorem should hold

$$\Rightarrow 12^2 = (6\sqrt{3})^2 + (6)^2$$

$$\Rightarrow 144 = 108 + 36$$

$\Rightarrow 144 = 144$. Therefore the $\triangle$ ABC is a right-angled triangle.

$\therefore \angle B = 90°$

OR

Two triangles are similar if their corresponding sides are proportional

14. The value of ($\tan 1° \tan 2° \ldots \tan 89°$) is equal to

Solution. Out of syllabus

15. In Fig. 3, the angles of depressions from the observing positions O_1 and O_2 respectively of the object A are_______

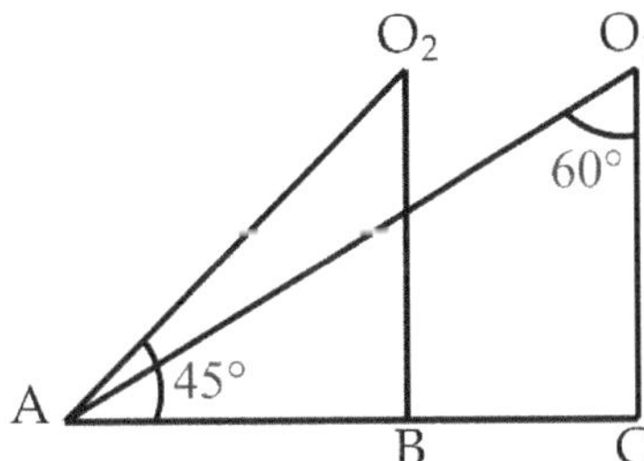

Solution. 30°&45°

Please refer to the adjoining diagram

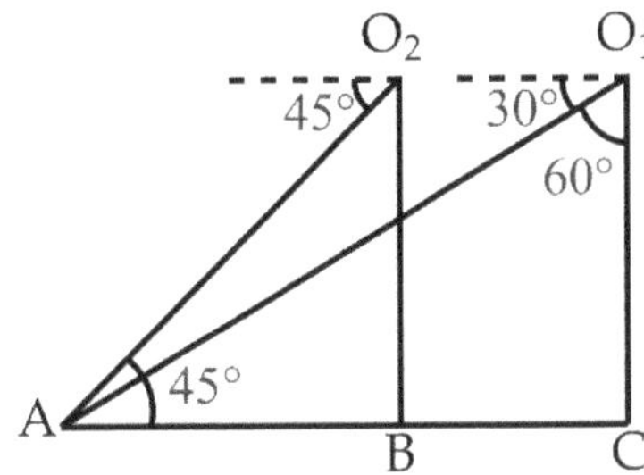

Therefore, the angle of depression is30°&45°.

SECTION C

(Questions No. 16 to 20 are short answer type questions of 1 mark each.)

16. If $\sin A + \sin^2 A = 1$, then find the value of the expression $(\cos^2 A + \cos^4 A)$.

Solution.

Given $\sin A + \sin^2 A = 1$

$\Rightarrow \sin A = 1 - \sin^2 A$

$\Rightarrow \sin A = \cos^2 A$

Now $\cos^2 A + \cos^4 A = \cos^2 A(1 + \cos^2 A)$

$= \sin A(1 + \sin A) = \sin A + \sin^2 A = 1$

Hence $(\cos^2 A + \cos^4 A) = 1$

17. In Fig. 4 is a sector of a circle of radius 10.5cm. Find the perimeter of the sector. (Take $\pi = \frac{22}{7}$)

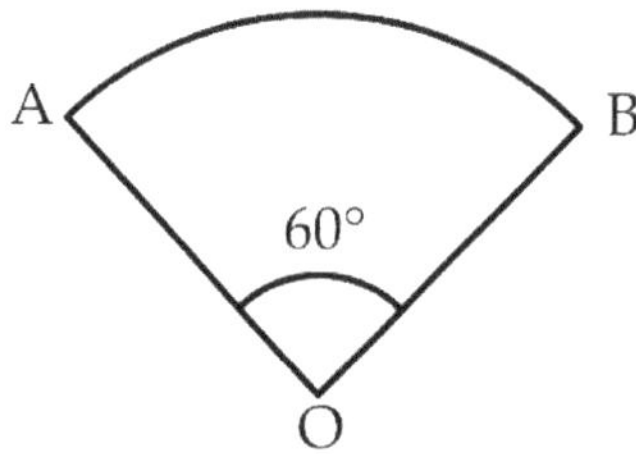

Solution.

Given: radius = 0A = 0B = 10.5cm

Central angle $(\theta) = 60^\circ$

We know, if the radius of the circle is r and the length of the arc is$l$, then

$$l = \frac{\theta}{360}2\pi r = \frac{\theta}{180}\pi r$$

$$\Rightarrow l = \frac{60}{180} \times \frac{22}{7} \times 10.5 = 11\text{cm}$$

Therefore, perimeter of the sector = 10.5 + 11 + 10.5 = 32cm

18. If a number x is chosen at random from the numbers $-3, -2, -1, 0, 1, 2, 3$ then find the probability of $x^2 < 4$,

OR

What is the probability that a randomly taken leap year has 52 Sundays?

Solution.

Total number of observations (s) = 7

If $x^2 < 4$, then x can be either -1,0,1 only.

Therefore, number of favourable events n(f) = 3

Therefore, the probability $\quad n(E) = \frac{n(f)}{n(s)} = \frac{3}{7}$

OR

There are 52 weeks in a way which means there will be 52 Sundays in a year.

There are 365 days in a year but we have 366 days in a leap year.

There are 7 days in a week.

If we multiply the weeks by the days, we have 52 × 7 which equals to 364. This means that there are 2 extra days in a leap year which will make it 366.

The probability of having 52 Sundays in a leap year is thus: the remaining two days can be any of these formations:

Sunday-Monday, Monday-Tuesday, Tuesday-Wednesday, Wednesday-Thursday, Thursday-Friday, Friday-Saturday, Saturday-Sunday.

However, to get 52 Sundays in a leap year, none of the remaining two days must be a Sunday. Therefore, out of the 7 combinations above, that can be only realized 5 out of 7 times. The connection "Sunday Monday and Saturday-Sunday" must be scraped off.

The probability of having 52 Sundays in a leap year is therefore $\frac{5}{7}$

19. Find the class - marks of classes 10 – 25 and 35 – 55.

Solution.

Given: classes 10 – 25 and 35 – 55

We know, Class Marks $(x) = \frac{\text{lower limit + upper limit}}{2}$

For Class interval (10 – 25) lower limit = 10, upper limit = 25

Therefore, Class Marks of $10 - 15 = \frac{10+25}{2} = 17.5$

Similarly, For Class interval (35 – 55) lower limit = 35, upper limit = 55

Therefore, Class Marks of $35 - 55 = \frac{35+55}{2} = 45$

20. A die is thrown once. What is the probability of getting a prime number?

Solution.

Total outcomes that are possible are 1, 2, 3, 4, 5, 6

Therefore, the number of possible outcomes n(s) = 6

No of the prime numbers on the dice are 2, 3, 5

Therefore, the number of favourable outcomes $n(f) = 3$

Hence the probability of getting a prime number

$$n(E) = \frac{n(f)}{n(s)} = \frac{3}{6} = \frac{1}{2}$$

SECTION D

(Questions Nos. 21 to 26 carry 2 marks each.)

21. A teacher asked 10 of his students to write a polynomial in one variable on a paper and then to hand over the paper. The following were the answers given by the students:

$2x + 3, 3x^2 + 7x + 2, 4x^3 + 3x^2 + 2, x^3 + \sqrt{3x} + 7$

$7x + \sqrt{7}, 5x^3 - 7x + 2, 2x^2 + 3 - \frac{5}{x^2}, 5x - \frac{1}{2}$

$$ax^3 + bx^2 + cx + d, x + \frac{1}{x}$$

Answer the following questions:

(i) How many of the above 10 are not polynomials?

(ii) How many of the above are quadratic polynomials?

Solution.

Definitions:

A polynomial is an expression consisting of variables and coefficients, that involves only the operations of addition, subtraction, multiplication, and non-negative integer exponents of variables

A quadratic polynomial, a polynomial of degree 2, or simply a quadratic, is a polynomial function with one or more variables in which the highest-degree term is of the second degree.

⇒ $2x + 3$: This is a polynomial.

⇒ $3x^2 + 7x + 2$: This is a polynomial. This is also a quadratic polynomial as the highest-degree term is of the second degree.

⇒ $4x^3 + 3x^2 + 2$: This is a polynomial.

$\Rightarrow x^3 + \sqrt{3x} + 7 \Rightarrow x^3 + (3x)^{\frac{1}{2}} + 7$: This is NOT a polynomial as one of the exponents is not an integer.

$\Rightarrow 7x + \sqrt{7}$: This is a polynomial.

$\Rightarrow 5x^3 - 7x + 2$: This is a polynomial.

$\Rightarrow 2x^2 + 3 - \frac{5}{x^2}$ This is NOT a polynomial as one of the exponents is a negative integer.

$\Rightarrow 5x - \frac{1}{2}$: This is a polynomial.

$\Rightarrow ax^3 + bx^2 + cx + d$: This is a polynomial.

$\Rightarrow x + \frac{1}{x}$: This is NOT a polynomial as one of the exponents is a negative integer.

Therefore:

(a) How many of the above 10 are not polynomials? - Three

(b) How many of the above are quadratic polynomials? - one

22. In Fig. 5, ABC and DBC are two triangles on the same base BC, If AD intersects BC at O, shows that

$$\frac{\text{ar}(\triangle \text{ABC})}{\text{ar}(\triangle \text{DBC})} = \frac{\text{AO}}{\text{DO}}$$

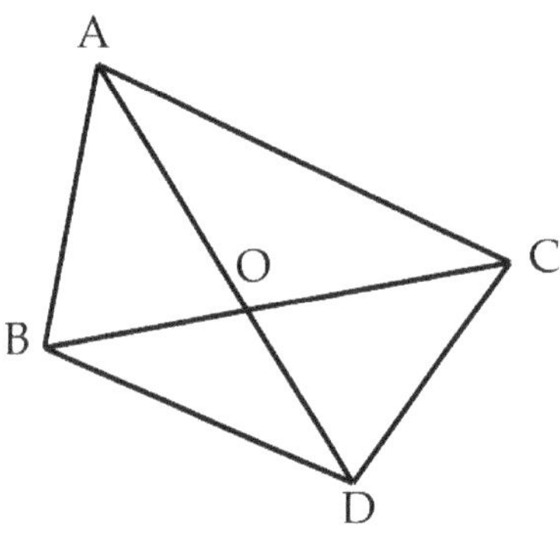

OR

In Fig. 6, if AD ⊥ BC, then prove that $AB^2 + CD^2 = BD^2 + AC^2$

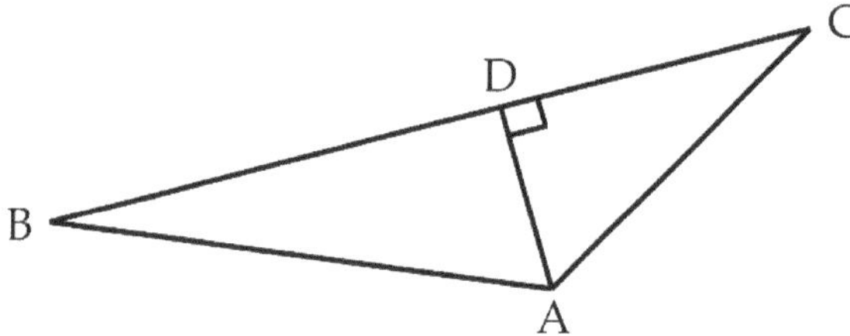

Solution.

Given: △ ABC and △ DBC have common bases.

To prove:

$$\frac{\text{ar}(\triangle \text{ABC})}{\text{ar}(\triangle \text{DBC})} = \frac{\text{AO}}{\text{DO}}$$

Construction: Draw AE ⊥ BC and DF ⊥ BC

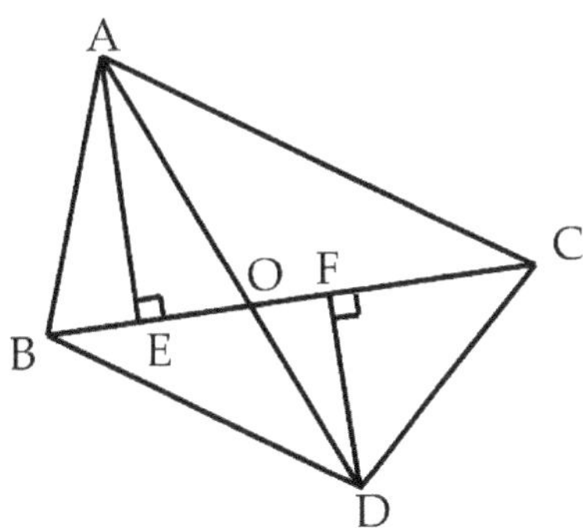

Proof: ar (△ ABC) $= \frac{1}{2} \times BC \times AE$ ....(i)

Similarly, ar (△ DBC) $= \frac{1}{2} \times BC \times DF$ ....(ii)

Therefore

$$\frac{ar(\triangle ABC)}{ar(\triangle DBC)} = \frac{AE}{DF}$$

In △ AOE and △ DOF

$\angle AEO = \angle DFO$ [90° each]

$\angle AOE = \angle DOF$ [vertically opposite angle]

∴△ AOE ~△ DOF (by AA similarity criterion)

$$\therefore \frac{AE}{DF} = \frac{AO}{DO} = \frac{OE}{OF} \quad \text{........(iv)}$$

Therefore from (iii) and (iv), we get

$$\frac{ar\ (\triangle ABC)}{ar\ (\triangle DBC)} = \frac{AO}{DO}$$

OR

Out of syllabus

23. Prove that $1 + \frac{\cot^2 \alpha}{1+\operatorname{cosec} \alpha} = \operatorname{cosec} \alpha$

OR

Show that $\tan^4 \theta + \tan^2 \theta = \sec^4 \theta - \sec^2 \theta$

Solution.

LHS:

$=1 + \frac{\cot^2 \alpha}{1+\operatorname{cosec}^?}$

$= 1 + \frac{\operatorname{cosec}^2 \alpha - 1}{1+\operatorname{cosec} \alpha}$ $[1 + \cot^2 \alpha = \operatorname{cosec}^2 \alpha]$

$= 1 + \frac{(\operatorname{cosec} \alpha+1)(\operatorname{cosec} \alpha-1)}{1+\operatorname{cosec} \alpha}$ $[a^2 - b^2 = (a = b)(a - b)]$

$= 1 + \operatorname{cosec} \alpha - 1$

$= \operatorname{cosec} \alpha$

RHS Hence proved.

OR

LHS:

$$= \tan^4\theta + \tan^2\theta$$
$$= \tan^2\theta(\tan^2\theta + 1)$$

Since $1 + \tan^2\theta = \sec^2\theta$

$$= (\sec^2\theta - 1)\sec^2\theta$$
$$= \sec^4\theta - \sec^2\theta$$

RHS   Hence proved

24. The volume of the right circular cylinder with its height equal to the radius is $25\frac{1}{7}\text{cm}^3$. Find the height of the cylinder. (Use $\pi = \frac{22}{7}$)

Solution.

Volume of the cylinder $= 25\frac{1}{7}\text{cm}^3$

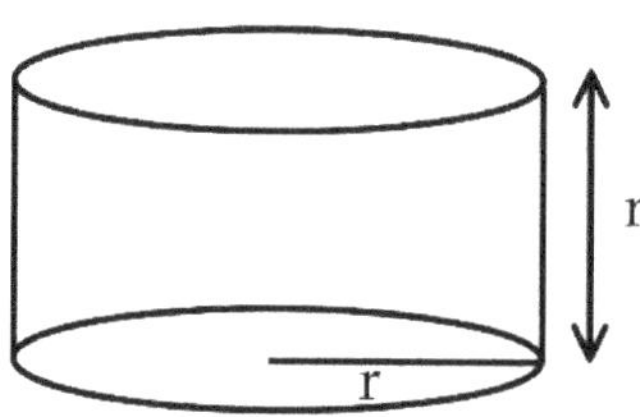

Let the radius = r. Therefore height = r

Volume of a right circular cylinder $= \frac{22}{7}\pi r^2$

Therefore $\frac{22}{7} \times r^2 \times r = 25\frac{1}{7}$

$$\Rightarrow \frac{22}{7}r^3 = \frac{176}{7}$$
$$\Rightarrow r^3 = 8$$
$$\Rightarrow r = 2\text{cm}$$

Therefore, the height of the cylinder is 2cm

25. A child has a die whose six faces show the letters shown below:

A	B	C	D	E	A

The Die is thrown once. What is the probability of getting (i)A(ii)D?

Solution.

Probability $n(E) = \frac{n(f)}{n(s)}$

Number of faces in the dice $n(s) = 6$

(i) The probability of getting A

$n(f) = 2$

∴ Probability $= \frac{2}{6} = \frac{1}{3}$

(ii) The probability of getting a D

$n(f) = 1$

∴ Probability $= \frac{1}{6}$

26. Compute the mode for the following frequency distribution:

Size of the items (in cm)	0 – 4	4 – 8	8 – 12	12 – 16	16 – 20	20 – 24	24 – 25
Frequency	5	7	9	17	12	10	6

Solution.

Here the maximum frequency is 17 and the corresponding modal class is 12 – 16

$\therefore$ 12 – 16 is the modal class

$\therefore l = 12, h = 4, f_1 = 17, f_0 = 9, f_2 = 12$

Mode $= l + \dfrac{f_1 - f_0}{2f_1 - f_0 - f_2} \times h$

$= 12 + \dfrac{17 - 9}{2 \times 17 - 9 - 12} \times 4$

$= 12 + \frac{8}{13} \times 4 = 12 + 2.4 = 14.4$ cm

SECTION - E

(Questions Nos. 27 to 34 carry 3 marks each.)

27. If $2x + y = 23$ an$4x - y = 19$, find the value of $(5y - 2x)$ and $\left(\frac{y}{x} - 2\right)$

OR

Solve for x: $\frac{1}{x+4} - \frac{1}{x+7} = \frac{11}{30}, x \neq -4,7$

Solution.

Given equations: $2x + y = 23$ and $4x - y = 19$

Adding the two equations we get $6x = 42 \Rightarrow x = 7$

Substituting it back we get $y = 23 - 2(7) = 23 - 14 = 9$

Hence $5y - 2x = 5(9) - 2(7) = 45 - 14 = 31$

$\frac{y}{x} - 2 = \frac{9}{7} - 2 \quad = -\frac{5}{7}$

OR

$$\frac{1}{x+4} - \frac{1}{x-7} = \frac{11}{30}, x \neq -4,7$$

$$\frac{x - 7 - x - 4}{(x+4)(x-7)} = \frac{11}{30}$$

$\Rightarrow 11[(x+4)(x-7)] = 30 \times (-11)$

$\Rightarrow [x^2 - 7x + 4x - 28] = -30$

$\Rightarrow x^2 - 3x - 28 + 30 = 0$

$\Rightarrow \quad x^2 - 3x + 2 = 0$

$\Rightarrow \quad x^2 - 2x - x + 2 = 0$

$\Rightarrow x(x - 2) - 1(x - 2) = 0$

$\Rightarrow \quad (x - 1)(x - 2) = 0$

$x = 1$ or $x = 2$

28. Show that the sum of all terms of an A.P. whose first term is a and the second term is b and the last term is c is equal to $\frac{(a+c)(b+c-2a)}{2(b-a)}$

OR

Solve the equation: $1 + 4 + 7 + 10 + \cdots + x = 287$

Solution.

First term $= a$

Second term $= b$

Therefore, Common difference $(d) = b - a$

We know n^{th} term $= c$

We know $T_n = a + (n-1)d$

$$\therefore c = a + (n-1)(b-a)$$

$$\Rightarrow \frac{c-a}{b-a} = n - 1$$

$$\Rightarrow n = \frac{c-a}{b-a} + 1$$

$$\Rightarrow n = \frac{c-a+b-a}{b-a}$$

$$\Rightarrow n = \frac{c+b-2a}{b-a}$$

We know that sum of n terms $= \frac{n}{2}$[first term + last term]

$$= \frac{c+b-2a}{2(b-a)}(a+c)$$

Hence proved.

OR

Given $1 + 4 + 7 + 10 + \cdots + x = 287$

First term$(a) = 1$

Common difference $(d) = 4 - 1 = 3$

$$S_n = \frac{n}{2}[2a + (n-1)d]$$

$$\Rightarrow \quad \frac{n}{2}[2(1) + (n-1)(3)] = 287$$

$$\Rightarrow \quad \frac{n}{2}[3n - 1] = 287$$

$$\Rightarrow \quad 3n^2 - n - 574 = 0$$

$$\Rightarrow \quad 3n^2 - 42n + 41n - 574 = 0$$

$$\Rightarrow \quad 3n(n-14) + 41(n-14) = 0$$

$$\Rightarrow \quad (n-14)(3n+41) = 0$$

$$\Rightarrow \quad n = 14 \text{ or } n = -\frac{41}{3} \text{[this is not possible]}$$

Hence $n = 14$

We know x is the 14th term

$\therefore x = T_{14} = 1 + (14-1)(3) = 40$

29. In a flight of 600km, an aircraft was slowed down due to bad weather. The average speed of the trip was reduced by 200km/hr and the time of the flight increased by 30 minutes. Find the duration of the flight.

Solution.

Distance travelled $= 600km$

Let the average speed $= xkm/hr$

Therefore $\frac{600}{x-200} - \frac{600}{x} = \frac{1}{2}$

$$\Rightarrow \quad 600\left[\frac{x - x + 20}{(x-200)x}\right] = \frac{1}{2}$$

$$\Rightarrow \quad x^2 - 200x - 24000 = 0$$

$$\Rightarrow \quad (x - 600)(x + 400) = 0$$

$$\Rightarrow \quad x = 600\text{km/hr or } x = -400\text{km/hr}$$

[this is not possible as speed cannot be negative]

Therefore, the normal duration of flight $= \frac{600}{600} = 1\text{hr}$

30. If the midpoint of the line segment joining the points A(3,4) and B(k, 6), is $P(x, y)$ and $x + y - 10 = 0$, find the value of k.

OR

Find the area of triangle ABC with A(1, −4) and the midpoints of the sides through A being (2, −1) and (0, −1) [Out of syllabus]

Solution.

If P is the midpoint, then

$x = \frac{k+3}{2}$ and $y = \frac{4+6}{2} = 5$

Also

$$x + y - 10 = 0$$

$$\Rightarrow \frac{k+3}{2} + 5 - 10 = 0$$

$$\Rightarrow \quad \frac{k+3}{2} = 5$$

$$\Rightarrow \quad k + 3 = 10$$

$$\Rightarrow \quad k = 7$$

31. In Fig. 7, if △ ABC ~△ DEF and their sides of the lengths (in cm) are marked along them, then find the length of the sides of each of the triangles.

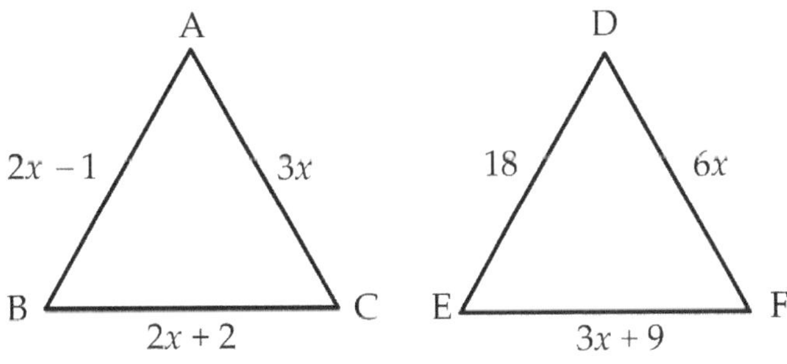

Solution.

Since △ ABC ~△ DEF

Therefore $\frac{AB}{DE} = \frac{BC}{EF} = \frac{AC}{DF}$ [corresponding sides of similar triangles are proportional]

$\Rightarrow = \dfrac{2x-1}{18} = \dfrac{2x+2}{3x+9} = \dfrac{3x}{6x}$

$\Rightarrow = \dfrac{2x-1}{18} = \dfrac{1}{2}$

$\Rightarrow 2x - 1 \quad = 9$

$\Rightarrow \qquad x = 5$

Therefore $AB = 2(5) - 1 = 9, BC = 2(5) + 2 = 12, AC = 3(5) = 15$

Similarly, $EF = 3(5) + 9 = 24, DF = 6(5) = 30$

AB = 9 units, BC = 12 units, and AC = 15 units

EF = 24 units, DF = 30 units

32. If a circle touches the side BC of a triangle ABC at P and the extended sides AB and AC at Q and R respectively, prove that

$$\text{AQ} = \frac{1}{2}(\text{BC} + \text{CA} + \text{AB})$$

Solution.

Given: A circle touching the side BC of $\triangle$ ABC at P and AB, AC produced at Q and R respectively.

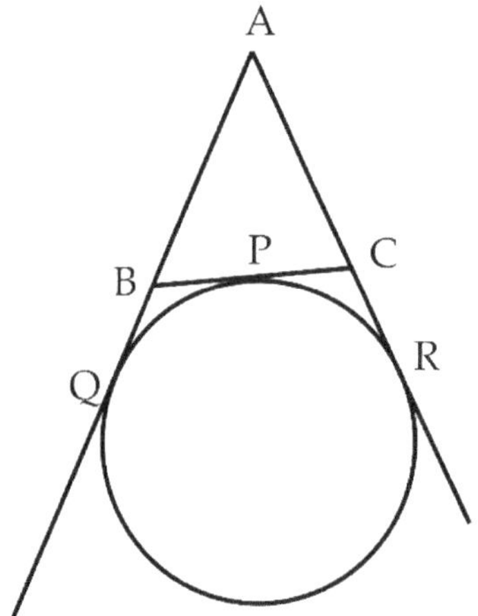

We know that tangents drawn from an external point to the same circle are equal.

Hence $\text{BP} = \text{BQ}$ and $\text{CP} = \text{CR}$

Also, $\text{AQ} = \text{AR}$

$\Rightarrow \text{AR} = \text{AC} + \text{CR}$

$\Rightarrow \text{AR} = \text{AC} + \text{CP}$ ....(i)

Also, $\text{AQ} = \text{AB} + \text{BQ}$

$\Rightarrow \text{AQ} = \text{AB} + \text{BP}$ ....(ii)

Adding (i) and (ii) we get

$\text{AR} + \text{AQ} = \text{AB} + \text{AC} + (\text{BP} + \text{CP})$

$2\text{AQ} = \text{AB} + \text{AC} + (\text{BP} + \text{CP})$ [as $AR = AQ$]

$\Rightarrow 2\text{AQ} = \text{AB} + \text{AC} + \text{BC}$

$\Rightarrow \text{AQ} = \frac{1}{2}(\text{AB} + \text{AC} + \text{BC})$ Hence proved

33. If $\sin\theta + \cos\theta = \sqrt{2}$, prove that $\tan\theta + \cot\theta = 2$

Solution.

Given $\sin\theta + \cos\theta = \sqrt{2}$

Squaring both sides

$$\sin^2\theta + \cos^2\theta + 2\sin\theta\cos\theta = 2$$

$$\Rightarrow \quad 2\sin\theta\cos\theta = 1$$

$$\Rightarrow \quad \sin\theta\cos\theta = \frac{1}{2} \quad ....(i)$$

Now, LHS = $\tan\theta + \cot\theta$

$$= \frac{\sin\theta}{\cos\theta} + \frac{\cos\theta}{\sin\theta}$$

$$= \frac{\sin^2\theta + \cos^2\theta}{\sin\theta\cos\theta}$$

$$= \frac{1}{\sin\theta\cos\theta}$$

$$= \frac{1}{1/2}$$

$= 2$ RHS. Hence proved.

34. The area of a circular playground is 22176 cm^2. Find the cost of fencing this ground at the rate of Rs. 50 per meter.

Solution.

Area $= 22176 cm^2$

Let the radius $= r cm$

$$\therefore \pi r^2 = 22176$$

$$\Rightarrow r^2 = \frac{7}{22} \times 22176 = 7056$$

$$\Rightarrow r = 84 cm$$

Circumference $= 2\pi r = 2 \times \frac{22}{7} \times 84 = 528 cm$

Per unit cost = Rs. 50 per meter

Therefore cost of fencing $= 50 \times \frac{528}{100}$ = Rs. 264

SECTION F

(Question Nos. 35 to 40 carry 3 marks each.)

35. Prove that $\sqrt{5}$ is an irrational number.

Solution.

Let's prove this by the method of contradiction.

Say, $\sqrt{5}$ is a rational number.

Therefore, It can be expressed in the form $\frac{p}{q}$ where $q \neq 0$ also p, and q are co-prime integers i.e. they do not have any common factors except 1.

$$\Rightarrow \sqrt{5} = \frac{p}{q}$$

$$\Rightarrow 5 = \frac{p^2}{q^2} \text{ (Squaring both the sides)}$$

$\Rightarrow 5q^2 = p^2$ ....(i)

4 divides p

$\Rightarrow$ 5 divides p [If p is a prime no and divies a^2 then p divides a also(by theorem)]

So 5 is a factor of p ....(i)

$\Rightarrow$ so p = $5m$ where m is a positive integer.

$\Rightarrow p^2 = 25m^2$ ....(ii)

From equations (i) and (ii), we get,

$$5q^2 = 25m^2$$

$\Rightarrow$ $q^2 = 5m^2$

$\Rightarrow$ Here 5 divides q^2

$\Rightarrow$ so 5 divides q[$\because$5 is a prime and divides q^2]

So, 5 is a factor of q..............................(ii)

Thus from (i) and (ii) p and q have a common factor 5.

This contradicts the fact that p and q have no common factor other than 1.

This contradiction has arisen because of our incorrect assumption that $\sqrt{5}$ is rational.

Hence, $\sqrt{5}$ is an irrational number. Hence proved

36. It takes 12 hours to fill a swimming pool using two pipes. If the pipe of the larger diameter is used for 4 hours and the pipe of the smaller diameter for 9 hours, only half of the pool can be filled. How long would it take for each of the pipes to fill the pool separately?

Solution.

Let the pipe with the larger diameter and the smaller diameter be pipe A and B respectively.

Let Pipe A works at x liters/hours and Pipe B works at y liters/hours.

Therefore, the capacity of the pool = $12x + 12y$ liters

Given, $4x + 9y = \frac{1}{2}(12x + 12y)$

$\Rightarrow$ $4x + 9y = 6x + 6y$

$\Rightarrow$ $3y = 2x$

For larger pipe to fill the swimming pool

$$= \frac{12x + 12y}{x} = 12 + 12\frac{y}{x}$$

$$= 12 + 12 \times \frac{2}{3}$$

$$= 12 + 8 = 20 \text{ hours}$$

For smaller pipe to fill the swimming pool

$$= \frac{12x + 12y}{y} = 12\frac{x}{y} + 12$$

$$= 12 \times \frac{3}{2} + 12$$

$$= 18 + 12 = 30 \text{ hours}$$

37. Draw a circle of 2cm radius with center 0 and take a point P outside the circle such that 0P is 6.5cm. From P, draw two tangents to the circle.

OR

Construct a triangle with sides of 5cm, 6cm, and 7cm, and then construct another triangle whose sides are $\frac{3}{4}$ times the corresponding sides of the first triangle.

Solution.

Out of syllabus

OR

Out of syllabus

38. From a point on the ground, the angles of elevation of the bottom and top of the tower fixed at the top of a 20m high building are 45° and 60° respectively. Find the height of the tower.

Solution.

Let the height of the tower be h m

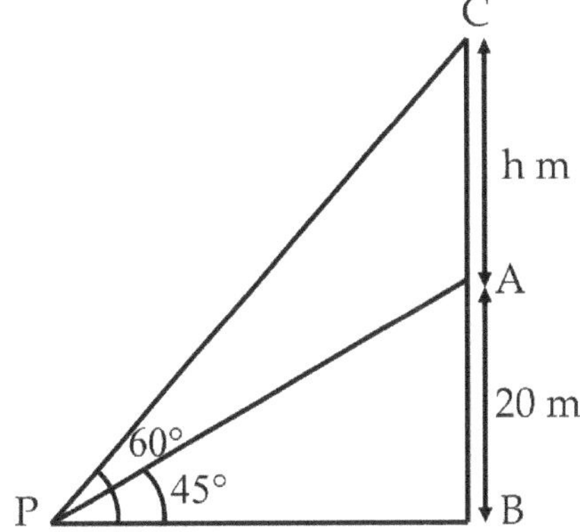

In $\triangle$ CBP

$\tan 60° = \frac{BC}{BP}$

$\Rightarrow \sqrt{3} = \frac{20+h}{BP}$ ....(i)

In $\triangle$ ABP

$\tan 45° = \frac{AB}{BP}$

$\Rightarrow \quad 1 = \frac{20}{BP}$

$\Rightarrow \quad BP = 20$ ....(ii)

Substituting in (i) we get

$$\sqrt{3} = \frac{20+h}{20}$$

$$\Rightarrow \quad 20\sqrt{3} = 20 + h$$

$$\Rightarrow \quad h = 20(\sqrt{3} - 1) = 20(1.73 - 1) = 20 \times 0.73 = 14.6\text{m}$$

39. Find the area of the shaded region in Fig. 8, if PQ = 24cm, PR = 7cm, and O is the center of the circle.

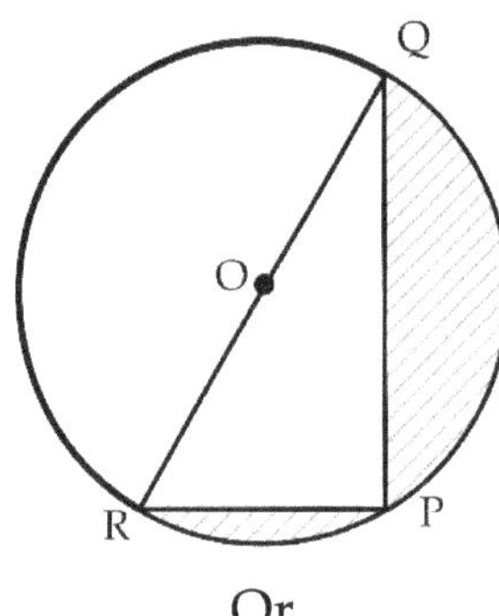

Or

Find the curved surface area of the frustum of a cone, the diameters of whose circular ends are 20m and 6m and its height is 24m.

Solution.

$\angle RPQ = 90°$ (Diameter or a circle subtends a right angle on any point of the circumference of the circle)

$\therefore QR = \sqrt{7^2 + 24^2} = \sqrt{625} = 25$ [Using 153 Pythagoras]

$\therefore$ Radius $= \frac{25}{2}$

$\therefore$ Area of semi-circle $= \frac{1}{2}(\pi r^2) = \frac{1}{2} \times \frac{22}{7} \times \left(\frac{25}{2}\right)^2 = 245.54 cm^2$

Area of $\triangle$ PQR $= \frac{1}{2} \times 7 \times 24 = 84 cm^2$

Therefore, the shaded area = $245.54 - 84 = 161.54 cm^2$

OR

Curved Surface Area $= \pi l(R + r)$ where l = slant height, R is the larger radius, r is the smaller radius

Solution. Out of syllabus

40. The mean of the frequency distribution is 18. The frequency f in the class interval 19 – 21 is missing. Determine f.

Class Interval	11 – 13	13 – 15	15 – 17	17 – 19	19 – 21	21 – 23	23 – 25
Frequency	3	6	9	13	f	5	4

OR

The following table gives the production yield per hectare of wheat of 100 farms of a village

Production yield	40 – 45	45 – 50	50 – 55	55 – 60	60 – 65	65 – 70
No. of farms	4	6	16	20	30	24

Change the distribution to a 'more than type distribution and draw an ogive.

Solution.

Class Interval	Frequency (f)	Class marks(x)	fx
$11-13$	3	12	36
$13-15$	6	14	84
$15-17$	9	16	144
$17-19$	13	18	234
$19-21$	f	20	20f
$21-23$	5	22	110
$23-25$	4	24	96
Total	$\Sigma f_1 = 40 + f$		$\Sigma f = 704 + 20f$

$$\text{Mean} = \frac{\Sigma f_i x_i}{\Sigma f_i}$$

$$\Rightarrow \quad 18 = \frac{704 + 20f}{40 + f}$$

$$\Rightarrow 720 + 18f = 704 + 20f$$

$$\Rightarrow \quad 16 = 2f$$

$$\Rightarrow \quad f = 8$$

OR

Production Yield	Number of Farms (f_i)	Production Yield (x –axis)	Number of Farms (y-axis)
$40-45$	4	More than 40	100
$45-50$	6	More than 45	96
$50-55$	16	More than 50	90
$55-60$	20	More than 55	74
$60-65$	30	More than 60	54
$65-70$	24	More than 65	24

Now plot (40,100), (45,96), (50,90), (55,74), (60,54), (65,24)

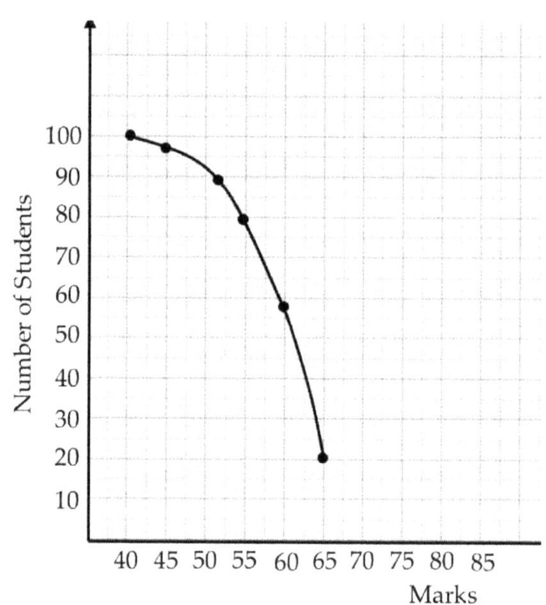

100
90
80
70
60
50
40
30
20
10
Number of Students
40 45 50 55 60 65 70 75 80 85
Marks

Class- X Session- 2022-23

PREVIOUS YEAR PAPER-2022

Sample Question Paper

Time Allowed: 3 Hrs. **Maximum Marks: 80**

General Instructions:

1. This Question Paper has 5 Sections A-E.
2. Section **A** has 20 MCQs carrying 1 mark each
3. Section **B** has 5 questions carrying 02 marks each.
4. Section **C** has 6 questions carrying 03 marks each.
5. Section **D** has 4 questions carrying 05 marks each.
6. Section **E** has 3 case-based integrated units of assessment (04 marks each) with subparts of the values of 1, 1, and 2 marks each respectively.
7. All Questions are compulsory. However, an internal choice in 2 Qs of 5 marks, 2 Qs of 3 marks, and 2 Questions of 2 marks has been provided. An internal choice has been provided in the 2marks questions of Section E
8. Draw neat figures wherever required. Take π =22/7 wherever required if not stated

SECTION – A

(Question Number 1 to 6 carries 2 marks each.)

1. Solve the quadratic equation: $x^2 + 2\sqrt{2}x - 6 = 0$for$x$

Solution

Compare the given equation to $ax^2 + bx + c = 0$

$$a = 1, b = 2\sqrt{2}, c = -6$$

use quadratic formula $x = \frac{-b\pm\sqrt{b^2-4ac}}{2a}$

$$x = \frac{-2\sqrt{2} \pm \sqrt{(2\sqrt{2})^2 - 4 \times (\times (-6)}}{2 \times 1}$$

$$= \frac{-2\sqrt{2} \pm \sqrt{8 + 24}}{2}$$

$$= \frac{-2\sqrt{2} \pm \sqrt{32}}{2}$$

$$= \frac{-2\sqrt{2} \pm 4\sqrt{2}}{2}$$

$$= \frac{-2(\sqrt{2} \mp 2\sqrt{2})}{2}$$

$$= -\sqrt{2} + 2\sqrt{2}, \leftarrow \sqrt{2} - 2\sqrt{2}$$

$$= \sqrt{2}, -3\sqrt{2}$$

2. (a) Which term of the A.P. $-\frac{11}{2}, -3, -\frac{1}{2}, \ldots$ is $\frac{49}{2}$?

Solution

$$a = -\frac{11}{2}$$

$$d = -3 - \left(-\frac{11}{2}\right)$$
$$= -\frac{3}{1} + \frac{11}{2}$$
$$= \frac{-6+11}{2} \Rightarrow \frac{5}{2}$$

Let $\frac{49}{2}$ is nth term

$$\therefore a_n = \frac{49}{2}$$
$$a_+(n-1)d = \frac{49}{2}$$
$$\frac{-11}{2} + (n-1) \times \frac{5}{2} = \frac{49}{2}$$
$$\frac{1}{2}(-11 + 5n - 5) = \frac{49}{2}$$
$$5n - 16 = \frac{49}{2} \times 2$$
$$5n - 16 = 49$$
$$5n = 49 + 16 \Rightarrow 65$$
$$n = \frac{65}{5} \Rightarrow 13$$

$\therefore$ 13 th term **Ans.**

(b) Find a and b so that the numbers: $a, 7, b, and$ 23 are in A.P.

Solution:

$\because$ These no. are in A.P.

First term= a

$$a_2 = 7$$
$$a + d = 7 \quad \text{.........(i)}$$
$$a_4 = 23$$
$$\therefore a + 3d = 23 \quad \text{.........(ii)}$$

let's solve equations (i) and (ii)

$$a + d = 7$$
$$\underline{a + 3d = 23}$$
$$2d = 16$$
$$d = \frac{16}{2}$$
$$d = 8$$

Put d in eq. (i)

$$a + 8 = 7$$
$$a = 7 - 8 \Rightarrow -1$$
$$a_3 = b$$
$$a + 2d = b$$
$$\therefore b = -1 + 2 \times 8$$
$$b = 15$$

$\therefore a = -1, b = 15$ **Ans.**

3. A solid piece of metal in the form of a cuboid of dimensions 11cm × 7cm × 7cm is melted to form ' n ' number of solid spheres of radii $\frac{7}{2}$ cm each. Find the value of n.

Solution:

Volume of cuboid

$$= l \times b \times h$$
$$= 11 \times 7 \times 7cm^3$$

Volume of sphere $= \frac{4}{3}\pi r^3$

$$= \frac{4}{3} \times \frac{22}{7} \times \frac{1}{2} \times \frac{1}{2} \times \frac{1}{2} \text{cm}^3$$

$\therefore n \times$ volume of 1 sphere = volume of Corrode

$$n \times \frac{4}{3} \times \frac{22}{7} \times \frac{7}{2} \times \frac{7}{2} \times \frac{7}{2} = 11 \times 7 \times 7$$

$$n = \frac{11 \times 7 \times 7 \times 3 \times 7 \times 2 \times 2 \times 2}{4 \times 22 \times 7 \times 7 \times 7} \Rightarrow 3$$

$$n = 3$$ **Ans.**

4. **(a)** In the given figure AB is the diameter of a circle centered at O. BC is tangent to the circle at B. If OP bisects the chord AD and ∠AOP = 60°, then find m∠C (angle C).

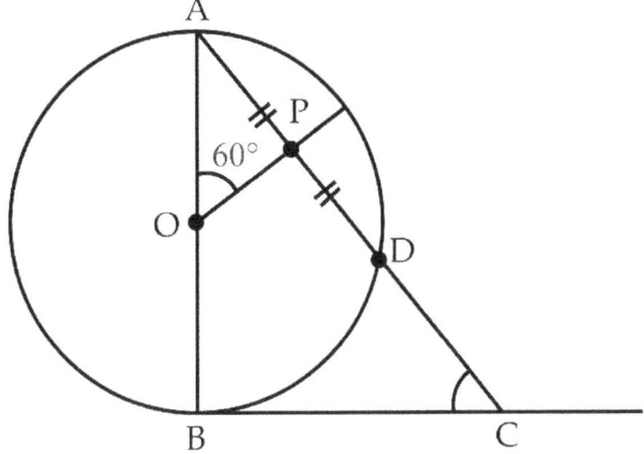

Solution:

In $\triangle OAP$

$OP \perp AD$ [Line segment from center bisects the chord]

$\therefore \angle OAP = 180 - (60 + 90)$ (Angle sum property of triangle)

$\angle OAP = 30°$

$\angle ABC = 90°$(tangent is perpendicular to a diameter at the point of contact)

so, In $\triangle ABC$

$$\angle C = 180 - (90 + 30)$$
$$\angle C = 60°$$ **Ans.**

(b) In the given figure, XAY is a tangent to the circle cantered at O. If ∠ABO = 40°, then find m∠BAY and m∠AOB.

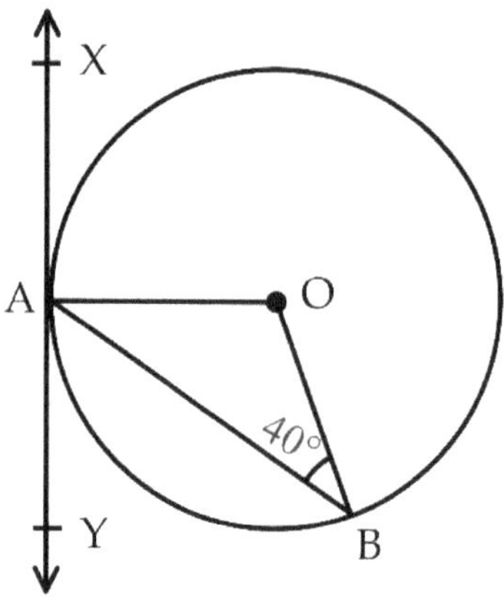

Solution:

$$\angle OAB = \angle OBA (OA = OB)$$
$$\angle OAB = 40°$$

So, In $\triangle AOB$

$$\angle AOB = 180 - (40 + 40)$$
$$= 180 - 80 = 100°$$ **Ans**

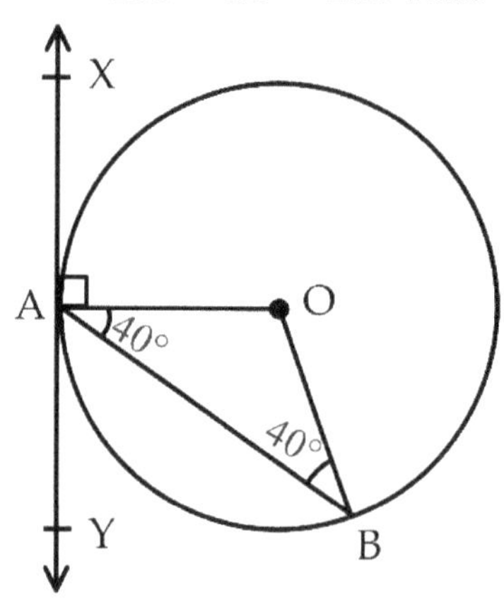

Fig. 2

$\angle OAY = 90°$[Radius make 90° with tangent at Point of content]

$\therefore \angle BAY = 90 - 40$

$\angle BAY = 50°$ **Ans.**

5. If the mode of the following frequency distribution is 55, then find the value of x.

Class	0 – 15	15 – 30	30 – 45	45 – 60	60 – 75	75 – 90
Frequency	10	7	x	15	10	12

Solution:

C.I	f
0 – 15	10

15 – 30	7
30 – 45	x
45 – 60	15
60 – 75	10
75 – 90	12

∵ Modo is 55

Modal Clam is 45 – 60

$$l = 45$$
$$h=15\text{-}0 \Rightarrow 15$$
$$f_1=15$$
$$f_2=10$$
$$f_0=x$$

∴ Mode

$$= l + \left(\frac{f_1-f_2}{2f_1-f_0-f_2}\right) \times h$$
$$55 = 45 + \left(\frac{15 - x}{30 - x - 10}\right) \times 15$$
$$55 = 45 + \left(\frac{15 - x}{20 - x}\right) \times 15$$
$$55 - 45 = \left(\frac{15 - x}{20 - x}\right) \times 15$$
$$\frac{10}{15} = \frac{15 - x}{20 - x}$$
$$\frac{2}{3} = \frac{15 - x}{20 - x}$$
$$45 - 3x = 40 - 2x$$
$$-3x + 2x = 40 - 45$$
$$x = 5$$
$$x = 5$$ **Ans.**

6. Find the sum of the first 20 terms of an A.P. whose n^{th} the term is given as $a_n = 5 - 2n$

Solution:

$$a_n = 5 - 2n$$
$$\text{let } n = 1 => a_1 = 5 - 2 \times 1 \Rightarrow 3$$
$$\text{n} = 2 => a_2 = 5 - 2 \times 2 \Rightarrow 1$$
$$\text{First term } a = 3$$
$$\text{Common difference } (d) = 1 - 3 \Rightarrow -2$$
$$n = 20$$
$$s_n = \frac{n}{2}[2a + (n - 1)d]$$
$$S_{20} = \frac{20}{2}[2 \times 3 + (20 - 1) \times (-2)]$$
$$= 10[6 - 38] \Rightarrow 10x - 32 \Rightarrow -320$$ **Ans.**

SECTION B
(Question Numbers from 7 to 10 carry 3 marks each.)

7. Draw two concentric circles of radii 2cm and 5cm. From a point on the outer circle, construct a pair of tangents to the inner circle.
   Solution: out of syllabus

8. In Fig., AB is a tower of a height of 50m. A man standing on its top, observes two cars on the opposite sides of the tower with angles of depression 30° and 45° respectively. Find the distance between the two cars.

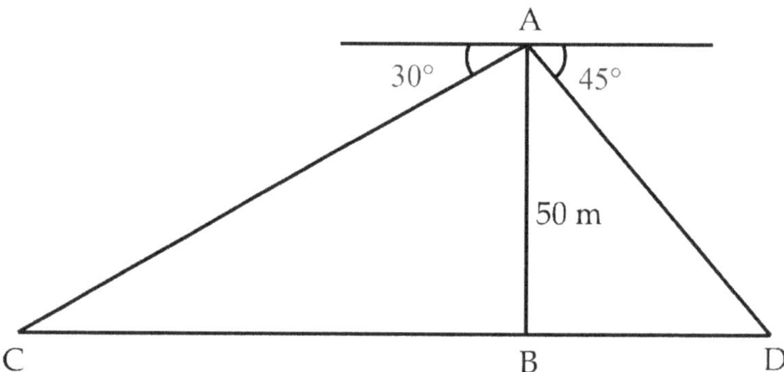

Solution:

$\angle ACB = 30°$ (alternate)

$\angle ADB = 45°$ (alternate)

In $\triangle ABD$

$$\tan 45 = \frac{AB}{BD}\left[\tan\theta = \frac{\text{Perpendiculs}}{Bace}\right]$$

$$1 = \frac{50}{BD} \Rightarrow BD = 50\text{m.}$$

In $\triangle ABC$

$$\tan 30 = \frac{AB}{CB}$$

$$\frac{1}{\sqrt{3}} = \frac{50}{CB}$$

$$CB = 50 \times \sqrt{3}$$
$$= 50 \times 1.732$$
$$= 86600$$

∴Distance between two Carn= 86.6 + 50

= 136.60m. **Ans.**

9. (a) The mean of the following frequency distribution is 25. Find the value of f.

Class	$0-10$	$10-20$	$20-30$	$3-40$	$40-50$
Frequency	5	18	15	f	6

Solution:

C.I	f	$x(clan\ mark)$	fx
$0-10$	5	$\frac{0+10}{2}=5$	25
$10-20$	18	15	270
$20-30$	15	25	375
$30-40$	f	35	$35f$
$40-50$	6	45	210
	$\Sigma f=44+f$		$\Sigma(fx)=940+25f$

$$\text{mean} = \frac{\Sigma(fx)}{\Sigma f}$$
$$25 = \frac{940+35f}{44+f}$$
$$35f+940 = 1100+25f$$
$$35f-25f = 1100-940$$
$$10f = 160$$
$$f = \frac{160}{10}$$
$$f = 16$$

(b) Find the mean of the following data using the assumed mean method:

Class	$0-5$	$5-10$	$10-15$	$15-20$	$20-25$
Frequency	8	7	10	13	12

Solution:

class intervals	**class marks (x)**	**frequency (f)**	**d $= x - A$**	***Fd***
0 - 5	2.5	8	-10	-80
5 - 10	7.5	7	-5	-35
10 - 15	$12.5 = A$	10	0	0
15 - 20	17.5	13	5	65
20 - 25	22.5	12	10	120
		$f = 50$		$fd = 70$

Mean in direct method $= A + \frac{\Sigma fd}{\Sigma f}$

$$= 12.5 + \frac{70}{50}$$

$= 12.5 + 1.4$
$= 13.9$ **Ans.**

10. Heights of 50 students of class **X** of a school are recorded and the following data is obtained:

Height (in cm):	130 – 135	135 – 140	140 – 145	145 – 150	150 – 155	155 – 160
Number of	4	11	12	7	10	6

Find the median height of the students.

Solution:

Height	No. of students	cumulative frequency
130 – 135	4	4
135 – 140	11	15
140 – 145	12	27
145 – 150	7	34
150 – 155	10	44
155 – 160	6	50
	$N = 50$	

$n = 50$(even), so$\frac{n}{2} = 25$, and median class $= 140 - 145$

so according to the formula media$= l + \left(\frac{\frac{n}{2} - cf}{f}\right) \times h$

the lower limit of median class $(l) = 140$

number of observations $(n) = 50$

cumulative frequency of class preceding the median class $(cf) = 15$

frequency of the median class $(f) = 12$

class size (assuming class size to be equal) $(h) = 5$

substituting these values in the formula above

median$= 140 + \left(\frac{25-15}{12}\right) \times 5$

median$= 140 + \left(\frac{10}{12}\right) \times 10$

median $= 140 + 8.33 = 148.33\ cm$ (approx.) **Ans.**

Question Numbers 11 to 14 carry 4 marks each.

11. In the given figure, PQ is a chord of length 8cm of a circle of radius 5cm. The tangents at P and Q meet at a point T. Find the length of TP.

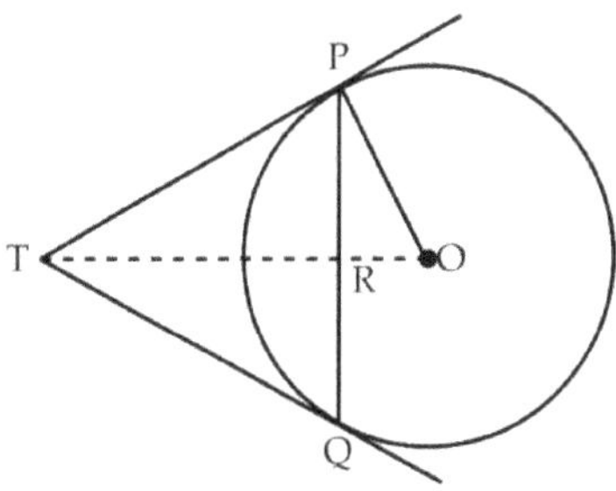

Solution:

∠TRP = 90°(From an external point if two targets are drawn then the line segment joining to the Centre is perpendicular to the chord)

$$\therefore OR = \sqrt{25-16} \Rightarrow 9cm. \text{ [Pythogoras]}$$

Now In △ TPO and $\triangle PRO$

$$\therefore TPO = \angle PRO \quad (90°)$$

$$\angle O = LO(\text{ common})$$

$\therefore \triangle TPO \sim \triangle PRO$ (AA similarity rule)

$$\therefore \frac{TP}{PR} = \frac{Po}{Ro}\left(\begin{array}{l}\text{corresponding sides of similar} \\ \text{Triangles are Proportional}\end{array}\right)$$

$$\frac{TP}{4} = \frac{5}{3}$$

$$TP = \frac{20}{3} \Rightarrow 6\frac{2}{3}\text{ cm.}$$ **Ans.**

12. (a) A 2-digit number is such that the product of its digits is 24. If 18 is subtracted from the number, the digits interchange their places. Find the number.

Solution:

let unit digit = y

$10'$s digit = x

$$xy = 24$$

$$y = \frac{24}{x}$$

$$\therefore No = 10x + y$$

$$= 10x + \frac{24}{x} \Rightarrow \frac{10x^2 + 24}{x}$$

$$\frac{10x^2 + 24}{x} - 18 = 10y + x$$

$$\frac{10x^2 + 24 - 18x}{x} = \frac{10 \times 24}{x} + x \Rightarrow \frac{240 + x^2}{x}$$

$$10x^2 + 24 - 18x = 240 + x^2$$

$$10x^2 - x^2 - 18x + 24 - 240 = 0$$

$$9x^2 - 18x - 216 = 0$$

$$x^2 - 2x - 24 = 0$$

$$x^2 - 6x + 4x - 24 = 0$$

$$\therefore x(x-6) + 4(x-6) = 0$$

$$(x+4)(x-6) = 0$$

$$x = -4, 6$$

$$\therefore \text{No} = \frac{10x^2+24}{x} = \frac{10 \times 36 + 24}{6} = 64.$$ **Ans.**

(b) The difference between the squares of the two numbers is 180. The square of the smaller number is 8 times the greater number. Find the two numbers.

Solution:

let the larger $No. = x$

Smaller $No. = y$

$$x^2 - y^2 = 180$$
$$y^2 = x^2 - 180$$
$$\therefore y^2 = 8 \times x$$
$$x^2 - 180 = 8x$$
$$x^2 - 8x - 180 = 0$$
$$x^2 - 8x - 180 = 0$$
$$x^2 - 18x + 10x - 180 = 0$$
$$(x - 18) + 10(x - 18) = 0$$
$$(x + 10)(x - 18) = 0$$
$$\therefore x = 18, 10 \text{(Not possible)}$$
$$\therefore y = \sqrt{18^2 - 180}$$
$$= \sqrt{324 - 180}$$
$$= \sqrt{144} = 12$$
$$\therefore \text{two no.} = 18, 12$$

13. Case Study - 1:

Kite Festival

The Kite festival is celebrated in many countries at different times of the year. In India, every year 14 January is celebrated as International Kite Day. On this day many people visit India and participate in the festival by flying various kinds of kites.

The picture given below, shows three kites flying together.

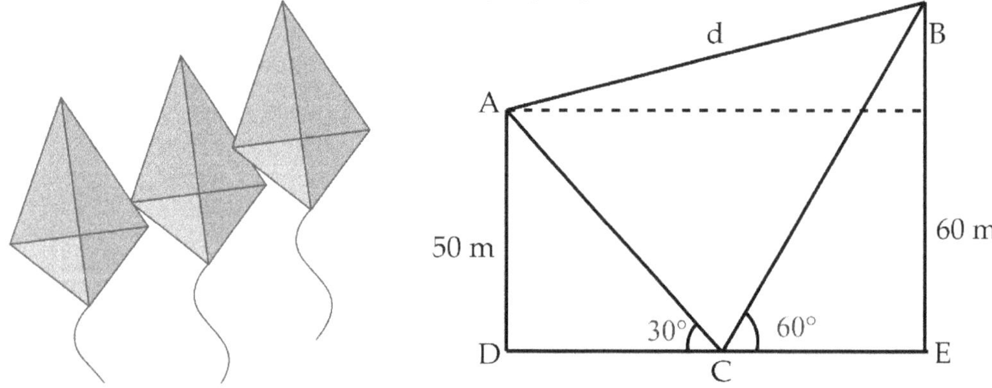

In the figure, the angles of elevation of two kites (Points A and B) from the hands of a man (Point C) are found to be 30° and 60° respectively. Taking AD = 50m and BE = 60m, find

(1) The lengths of strings used (take them straight) for kites A and B as shown in the figure. 2

(2) The distance 'd' between these two kites 2

Solution:

(1) In $\triangle ADC$

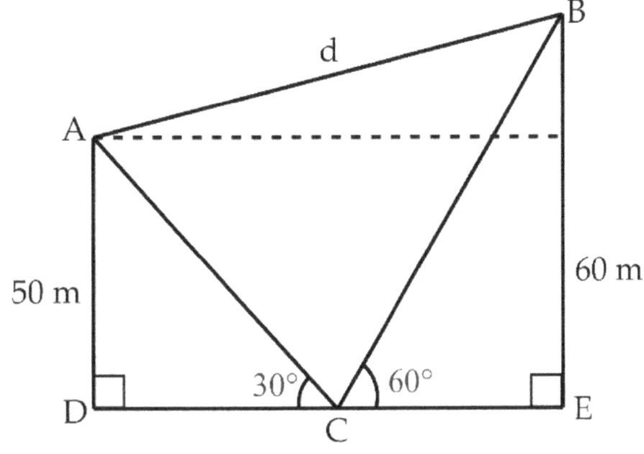

$$\sin 30^o = \frac{AD}{AC}\left(\sin\theta = \frac{\text{Peoprecicien}}{\text{Hypotenuse}}\right)$$

$$\frac{1}{2} = \frac{50}{AC}$$

$$AC = 100\text{m}$$

length of String $A = 100\text{m}.$ Ans.

In $\triangle BEC$

$$\sin 60^o = \frac{60}{BC}$$

$$\frac{\sqrt{3}}{2} = \frac{60}{BC} \Rightarrow BC = \frac{120}{\sqrt{3}} \times \frac{\sqrt{3}}{\sqrt{3}}$$

$$= 40\sqrt{3}$$

$$= 40 \times 1.732 \Rightarrow 69.280$$

$$= 69.28\text{m}$$ **Ans.**

(2) $LACB = 180 - (30 + 60)$ Angles on a straight line]

$= 90^o$

$AB^2 = AC^2 + BC^2$(Pythagoras theorem)

$$d^2 = (100)^2 + (40\sqrt{3})^2$$

$$= 10000 + 4800$$

$$= 14800$$

$$d = 20\sqrt{37}\text{m}$$ **Ans.**

14. Case Study –2

A 'circus' is a company of performers who put on shows of acrobats, clowns, etc. to entertain people started around 250 years back, in open fields, is now generally performed in tents. One such 'Circus Tent' is shown below.

The tent is in the shape of a cylinder surmounted by a conical top. If the height and diameter of a cylindrical part are 9m and 30m respectively and the height of the conical part is 8m with the same diameter as that of the cylindrical part, then find

(1) The area of the canvas used in making the tent; 3

(2) The cost of the canvas bought for the tent at the rate of Rs. 200 per sq m, if 30sq m of can vas was wasted during stitching. 1

Solution:

The radius of cylinder and cone $r = \frac{30}{2} \Rightarrow 15\text{m}.$

(1) Area of canvas= CSA of cylinder + CSA of cone

$= 2\pi rh + \pi rl$

$= 2 \times \pi \times 15 \times 9 + \pi \times 15 \times 17$ $\left[\begin{array}{l} l = \sqrt{15^2 + 8^2} \\ = \sqrt{209} \\ = 17\text{m.} \end{array} \right]$

$= 270\pi + 255\pi$

$= 525\pi$

$= 525 \times \frac{22}{7} \Rightarrow 75 \times 22 \Rightarrow 1650\text{m}^2$ **Ans.**

(2) Total required canvas $= 1650 + 30$

$= 1680\text{m}^2$

Cost of canvas $= 1680 \times 200$

$= \text{Rs.}\, 2336000$

MOST EXPECTED QUESTIONS PAPER

Class- X Session- 2022-23

SAMPLE PAPER-1

Sample Question Paper

Time Allowed: 3 Hrs. **Maximum Marks: 80**

General Instructions:

1. This Question Paper has 5 Sections A-E.
2. Section **A** has 20 MCQs carrying 1 mark each
3. Section **B** has 5 questions carrying 02 marks each.
4. Section **C** has 6 questions carrying 03 marks each.
5. Section **D** has 4 questions carrying 05 marks each.
6. Section **E** has 3 case based integrated units of assessment (04 marks each) with subparts of the values of 1, 1 and 2 marks each respectively.
7. All Questions are compulsory. However, an internal choice in 2 Qs of 5 marks, 2 Qs of 3 marks and 2 Questions of 2 marks has been provided. An internal choice has been provided in the 2marks questions of Section E
8. Draw neat figures wherever required. Take π =22/7 wherever required if not stated

SECTION A

(Section A consists of 20 questions of 1 mark each)

1. If HCF of 65 and 117 is expressible in the form $65\,m - 117$, then the value of m is

(a) 1

(b) 21

(c) 3

(d) 4

Answer: (b)

2. The quadratic polynomial whose sum of zeroes is 3 and product of zeroes is -2 is

(a) $x^2 + 3x - 2$

(b) $x^2 - 2x + 3$

(c) $x^2 - 3x + 2$

(d) $x^2 - 3x - 2$

Answer:(d)

3. Number of solution of pair of equations $x = 0$ and $x = 5$

(a) Many solutions

(b) One solution at (0, 5)

(c) No solution

(d) None of these

Answer: (c)

4. If the discriminant of $3x^2 + 2x + a = 0$ is double the discriminant of $x^2 + 4x + 2 = 0$ then the valueof a is:
   (a) 2
   (b) −2
   (c) 1
   (d) −1
   Answer:(d)

5. A vertical stick 20m long casts a shadow 10m long on the ground. At the same time, a tower casts a shadow 50m long on the ground. The height of the tower is
   (a) 100m
   (b) 120m
   (c) 25m
   (d) 200m
   Answer:(a)

6. In the given figure, ABCD is a rectangle with AD = 12cm and DC = 20cm, and line-segment DE is drawn making an angle of 30° with AD, intersecting AB in E. The length of DE is:

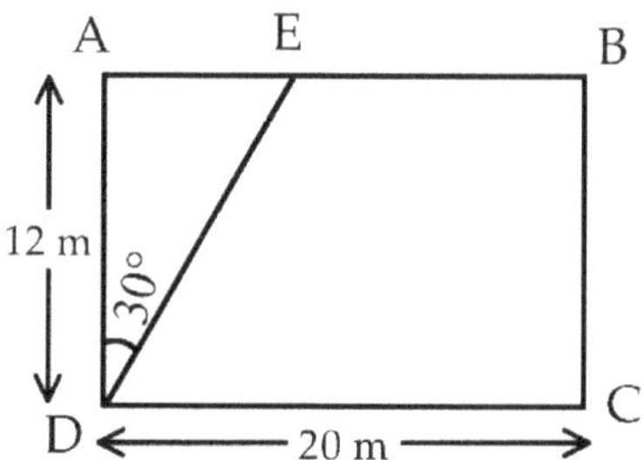

   (a) $4\sqrt{3}$cm
   (b) $8\sqrt{3}$cm
   (c) 13 cm
   (d) 24cm
   Answer:(b)

7. The ratio in which the line segment joining P (x_1, y_1) and Q (x_2, y_2) is divided by x – axis is
   (a) $y_1 : y_2$
   (b) $-y_1 : y_2$
   (c) $x_1 : x_2$
   (d) $-x_1 : x_2$
   Answer:(b)

8. A pair of tangents are drawn from the endpoints of two radii which are making an angle of 60° at the centre, then the tangents are inclined at an angle:
   (a) 120°
   (b) 60°

(c) 30°
(d) 90°
Answer: (a)

9. The perimeters of circular and square fields are equal. If the area of the square field is $484m^2$, then the diameter of the circular field is:
(a) 14m
(b) 21m
(c) 28m
(d) 7m
Answer: (c)

10. $\frac{1+\tan^2 A}{1+\cot^2 A}$ is equal to:
(a) $\sec^2 A$
(b) -1
(c) $\cot^2 A$
(d) $\tan^2 A$
Answer: (d)

11. The radius of a wire is decreased to one-third. If volume remains the same, the length will become:
(a) 3 times
(b) 6 times
(c) 9 times
(d) 27 times
Answer:(c)

12. In Fig. 4.243, the value of x for which $DE \parallel BC$ is

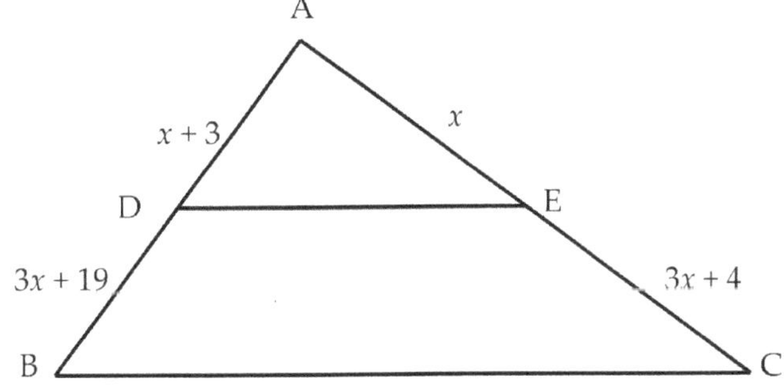

(a) 4
(b) 1
(c) 3
(d) 2
Answer: (d)

13. If the median of the data: $6, 7, x-2, x, 17, 20$, written in ascending order, is 16. Then $x =$

(a) 15

(b) 16

(c) 17

(d) 18

Answer: (c)

14. The circumferences of two concentric circles forming a ring are 88cm and 66cm. Taking $\pi = \frac{22}{7}$, the width of the ring is:

(a) 14cm

(b) 7cm

(c) $\frac{7}{2}$cm

(d) 21cm

Answer: (c)

15. If the common difference of an A.P. is 5, then the value of $a_{18} - a_{13}$is:

(a) 5

(b) 20

(c) 25

(d) 30

Answer: (c)

16. Mid value of class intervals is called:

(a) Class mark

(b) Assumed mean

(c) Class height

(d) Adjustment factor

Answer: (a)

17. A single letter is selected at random from the word 'PROBABILITY'. The probability that it is a vowel is:

(a) $\frac{3}{11}$

(b) $\frac{4}{11}$

(c) $\frac{2}{11}$

(d) $\frac{5}{11}$

Answer: (b)

18. If $\frac{x \operatorname{cosec}^2 30° \sec^2 45°}{8 \cos^2 45° \sin 60°} = \tan^2 60° - \tan^2 30°$, then $x =$

(a) 2

(b) 1

(c) -1

(d) 0

Answer: (b)

Direction: In the following questions, a statement of Assertion (A) is followed by a statement of Reason (R). Mark the correct choice as:

(a) Both Assertion (A) and Reason (R) are true, and Reason (R) is the correct explanation of Assertion (A).

(b) Both Assertion (A) and Reason (R) are true, but Reason (R) is not the correct explanation of Assertion (A).

(c) Assertion (A) is true, but Reason (R) is false.

(d) Assertion (A) is false, but Reason (R) is true.

19. Assertion: If $x = 2\sin^2\theta$ and $y = 2\cos^2\theta + 1$ then the value of $x + y = 3$.

Reason: For any value of θ, $\sin^2\theta + \cos^2\theta = 1$

Answer. (a)

20. Assertion: In a right ΔABC, right angled at B, if $\tan A = 1$, then $2\sin A.\cos A = 1$

Reason: cosec A is the abbreviation used for cosecant of angle A.

Answer. (b)

Section B

Section B consists of 5 questions of 2 marks each

21. For what value of m, will the equations: $x + 2y + 7 = 0$ and $2x + my + 14 = 0$ represent coincident lines.

22. In $\triangle ABC, P$ and Q are points on sides AB and AC respectively, such that $PQ \parallel BC$. If $AP = 3\text{cm}, PB = 5\text{cm}$, and $AC = 8\text{cm}$, then find the value of AQ.

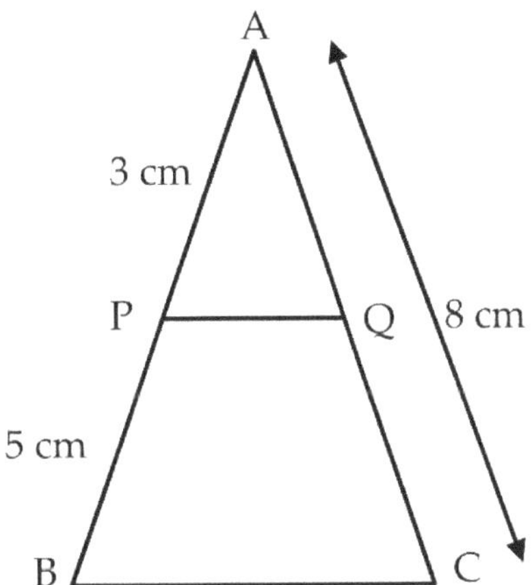

23. If $(1 + \cos\theta)(1 - \cos\theta)\, cosec^2\,\theta = k$, then find the value of k

OR

Find angle ' x ' if:

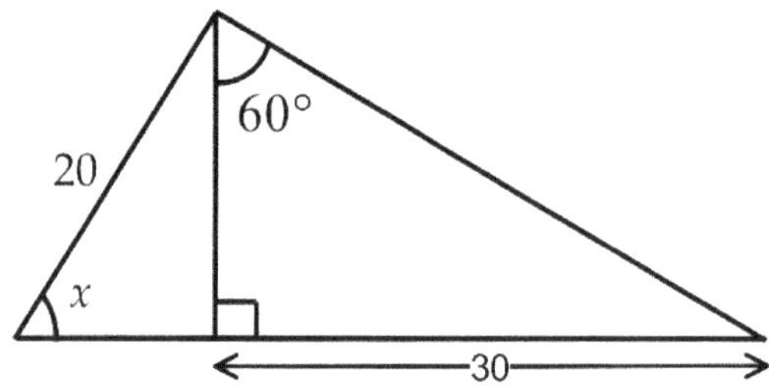

24. TC is a tangent drawn to a circle with centre O. If $\angle ACS = 60°$, find $\angle TAC$, $\angle AOC$ and $\angle AOB$

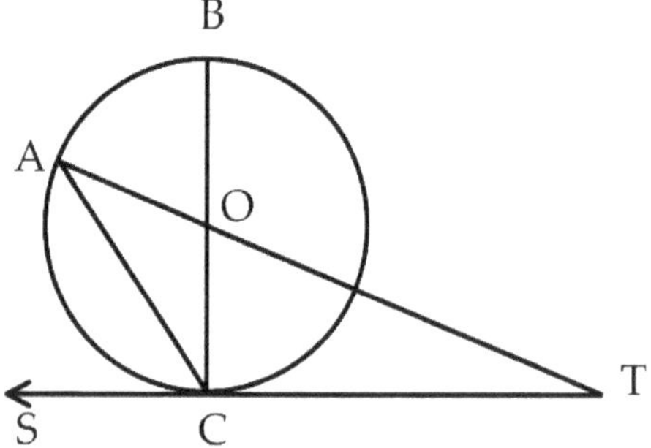

25. The boundary of the shaded region in the given figure consists of three semicircles, the smaller being equal. If the diameter of the larger one is 28cm, find

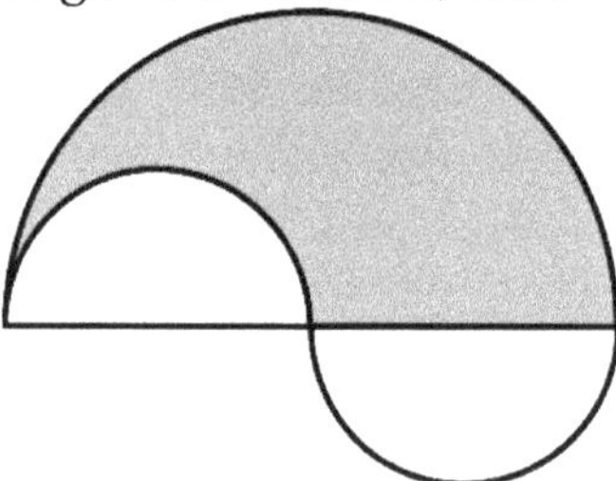

(i) The length of the boundary.
(ii) The area of region.

SECTION C

(Section C consists of 6 questions of 3 marks each)

26. Prove that $\sqrt{5}$ is an irrational number.

27. Prove the identity: $\frac{\sin A+\cos A}{\sin A-\cos A}+\frac{\sin A-\cos A}{\sin A+\cos A}=\frac{2}{sin^2 A-cos^2 A}=\frac{2}{1-2\,cos^2 A}$

28. If the square of difference of the zeroes of the quadratic polynomial $x^2 + ax + 45$ is equal to 144, then find the value of 'a'.

29. A boat goes 30km upstream and 44km downstream in 10 hours. In 13 hours, it goes 40km upstream and 55km downstream. Determine the speed of the stream and that of the boat in still water.

30. Prove that the tangents to a circle from an external point are equal.

31. A dice has 6 faces marked by the given numbers as shown below:

1	2	3	-1	-2	-3

The dice are thrown once. What is the probability of getting

(i) A positive integer?

(ii) An integer greater than -3?

(iii) The smallest integer?

SECTION D

(Section D consists of 4 questions of 5 marks each)

32. An airplane travelled a distance of 400km at an average speed of $x$km/hr. On the return journey, the speed was increased by 40km/hr. Write down an expression for the time taken for:

(i) The onward journey:

(ii) The return journeys.

33. If the return journey took 30 minutes less than the onward journey, write down an equation in x and find its value.

34. In the given figure AB | | CR and LM | | QR.

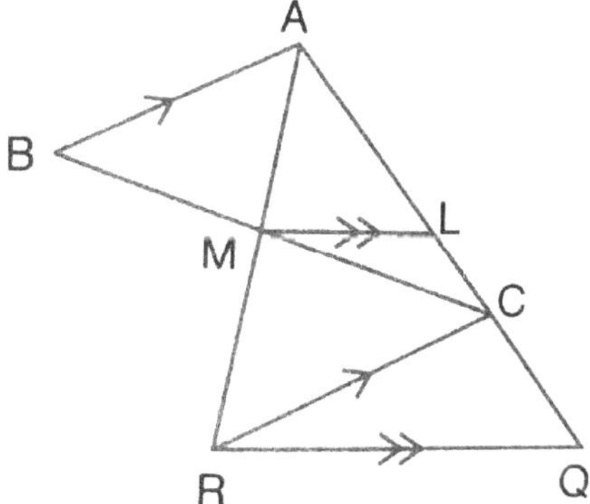

(i) Prove that $\frac{BM}{MC} = \frac{AL}{LQ}$

(ii) Calculate LM: QR, given that $BM : MC = 3 : 4$

35. A hemispherical bowl of an internal diameter of 36cm is full of some liquid which is to be filled in cylindrical bottles of a radius of 3cm and height of 6cm. Find the number of bottles needed to empty the bowl.

36. If the median of the following frequency distribution is 27.5, then find the missing frequencies.

Class intervals	0 – 10	10 – 20	20 – 30	30 – 40	40 – 50	50 – 60	Total
Frequency	3	$f1$	20	15	$f2$	5	60

Section E

3 Case study-based question of 4 (1 + 1 + 2) marks each

37. Case Study based – 1 (Toffees and Candies)

Raj's mother gave him a packet of toffees and candies. The packet he had was having 120 toffees and candies. He started arranging toffees and candies in such a way that there were 3 in row 1, 5 in row 2, 7 in row 3 and so on. Answer the following questions using the above passage:

(i) What is the total number of rows formed by the number of candies he had?
(a) 12
(b) 10
(c) 8
(d) 14

(ii) How many candies are there in the last row?
(a) 21
(b) 23
(c) 19
(d) 17

(iii) How many candies would Raj require more, if he wishes to add two more rows to his pattern?
(a) 46

(b) 48
(c) 50
(d) 44

(iv) What is the difference of the candies between row 4th and row 8th?
(a) 9
(b) 7
(c) 6
(d) 8

38. Case Study based – 2

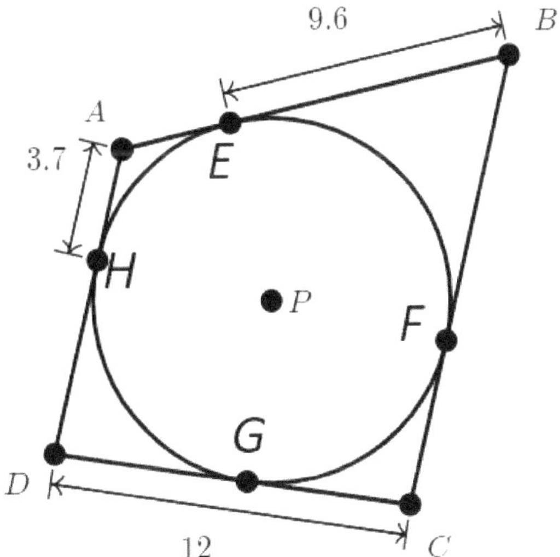

The above figure shows a circular field, which has road on all sides. Due to restriction the roads touch the circular field at one point.

(i) How many tangents are there in the figure?
(a) 1
(b) 2
(c) 3
(d) 4

(ii) The tangents are drawn from an external point to a circle are:
(a) Equal
(b) perpendicular
(c) Unequal
(d) None of the above

(iii) In the figure EB = 9.6 cm, then what is the value of FB?
(a) 3.7 cm
(b) 12 cm
(c) 9.6 cm
(d) 10 cm

(iv) What is the perimeter of the road ABCD?

(a) 50 cm
(b) 50.6 cm
(c) 60 cm
(d) 60.6 cm

39. The below picture are few natural examples of parabolic shape which is represented by a quadratic polynomial. A parabolic arch is an arch in the shape of a parabola. In structures, their curve represents an efficient method of load, and so can be found in bridges and in architecture in a variety of forms.

(i) In the standard form of quadratic polynomial $ax^2 + bx + c$,which is true

(a) $b \neq 0$
(b) $a \neq 0$
(c) $c \neq 0$
(d) None

(ii) If the roots of the quadratic polynomial are equal, where the discriminant $D = b^2 - 4ac$, then

(a) $D < 0$
(b) $D \geq 0$
(c) $D = 0$
(d) $D > 0$

(iii) If both the zeroes of a quadratic polynomial $ax^2 + bx + c$ are equal and opposite in sign, then b is:

(a) 1
(b) 0
(c) – 1
(d) 5

(iv) The graph of $p(x) = x^2 + 5x + 6$

(a) Intersects x - axis at two distinct points.

(b) Touches y axis at a point

(c) Touches x - axis at a point

(d) Intersect x - axis at more than two points

Answers:

Section B
21. m = 4
22. 3cm
23. 1 or 60^0
24. $30^0, 120^0, 60^0$
25. (i) 88 cm (ii) 308 cm^2
Section C
28. A = ± 18
30. 2 cm
29. Boat 8 km/hr and stream 3 km/hr
31. (i) $\frac{1}{2}$ (ii) $\frac{5}{6}$ (iii) $\frac{1}{6}$
Section D
32. (i) $\frac{400}{x}$ *hrs*. (ii) $\frac{400}{x+40}$ *hrs*., (iii) $\frac{400}{x} - \frac{400}{x+40} = \frac{1}{2}$ and $x = 160$
33. (ii) $\frac{3}{7}$
34. 72
35. f1 = 10, f2 = 5
Section E
36. (a) 10 (b) 21 (c) 48 (d) 8
37. (a) 4 (b) Equal (c) 9.6 cm (d) 50.6 cm
38. (a) a $\neq$ 0 (b) D = 0 (c) 0 (d) Intersects x – axis at two distinct points.

Class- X Session- 2022-23
SAMPLE PAPER-2
Sample Question Paper

Time Allowed: 3 Hrs. **Maximum Marks: 80**

General Instructions:

1. This Question Paper has 5 Sections A-E.
2. Section **A** has 20 MCQs carrying 1 mark each
3. Section **B** has 5 questions carrying 02 marks each.
4. Section **C** has 6 questions carrying 03 marks each.
5. Section **D** has 4 questions carrying 05 marks each.
6. Section **E** has 3 case based integrated units of assessment (04 marks each) with subparts of the values of 1, 1 and 2 marks each respectively.
7. All Questions are compulsory. However, an internal choice in 2 Qs of 5 marks, 2 Qs of 3 marks and 2 Questions of 2 marks has been provided. An internal choice has been provided in the 2marks questions of Section E
8. Draw neat figures wherever required. Take π =22/7 wherever required if not stated

SECTION A
(Section A consists of 20 questions of 1 mark each)

1. ' a ' and ' b ' are two +ve integers, where $a > b$ and ' b ' is a factor of ' a ', then HCF(a, b) is
(a) b
(b) a
(c) ab
(d) $\frac{a}{b}$
Answer:(a)

2. The graph of a polynomial p(x) is shown in the figure. The number of zeroes of p(x) is

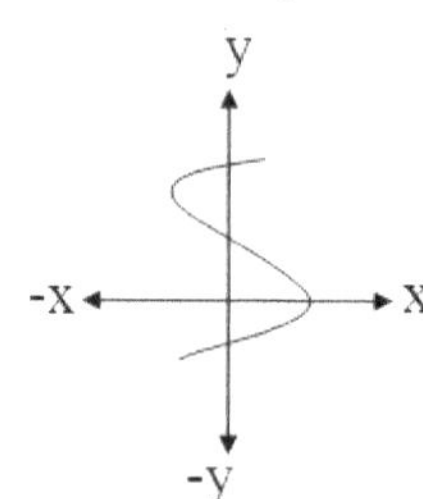

(a) 2
(b) 1
(c) 3
(d) 4
Answer: (b)

3. The point at which line $4x - 3y - 5 = 0$ meets x - axis.
   (a) $(\frac{5}{4}, 0)$
   (b) $(0, \frac{5}{4})$
   (c) $(\frac{3}{5}, 0)$
   (d) $\left(-\frac{5}{4}, 0\right)$
   Answer:(a)

4. The value of k for which the roots of the equation $8kx\,(x - 1) + 1 = 0$ are real and equal.
   (a) 0
   (b) 1/2
   (c) 2
   (d) 3
   Answer:(b)

5. If $\triangle ABC$ and $\triangle DEF$ are similar such that $2AB = DE$ and $BC = 8$cm, then $EF =$
   (a) 16cm
   (b) 12cm
   (c) 8cm
   (d) 4cm
   Answer:(a)

6. If $(1 + \cos\theta)\,(1 - \cos\theta)\,\mathrm{cosec}^2\,\theta = \mathrm{k}$, then the value of k
   (a) 2
   (b) 1
   (c) -1
   (d) -2
   Answer:(b)

7. If the centroid of the triangle formed by the points $(a, b), (b, c)$ *and* (c, a) is at the origin, then $a^3 + b^3 + c^3 =$
   (a) abc
   (b) 0
   (c) $3abc$
   (d) $a + b + c$
   Answer:(c)

8. The length of the minute hand of a clock is 14cm. Area swept by the minute hand in 30 minutes $\left(\text{taking } \pi = \frac{22}{7}\right)$ is:
   (a) 308cm^2
   (b) 44cm^2
   (c) $\frac{154}{3}\text{cm}^2$
   (d) 18480cm^2

Answer:(a)

9. In the given figure, if $\angle AOQ = 55°$, then $\angle PAQ$ is:
   (a) 35°
   (b) 70°
   (c) 110°
   (d) 80°
   Answer:(b)

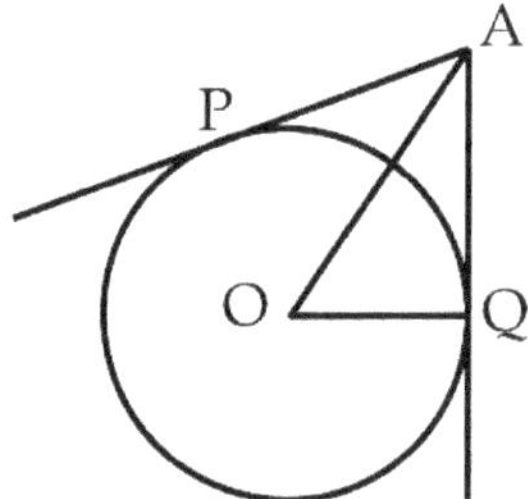

10. If two towers of height h_1 and h_2 subtend angles of 60° and 30° respectively at the mid-point of the line segment joining their feet, then $h_1 : h_2$ is:
   (a) $3:1$
   (b) $\sqrt{3}:1$
   (c) $1:\sqrt{3}$
   (d) $1:3$
   Answer:(d)

11. The volume of a right circular cylinder is 345cm^3. Then the volume of a right circular cone whose radius of the base and height is the same as that of a circular cylinder will be:
   (a) 345cm^3
   (b) 690cm^3
   (c) 115cm^3
   (d) 230cm^3
   Answer:(c)

12. The mode of a frequency distribution can be determined graphically from
   (a) Ogive
   (b) Histogram
   (c) Frequency polygon
   (d) Frequency curve
   Answer:(b)

13. In a circle of diameter 42cm, if an arc subtends an angle of 60° at the center, where $\pi = \frac{22}{7}$, then the length of the arc is:
   (a) 11cm

(b) $\frac{22}{7}$cm

(c) 22cm

(d) 44cm

Answer:(c)

14. If ABC and DEF are similar triangles such that $\angle A = 47°$ and $\angle E = 83°$, then $\angle C$ =

(a) 50°

(b) 80°

(c) 70°

(d) Not possible to find

Answer:(a)

15. If θ is an acute angle and sin θ = cos θ, the value of: $2\, sin^2\, \theta - 3\, cos^2\, \theta + \frac{1}{2} cot^2\, \theta$

(a) 1

(b) –1

(c) 0

(d) 2

Answer:(c)

16. The following data have been arranged in ascending order. If their median is 66, find the value of x: 35, 38, 52, 55, x, x + 2, 75, 83, 85, 100

(a) 62

(b) 66

(c) 65

(d) 64

Answer:(c)

17. $37th$ term of the A.P.:$\sqrt{x}$, $3\sqrt{x}$, $5\sqrt{x}$, ... is:

(a) $37\sqrt{x}$

(b) $39\sqrt{x}$

(c) $73\sqrt{x}$

(d) $75\sqrt{x}$

Answer:(c)

18. If P(E) = 0.05, then P(not E) is equal to:

(a) -0.05

(b) 0.5

(c) 0.9

(d) 0.95

Answer:(d)

Direction: In the following questions, a statement of Assertion (A) is followed by a statement of Reason (R). Mark the correct choice as:

(a) Both Assertion (A) and Reason (R) are true, and Reason (R) is the correct explanation of Assertion (A).

(b) Both Assertion (A) and Reason (R) are true but Reason (R) is not the correct explanation of Assertion (A).

(c) Assertion (A) is true but Reason (R) is false.

(d) Assertion (A) is false, but Reason (R) is true.

19. Assertion: If ΔABC and ΔPQR are congruent triangles, then they are also similar triangles.
Reason: All congruent triangles are similar, but the similar triangles need not be congruent.
Answer. (a)

20. Both assertion and reason are correct, but reason is not correct explanation for assertion.
Assertion: the mode of the call received on 7 consecutive day 11,13,13,17,19,23,25 is 13.
Reason: Mode is the value that appears most frequent.
Answer. (a)

SECTION B

(Section B consists of 5 questions of 2 marks each)

19. Find the value of 'k' for which the pair of lines: $kx + 3y = k - 3$ and $12x + ky = k$ has infinitely many solutions.

20. In the given figure, DE || BC.

(i) Prove that: $\Delta ADE \sim \Delta ABC$

(ii) Given that$AD = \frac{1}{2}BD$, calculate DE, if BC = 4.5 cm.

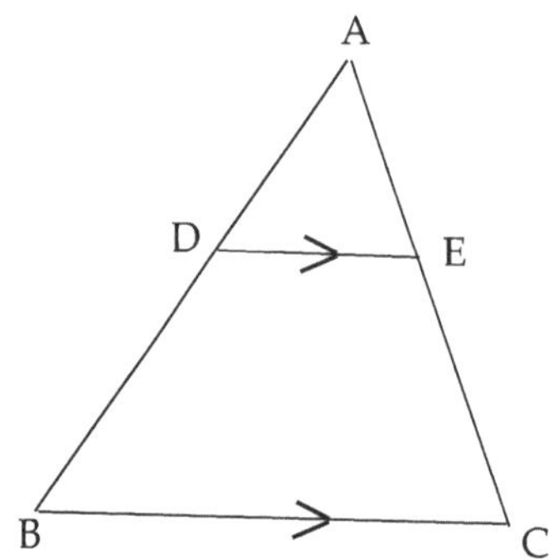

21. Find AD if:

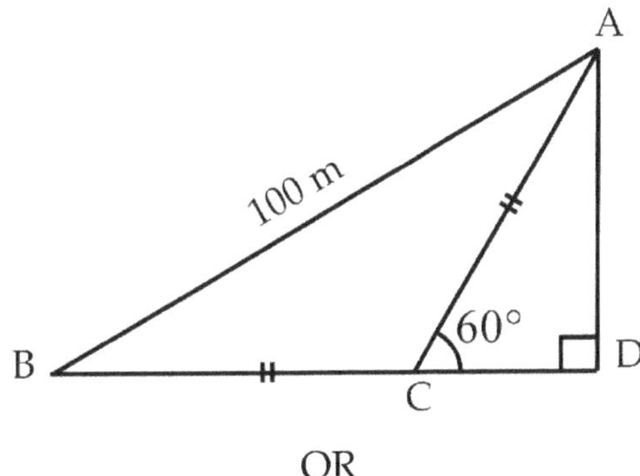

OR

Find the value of: $\frac{4}{3} tan^2 30^o + sin^2 60^o - 3\ cos^2\ 60^o + \frac{3}{4} tan^2\ 60^o - 2\ tan^2\ 45^o$

22. Prove that the angle between the two tangents to a circle drawn from an external point is supplementary to the angle subtended by the line segment joining the points of contact at the center.

23. A rectangular sheet of paper is 22 cm long and 6 cm wide. Circular pieces 2 cm in diameter are cut from it to prepare discs. Calculate the maximum number of discs that can be prepared. Also find the area of the sheet left after cutting circular pieces. (Take $\pi = 3.14$)

SECTION C

(Section C consists of 6 questions of 3 marks each)

24. If two positive integers x and y can be expressed as x = $a^2 b^3$ and $y = ab^2 c$; x and y being prime numbers. Find the $LCM\ (x, y)$ and $HCF\ (x, y)$

25. Prove that: $\frac{(1+\cot A+\tan A)(\sin A-\cos A)}{sec^3 A-cosec^3 A} = sin^2 A. cos^2 A$

OR

Solve for x:$\sin^2\ 60° + \cos^2\ (3x - 9°) = 1$

26. If α and β are zeroes of the quadratic polynomial p(x) = $x^2 - (k + 6)x + 2(2k - 1)$, find the value of k, if $\alpha + \beta - \frac{\alpha\beta}{2}$.

27. The students of a class are made to stand in (complete) rows. If one student is extra in a row, there would be 2 rows less, and if one student is less in a row, there would be 3 rows more. Find the number of students in the class.

28. The radius of the in – circle of a triangle is 4 cm and the segments into which one side is divided by the point of contact are 6 cm and 8 cm. Determine the other two sides of the triangle.

29. Sixteen cards are labelled as $a, b, c, \dots\dots\dots, m, n, o, p$. They are put in a box and shuffled. A boy is asked to draw a card from the box. What is the probability that the card drawn is:
(i) A vowel
(ii) A consonant
(iii) None of the letters of the word median?

SECTION D
(Section D consists of 4 questions of 5 marks each)

30. Some students arranged a picnic in metro walk. The budget for food was Rs. 1200. Due to some reason 3 students failed to go. Now the cost of food to each student got increased by Rs. 20. How many students went for the picnic?

OR

A boat can go 24 km downstream and 12 km upstream in a total of 4 hours. If speed of boat in still water is 9 km/hr, find the speed of the stream.

31. In given figure PS is the bisector of $\angle QPR$ of Δ PQR, prove that.

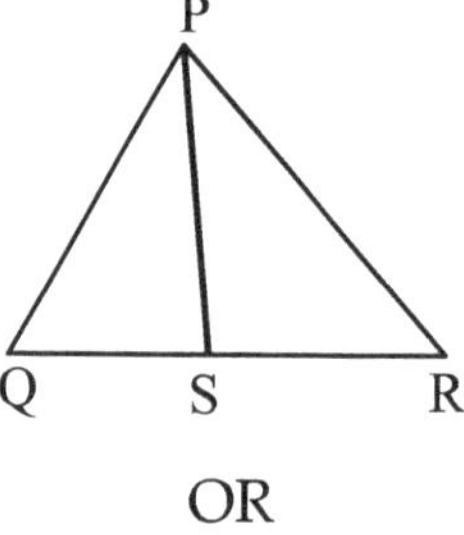

OR

In the given figure, DE || BC.
(i) Prove that: $\Delta ADE \sim \Delta ABC$
(ii) Given that $AD = \frac{1}{2}BD$, calculate DE, if BC = 4.5 cm.

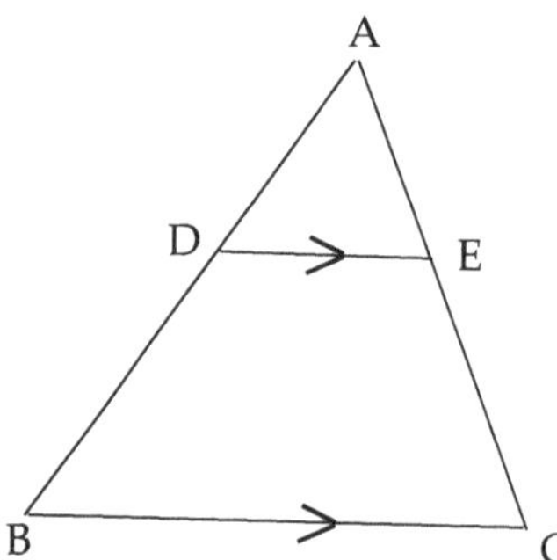

32. A toy is in the shape of a right circular cylinder with a hemisphere on one end and a cone on the other. The radius and height of the cylindrical parts are 5cm and 13cm respectively. The radii of hemispherical and conical parts are the same as that of the cylindrical part. Find the surface area

of the toy if the total height of the toy is 30cm and the cost of painting the toy at the rate of RS. 5.50 per cm^2.

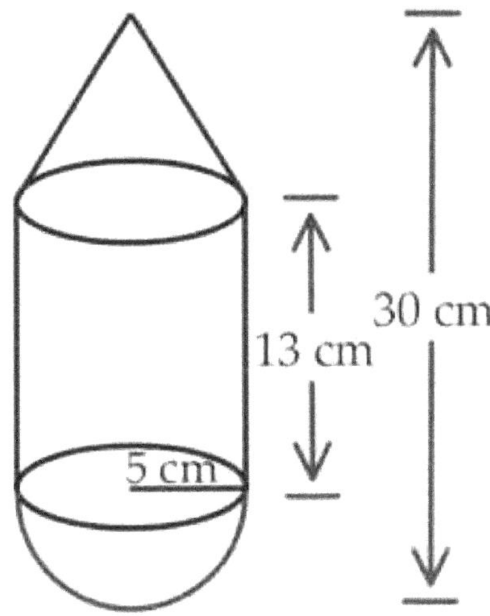

33. The data on the number of patients attending a hospital in the morning are given below. Find the average (mean) number of patients attending the hospital in a month by using the shortcut method.

No. of patients	10 – 20	20 – 30	30 – 40	40 – 50	50 – 60	60 – 70
No. of days	5	2	7	9	2	5

Take the assumed mean as 45. Give your answer correct to 2 decimal places.

SECTION E

(3 Case study-based question of 4 (1 + 1 + 2) marks each)

34. Case Study based – 1 (Train)

Two trains, train A and train B, departs from a station in 2 opposite direction Train A travels 360 km at a uniform speed. However, if the speed had been 5 km/h more, it would have taken 1 hour less for the same journey. On the other hand, train B covers a distance of 90 km at a uniform speed. But, if the speed had been 15 km/hr more, it would have taken 30 minutes less for the journey. Based on this information, answer the following questions:

(i) Find the speed of f train A:
(a) 44 km/hr
(b) 40 km/hr
(c) 30 km/hr
(d) 34 km/hr

(ii) Find the speed of train B:
(a) 44 km/hr
(b) 50 km/hr
(c) 45 km/hr
(d) 40 km/hr

(iii) If train A had covered 90 km instead of 360 km, then what would have been its speed (approximate)?
(a) 10 km/hr
(b) 32 km/hr
(c) 24 km/hr
(d) 19 km/hr

(iv) If train B had covered 360 km instead of 90 km, then what would have been its speed (approximate)?
(a) 66 km/hr
(b) 70 km/hr
(c) 34 km/hr
(d) 97 km/hr

35. Case Study based – 1 (Class Test)

In a class test, the sum of Ranjana's marks in mathematics and English is 40. Had she got 3 marks more in mathematics and 4 marks less in English, the product of the marks would have been 360. On the other hand, Ranjana's friend, Maya scored 3 marks less in mathematics and 2 marks more in English than what Ranjana scored. Based on this information, answer the following questions:

(i) How much did Ranjana score in mathematics?

(a) 12
(b) 21
(c) 26
(d) Both (a) and (b)

(ii) How much did Ranjana score in English?

(a) 19
(b) 28
(c) 20
(d) Both (a) and (b)

(iii) How much did Maya score in Mathematics?

(a) 9 or 18
(b) 15 or 24
(c) 23 or 29
(d) None of the above

(iv) How much did Maya score in English?

(a) 26 or 71
(b) 30 or 21
(c) 30 or 17
(d) 26 or 21

(v) Overall adding the marks of both the subjects, who scored more: Ranjana or Maya?

(a) Ranjana
(b) Maya

36. India is a leading manufacturing company due to the low cost of manpower and strong technical and engineering capabilities contributing to higher quality production runs. The production of TV sets in a factory increases uniformly by a fixed number every year. It produced 14000 sets in 5th year and 26500 in 10th year.

(a) Find the production during first year.
(b) Find the production during 9th year.
(c) Find the total production during first 4 years.
(d) In which year, the production is Rs 34000.

Answers:

Section B
21. $K = 6$
22. 1.5cm
23. 50 cm or $\frac{25}{36}$
25. 33,28.38cm^2
Section C
26. $LCM = a^2b^3c, HCF = ab^2$
27. 23^0
28. 7
29. 60
Section D
30. 13 cm and 15 cm
31. (i) $\frac{1}{4}$ (ii) $\frac{3}{4}$ (iii) $\frac{5}{8}$
32. 12 students or 3 km/hr
33. 1.5cm
34. 770cm^2, Rs. 4235
35. 40.33
Section E
36. (a) 40 km/hr (b) 45 km/hr (c) 19 km/hr (d) 97 km/hr
37. (a) both (a) and (b) (b) both (a) and (b) (c) 9 or 18 (d) 30 or 21
38. (a) 5000 (b) 24000 (c) 31000(d) 13th year

www.ingramcontent.com/pod-product-compliance
Ingram Content Group UK Ltd.
Pitfield, Milton Keynes, MK11 3LW, UK
UKHW061958290726
14090UKWH00021B/1279

9 789355 564887